Accounting Standards

Fourth Edition

John Blake

Professor of Accounting,
University of Central Lancashire

PITMAN
PUBLISHING

Pitman Publishing
128 Long Acre, London WC2E 9AN

A Division of Longman Group Ltd

First published in Great Britain in 1981
Second edition 1988
Third edition 1991
Fourth edition 1994
Reprinted 1994 (twice)
© Longman Group UK Limited 1981, 1988, 1991, 1994

British Library Cataloguing in Publication Data
A CIP catalogue record for this book can be obtained from the British Library

ISBN 0 273 60102 4

Typeset by Avocet Typesetters, Bicester, Oxon
Printed and bound in Great Britain by Clays Ltd, St Ives, Plc

Contents

Preface

Accounting standards are now emerging from a new authority, the Accounting Standards Board (ASB), under a new name, Financial Reporting Standards (FRSs). This text, therefore, includes chapters on these new FRSs as well as the extant Statements of Accounting Practice (SSAPs). The new ASB is endowed with greater authority than its predecessor, and is using that authority to tackle some long-standing abuses. Thus FRS 3, discussed in Chapter 4, should eliminate abuse of 'extraordinary item' treatment. One unavoidable consequence of this approach is that the new standards are more detailed, in order to avoid ambiguity and consequent abuse.

The structure of each chapter varies, but in relation to each standard this book covers:

(a) the basic problems addressed by the standard;
(b) the detailed requirements laid down in the standard;
(c) practical problems of compliance with the standard;
(d) controversy over the standard.

A study of the controversy over each standard is important for two reasons. First, thinking accountants will wish to understand not only *what* rules they have to follow, by *why* the rules have evolved in that way. Second, users of accounts may well find an appreciation of how accounting regulations have emerged helpful in their assessment of accounts prepared in compliance with those regulations. For instance, in discussing SSAP 15 it is observed that the standard is an example of the predominant influence of preparers rather than users of accounts on the Accounting Standards Committee (ASC). Users who are aware of the deficiencies of SSAP 15 are thereby equipped to make their own adjustments to accounts.

John Blake
July 1993

Acknowledgements

I would like to express my thanks to the Institute of Chartered Accountants in England and Wales, the Chartered Association of Certified Accountants, the Chartered Institute of Management Accountants and the Institute of Company Accountants for giving their permission to use questions from their examinations, and to the International Accounting Standards Committee for being helpful with enquiries.

1 The Origins and Development of the Accounting Standards Programme

Background

Accounting Standards, being Statements of Standard Accounting Practice (SSAPs) and Financial Reporting Standards (FRSs), have become one of the major sources of authority for accountants, covering the major areas of accounting controversy. The first such statement was issued in 1971, following the issue by the Institute of Chartered Accountants in England and Wales (ICAEW) of a 'Statement of Intent' promising to issue SSAPs in December 1969.

Prior to the establishment of the accounting standards programme the ICAEW gave guidance to its members in a series of statements, 'Recommendations on Accounting Principles'. The issue of such recommendations started with the establishment of the Taxation and Financial Relations Committee (later renamed Taxation and Research Committee) in 1942, and by 1969 twenty-nine recommendations had been issued. The Taxation and Research Committee would prepare draft recommendations which would be circulated to advisory committees of each of the Institute's district societies and then forwarded to the Council of the Institute, which would decide whether to issue a recommendation, and if so the exact content of the recommendation to be issued. The following features of this procedure should be noted:

(a) There was no system for consultations with other professional bodies on topics under consideration.
(b) While the recommendations offered guidance on 'best practice', members of the institute were under no obligation to follow that guidance.
(c) There was no public announcement of topics under consideration nor was there any system for exposing proposed recommendations to public comment.
(d) While the Council of the Institute would normally accept the guidance of the Taxation and Research Committee, it retained, and on occasion exercised, the power to reject or substantially amend proposed recommendations.

'Recommendations on Accounting Principles' generally consisted of summaries of current practice rather than giving a lead in new developments, and were rarely backed up by formal research. During the 1960s a number of cases where existing accounting and auditing practice seemed to lead to an unsatisfactory result led to considerable criticism of the accounting profession.

In the USA critics of the extent of the variety in accounting practice pointed to the example of the sale of the shares in Ethyl Corporation by its joint owners General Motors and Standard Oil; each company made a profit of some $40 million on the sale of its half share in the corporation. General Motors showed the proceeds as part of its trading income for the year, while Standard Oil did not bring in the surplus at any stage in the profit and loss account and instead took the surplus direct to the reserves. Thus, two of the largest industrial organisations in the world, audited by two of the most highly respected international firms of accountants, produced totally different treatments of earnings from identical transactions. In the UK a similar controversy arose following the takeover of AEI by GEC. While fighting the takeover, AEI had produced a forecast, in the tenth month of their financial year, that profit before tax for that year would come to £10 million. Following the takeover the accounts for AEI showed a loss of £4½ million. A report on the difference of £14½ million attributed £5 million to 'matters substantially of fact' and £9½ million to 'adjustments which remain matters substantially of judgement' arising from variations in accounting policies.

A number of articles in the City pages of the national press severely criticised the failure of the accounting profession to give a lead in developing a set of consistent principles for the presentation of financial reports. The case for reform was presented with particular clarity and vigour in a number of articles by Professor Edward Stamp published in 1969, followed up by a book *Accounting Principles and the City Code: The case for reform* (Stamp and Marley) published in 1970. While leading members of the accounting profession publicly rejected many of these criticisms, clearly in private there was a realisation that at least some of the criticism was justified.

On 12 December 1969 the ICAEW issued a 'Statement of Intent on Accounting Standards in the 1970s' laying down a five-point plan to advance accounting standards by:

(a) narrowing the areas of difference and variety in accounting practice by publishing authoritative, and where possible definitive, statements of best accounting practice;

(b) recommending disclosure of accounting bases used in arriving at the amount attributed to significant items depending on judgements of value or estimates of future events;

(c) requiring disclosure of departures from definitive accounting standards in the notes to the accounts;

(d) introducing a system for wide exposure of draft proposals for accounting standards to appropriate representative bodies for discussion and comment;

(e) continuing to suggest improvements in the accounting disclosure requirements laid down by company law and regulatory bodies such as the Stock Exchange.

Professor Stamp wrote 'What is really important about this Statement of Intent is the fact that it has been made and that things will never be the same again in British accountancy. The English Institute has stood up and declared itself foursquare for progress and improvement and it deserves the greatest possible credit for having done so'. There is reason to believe that, if the ICAEW had not set up the accounting standards programme, the government would have felt it necessary to set up some form of regulatory body to deal with the problem.

Thus it can be seen that the accounting standards programme originated in response to a demand for a lead from the accounting profession in developing improved and more consistent standards in financial reporting.

The ASC and the standard setting process

As we have seen the accounting standards programme was announced by the ICAEW in December 1969. The Institute immediately set up an Accounting Standards Steering Committee (ASSC) with 11 members, later renamed the Accounting Standards Committee (ASC); to avoid confusion the latter term will be used throughout this book. In April 1970 representatives from the Scottish (ICAS) and one from the Irish (ICAI) Institutes of Chartered Accountants joined the committee, followed by representatives of the Association of Certified Accountants (ACCA) and the Institute of Cost and Management Accountants (ICMA) in 1971 and the Chartered Institute of Public Finance and Accountancy (CIPFA) in 1976. One reason for the decision of the ICAEW to set up the ASC alone originally may well have been that at that time there were proposals to merge the major accounting bodies; following the rejection of these proposals by members of the ICAEW in June 1970 the Consultative Committee of Accounting Bodies (CCAB) was set up to enable the profession to co-ordinate activities in certain areas. From 1 February 1976 the ASC was reconstituted as a joint committee of the six governing bodies of the CCAB, committee members being nominated by the professional bodies.

The ASC's constitution defined its objectives as follows:

'Bearing in mind the intention of the governing bodies to advance accounting standards and to narrow the areas of difference and variety in accounting practice by publishing authoritative statements on best accounting practice which will wherever possible be definitive—

(a) To keep under review standards of financial accounting and reporting.
(b) To publish consultative documents with the object of maintaining and advancing accounting standards.
(c) To propose to the Councils of the governing bodies statements of standard accounting practice.
(d) To consult as appropriate with representatives of finance, commerce, industry and government and other persons concerned with financial reporting.

The Accounting Standards Committee, as we have seen, was composed entirely from nominees of the professional accounting bodies; in order to allow some measure of influence to the major groups the ASC set up a consultative committee of nominees from the major organisations representing those who use published accounts, including the CBI and the TUC.

In 1982 the organisational structure of the ASC was revised to reduce the number of members to 20, including five users of accounts who need not be accountants. Members were chosen with an eye to balancing various interest groups rather than purely to represent professional accounting bodies.

The procedure for developing a statement of standard accounting practice (SSAP) developed over the years. In 1990 the following stages were involved:

(a) The ASC identified a topic as requiring consideration for the possible issue of a SSAP. Identification was undertaken by a planning subcommittee which took into account suggestions from a range of sources.
(b) The planning subcommittee advised on the setting-up of working parties to prepare consultative documents.
(c) One or more research studies on a topic were commissioned, involving a review of the literature, consideration of potential problems, and tentative suggestions.

On the basis of the research the ASC would decide whether to proceed towards a SSAP or other statement on a topic, and if so set up a working party.

Consultative documents on a proposed statement were to be published by the ASC. These can be of three types:

(i) A discussion paper, designed to explore the issues and stimulate debate.

(ii) A statement of intent (SOI), summarising the way in which the ASC plans to proceed.

(iii) An exposure draft (ED), more detailed than a SOI, and providing a draft of a proposed standard.

Discussion papers and SOIs were optional, but an exposure draft always preceded the issue of a SSAP.

(f) The working party provided initial feedback to the ASC on its thinking at an early stage, so that an exchange of views could take place.

(g) A consultation plan would be drawn up, identifying groups with a special interest, considering any legal problems, planning full press exposure, and providing for public hearings if necessary.

(h) Technical drafting by the working party proceeded in parallel with widespread private consultations on the issues. At the same time each of the CCAB bodies would also be consulted.

(i) The ASC as a whole would be involved in finally approving issue of an exposure draft to the public. In practice over 100 000 copies of an ED would be distributed.

(j) An 'exposure period' of some six months was allowed for the collection of comment, possibly accompanied by public hearings.

(k) Following exposure the working party prepared a standard, often with the benefit of further private consultations. Where fundamental changes were considered a further ED may be issued.

(l) When the ASC agreed on a standard this was finally subject to approval by each of the CCAB member bodies on whose authority the SSAP was to be issued.

If an issue was not of sufficiently widespread significance to justify a SSAP, a Statement of Recommended Practice (SORP) might be issued instead. Such a SORP would have relevance and apply only to a particular industry or business sector.

The enforcement of accounting standards

Statements of Standard Accounting Practice, as we have seen, have been formulated by the Accounting Standards Committee and issued on the authority of the individual CCAB bodies. There has been no requirement in company law to comply with SSAPs; this contrasts with the situation in the USA where a government agency, the Securities Exchange Commission, effectively compels listed corporations to adopt accounting standards set by the Financial Accounting Standards Board. In certain parts of Canada there is a legal requirement that company accounts should conform to the recommendations of the Canadian Institute of Chartered Accountants. In the UK there is a strong tradition of securing improvements in standards of commercial practice by a system of voluntary self-regulation through the appropriate professional organisations rather than by legislation.

The professional bodies themselves impose compliance with SSAPs by means of their own internal disciplinary procedures. Each of the CCAB bodies has issued to its members an explanatory foreword which lays down a duty to observe accounting standards. For example, the ICAEW states that 'The Council, through its Professional Standards Committee, may inquire into apparent failures by members of the Institute to observe accounting standards or to disclose departures therefrom'. There have in fact been instances of the disciplinary committee of the ICAEW upholding complaints against members on these grounds. Members of the CCAB bodies are expected to ensure that, where they have a responsibility as directors or officers of a company for the publication of accounts, their fellow directors are fully aware of the existence and purpose of accounting standards; they should also use their best endeavours to ensure that the accounts comply with SSAPs and that the nature and effect of any departure from accounting standards is disclosed.

Where members of the CCAB bodies act as auditors or as reporting accountants they are required to ensure that any significant departures from accounting standards are disclosed, and if they concur in the disclosure to justify the departures. Since in the UK only members of the three institutes of chartered accountants and members of the association of certified accountants may become limited company auditors (apart from a diminishing number of persons who were already in practice when the relevant legislation came into force and are therefore allowed to continue) this is a highly significant requirement.

The basic rules for auditors (see Fig. 1.1) are:

(a)   All significant departures from accounting standards should be referred to in the auditor's report 'unless the auditor agrees therewith', the extent of the detail necessary depending on whether the departure is fully explained in the note to the accounts.

(b)   Where the auditors are of the opinion that the directors have necessarily departed

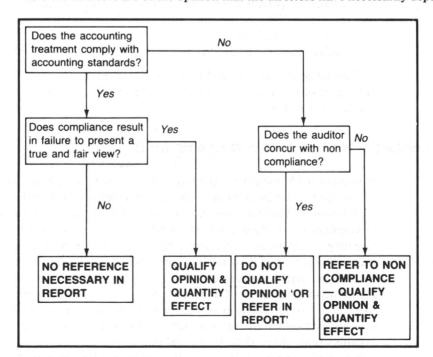

Fig. 1.1   SSAPs and the auditor.

from an accounting standard in order to present a true and fair view then 'no reference in the audit report is necessary'.

(c)   Where the auditors are of the opinion that the departure from an accounting standard is not justified they should express a qualified opinion on the accounts and quantify the financial effect of the departure if practical.

(d)   In 'rare circumstances' it may happen that the auditors come to the conclusion that adherence to an accounting standard results in a failure to produce a true and fair view; in that case they should express a qualified opinion and quantify the effect on the accounts 'if practical'.

Technically 'clean' audit reports in the UK are deliberately brief so as to highlight any reservations expressed by the auditor. Consequently there is a reluctance on the part of companies to incur the qualified opinion expressed when the auditor does not concur. The desire to avoid any such reference in the audit report has been one of the most significant factors leading to the acceptance of SSAPs by companies.

The Stock Exchange expects the accounts of listed companies to conform with SSAPs, and to disclose and explain any significant departures. In practice listed companies, which are subject to public comment and criticism, tend to comply with SSAPs.

The Dearing reforms

In 1987 the CCAB set up a committee under the Chairmanship of Sir Ron Dearing 'to review and make recommendations on the standard setting process'. The committee reported in 1988 and in 1990 a new standard setting organisation, structured largely along the lines suggested by the Dearing Report, was established to replace the ASC.

Figure 1.2 shows the new structure. The process of accounting standard setting is overseen by the 'Financial Reporting Council' (FRC). The chairman and three deputy chairmen of this body are appointed jointly by the Governor of the Bank of England and the Secretary of State for Trade and Industry. The other 21 members

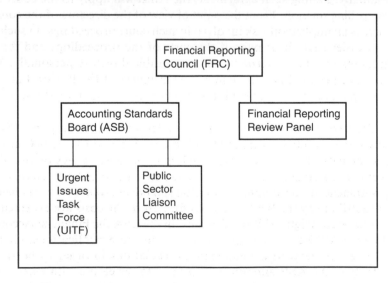

Fig. 1.2   The accounting standard regulatory structure.

are nominated by a range of interested groups including the professional accounting bodies.

The FRC's role is:

(a) To promote good accounting and to make representations to government on how accounting legislation might be improved.

(b) To guide the Accounting Standards Board on work programmes and broad policy issues.

(c) To oversee the conduct of arrangements, arrange funding, and make appoint-ments to the ASB and the review panel.

The Accounting Standards Board has a full-time chairman, a full-time technical director and seven part-time members, all of whom are paid. The ASB has taken over the role of the ASC in formulating accounting standards, following a similar consultative procedure but using the terms 'Financial Reporting Exposure Draft' (FRED), and 'Financial Reporting Standard' (FRS) in place of EDs and SSAPs. Initially the ASB adopted all the extant SSAPs. Unlike the ASC, the ASB has the authority to issue standards directly.

The Urgent Issues Task Force (UITF) is a sub-committee of the ASB. The UITF has some 15 members, and seeks to find consensus on how to deal with new accounting issues that emerge so as to offer an authoritative pronouncement. The Public Sector Liaison Committee is a smaller sub-committee which has the job of advising the ASB on the public sector implications of its work, with a view to minimising the differences between public and private sector practices.

The Company Act 1989 introduced a new form of legal backing for accounting standards. Public and large private companies are required to state in their accounts whether they have been prepared in accordance with accounting standards, and to describe and explain any material departures. The Financial Reporting Review Panel examines company accounts and forms a view as to whether there is a failure to provide a true and fair view as a result of departure from an accounting standard. Where such a failure is identified the Panel seeks to agree revision of the accounts with the company. Failing such agreement, the Panel will apply to the court to seek an order compelling revision. From the point of view of the directors of the company concerned there is an unpleasant risk involved in such court proceedings; in such a case the court may order that all or part of the costs of the proceedings and the revision of the accounts should be borne by the responsible directors personally. Since no similar threat of personal liability hangs over members of the Review Panel in the event of a complaint not being upheld, this can be seen as a somewhat one-sided enforcement tool.

The new system is an expensive one. The cost of running the ASC in its last year was some £400 000, compared with a cost of some £3 300 000 in running the new system in its first year. The Dearing Report proposed a levy on the filing of company accounts to finance this structure. Instead, contributions come equally from the government, the accounting profession and private sources (mainly banks 'encouraged' to contribute by the Bank of England). Part of the costs are expected to be recovered by sale of copyright ASB publications. In the USA the Financial Accounting Standards Board (FASB) derives a substantial income from publications, giving rise to a fear of excessive detailed amendments to regulations in order to boost such income.

In 1991 the ASB announced a project to develop a 'Statement of Principles' in seven chapters. Drafts have appeared, or are in the course of production, on:

(a) Objectives
(b) Qualitative characteristics
(c) Elements
(d) Recognition
(e) Valuation and measurement
(f) Presentation
(g) The reporting entity.

When developed, this framework should provide the basis for achieving a greater degree of consistency between accounting standards. It should also be useful to those involved in the preparation of accounts, helping them to understand accounting standards.

Comparing the ASC with the ASB a number of key areas of difference emerge:

(a) The ASB is answerable to, and appointed by, the FRC. This in turn is a body appointed by a range of interested parties. By contrast the ASC was under the control of the accounting profession. Thus accounting standard setting has moved from being an initiative of the accounting profession to being under the control of a broader based body with government input.

(b) The ASB issues standards in its own right rather than, as the ASC did, formulating standards for final approval, and possible amendment, by the CCAB bodies.

(c) The ASB is a smaller body than the ASC with two full-time members and payment for the other seven part-time members.

(d) The UITF offers a mechanism for addressing new issues rapidly.

(e) A potentially powerful new enforcement mechanism for ensuring compliance by large and listed companies has emerged.

(f) The new system is provided with resources at a level some eight times higher than the previous system.

(g) A statement of principles is being developed to underpin accounting standards and promote consistency.

Economic consequences

Observers of the work of the old ASC have noted that debate over accounting practice does not focus exclusively on technical issues. In practice, various affected parties perceive accounting standards as likely to have economic consequences, and lobby accordingly. Economic consequences can work in two ways:

(a) Various user groups may respond to changes in the information in the accounts with a changed view of the business, and change their economic behaviour accordingly.

(b) A business may be subject to some form of regulation or contract which uses the accounts as a measure of rights or obligations. As an example, the equity figure reported in the accounts is commonly used in measuring a company's borrowing powers.

It will be interesting to see how the new ASB copes with such issues.

International accounting standards

The International Accounting Standards Committee (IASC) was established in 1973, a revised constitution being agreed in 1977. As presently constituted the IASC has two classes of membership:

(a) Founder members, being the professional accounting bodies of the following nine countries:

Australia	Mexico
Canada	Netherlands
France	UK and Ireland*
Germany	USA
Japan	

Treated as one country for this purpose.

(b) Members, being accountancy bodies from countries other than the nine above which seek and are granted membership.

The business of the IASC is conducted by a Board comprising representatives:

(a) of each of the founder member countries;
(b) from two other member countries nominated by the nine founder members.

Each country represented on the Board shall have one vote.

The need for an International Accounting Standards Programme has been attributed to three factors:

(a) The growth in international investment. Investors in international capital markets are currently faced with making decisions based on published accounts based on accounting policies which will vary very widely according to the country of production. The harmonisation of International Accounting Standards will help investors to make more efficient decisions.
(b) The increasing prominence of multinational enterprises; such enterprises must produce accounts for the countries in which their shareholders reside and in the local country in which they operate. A harmonisation of accounting standards will help to avoid confusion and reduce the cost of producing multiple sets of accounts.
(c) The growth in the number of accounting standard setting bodies. It is hoped that the IASC can harmonise these separate rule-making efforts.

An additional benefit of the work of the IASC has been to make available to countries, which may be poor in human or financial resources necessary to operate their own accounting standards programmes, standards which they can republish for local domestic use.

IAS procedures

The procedure for publishing an international standard involves the following stages:

(a) The IASC selects a topic for consideration.
(b) The Board sets up a steering committee.

(c)   The steering committee prepares a draft standard.

(d)   The Board considers the draft at various stages; the accounting research committees of the founder member bodies offer guidance, finally a proposed exposure draft is approved by a two-thirds majority of the Board.

(e)   Comments are received over an exposure period of some six months.

(f)   The steering committee submits a revised draft standard to the IASC.

(g)   The Board approves a standard by a three to four majority.

Thus, as in the UK, there is a well-established procedure for consultation in drafting each accounting standard.

The members of the ASB are committed to use their best endeavours:

(a)   to ensure that accounts either comply or reveal non-compliance with international standards, and to recommend these to the appropriate authorities;

(b)   to ensure that where accounts fail to comply, or disclose non-compliance, auditors refer to this fact in the accounts.

In the UK and Republic of Ireland most IASs are covered by domestic SSAPs.

Conclusion

Accounting standards emerged in order to respond to demands from those who use company accounts for financial reports which are:

(a)   Comparable with those of other companies, an objective which can be met by narrowing the areas of difference and variety of accounting practice.

(b)   More informative in explaining the ways in which judgement is exercised in preparing the accounts, an objective which can be met by requiring fuller disclosure.

(c)   More meaningful, an objective which is difficult to achieve because of the subjectivity of the requirement. By a system of discussion and consultation prior to the issue of an SSAP the ASC tried to find some sort of consensus on what does constitute the most meaningful accounting practice.

In 1990 a new accounting regulatory framework was introduced. This draws on a wider base of sponsoring organisations, is more fully resourced, and has been endowed with greater authority. Some argue that this demonstrates some kind of failure of the old system. An alternative view is that the accounting standards developed by the ASC were successful in demonstrating the value of such a source of authority, leading to the more generously resourced and supported new system.

EXAMINATION PRACTICE

1.1   Compliance with accounting standards
By what means is compliance with accounting standards enforced?

2 | FRS 1: Now REVISED
Cash Flow Statements

Introduction

The two traditional accounting statements are the balance sheet, showing the position of the business at one point in time, and the profit and loss account, showing increases or decreases in the wealth of the business between two points in time. Accounting standard setters in the UK, as in many other countries, have seen a need for a third type of statement to focus on the flow of resources through a business between two balance sheet dates. Two types of statement have been put forward:

(a) In September 1991 the ASB issued its first standard, FRS 1: Cash Flow Statements, which analyses cash flows under five key headings.

(b) Previously, in July 1975, the ASC had issued SSAP 10: Statements of Source and Application of Funds, which focused on working capital movements. In July 1990 the ASC had issued ED 54: Cash Flow Statements, which proposed the move from the old SSAP 10 to the approach taken in FRS 1.

Summary of the statement

Definitions

FRS 1 defines 'cash flow' as:

> An increase or decrease in an amount of cash or cash equivalent resulting from a transaction.

Thus the focal point of the cash flow statement is identified as the total of 'cash' and 'cash equivalent'. These two terms are defined:

(a) *Cash:* 'Cash in hand and deposits repayable on demand with any bank or financial institution. Cash includes cash in hand and deposits denominated in foreign currencies.'

(b) *Cash equivalents:* 'Short-term, highly liquid investments which are readily convertible into known amounts of cash without notice and which were within three months of maturity when acquired; less advances from banks repayable within three months from the date of the advance. Cash equivalents include investments and advances denominated in foreign currencies provided that they fulfil the above criteria.'

Scope of the statement

While requiring in principle that accounts intended to give a true and fair view should include a cash flow statement, FRS 1 provides for an extensive range of exemptions:

(a)   All entities falling within the size limits provided under the Companies Act 1985 for classification as a small company. This exemption applies both to companies and other entities.

(b)   Wholly owned subsidiaries of European Community parent companies provided:
  (i)   the parent company publishes, in English, consolidated accounts which include the subsidiary and comply with UK, Irish, or EC Seventh Directive requirements;
  (ii)   the consolidated accounts include a consolidated cash flow statement;
  (iii)   the consolidated cash flow statement is in sufficient detail to identify the totals to be shown under FRS 1.

(c)   Building societies, as long as the law requires them to present a funds flow statement, and mutual life assurance companies.

Group accounts should include a cash flow statement for the group as a whole.

An insurance company should only include cash flows for the company itself, excluding flows relating to funds which the company manages.

Headings in the cash flow statement

FRS 1 requires cash flows to be analysed under five standard headings:

(a)   *Operating activities.* These are the cash flows relating to operating or trading activities. They may be reported on either a 'net' or a 'gross' basis as discussed below.

(b)   *Returns on investments and servicing of finance.* These are receipts resulting from owning an investment and payments made for the provision of finance. Examples of such inflows include interest received including tax recovered and dividends received net of related tax credits. Dividends received from associated companies should be shown separately. Examples of such outflows include interest paid, irrespective of whether or not it is capitalised, dividends paid excluding related ACT, and the interest element in finance lease rentals.

(c)   *Taxation.* This heading covers flows to and from the tax authorities relating to profits and capital gains, including ACT and purchases of certificates of tax deposit. It does not include other forms of tax such as VAT. VAT payments or receipts normally form part of operating cash flows. Irrecoverable VAT forms part of the related expense.

(d)   *Investing activities.* This heading covers cash flows from acquiring or disposing of fixed assets or current asset investments other than cash or cash equivalents.
  Cash inflows/outflows from investing activities include those arising from disposal/acquisition of:
  (i)   fixed assets;
  (ii)   subsidiaries, excluding cash balances included in the sale;
  (iii)   investments in other entities, with separate disclosure of associates;
  (iv)   loans to other entities.

(e) *Financing*. This heading covers cash flows from receipts of or repayments to external providers of finance in respect of amounts of principal. Inflows include receipts from share issues, debentures, loans, and other borrowings than cash or cash equivalents. Outflows include repayments of borrowings, the capital element of finance lease payments, expenses on issues of finance, and payments to redeem shares.

Operating cash flows – net or gross

There are two ways in which FRS 1 allows operating cash flows to be shown:

(a) The *net method*, otherwise called the *indirect method*, involves computation of the operating cash flows by adjusting the operating profits for non-cash charges and credits so that one figure of operating cash flow is shown.

(b) The *gross method*, otherwise called the *direct method*, involves showing individual operating cash receipts and payments such as cash receipts from customers, cash payments to suppliers, and cash payments for employees.

Whichever method is used, a note to the cash flow statement must show a reconciliation between operating profit and operating cash flow. Thus the information required by the indirect method must be given, while the information required by the direct method is optional.

Other requirements

Exceptional items

Cash flows relating to what are classified as exceptional items in the profit and loss account should be classified under the appropriate heading in the cash flow statement, with a note to the statement giving sufficient supporting detail for their effect to be understood.

Extraordinary items

Following the issue of FRS 3 (see Chapter 4) these should rarely, if ever, arise. Where they do, then, in extremely rare cases, it may be necessary to show them under a separate heading in the cash flow statement.

Foreign currency items

These should be translated in the cash flow statement on the same basis as in the profit and loss account. Cash flows on hedging transactions should be reported together with the related hedged item.

Group accounts

The cash flow statement of a group should only deal with cash flows in and out of the group. Thus cash flows within the group should cancel out in the group accounts. Dividends paid to the minority interest are an outflow under the heading 'returns on investments and servicing of finance', to be disclosed separately. Where equity accounting is applied, as for associated companies, only cash flows between the entity and the group should be reported.

When a subsidiary is acquired or disposed of, the amounts of cash or cash equivalents paid should be shown net of cash and cash equivalent balances within the subsidiary. A note to the cash flow statement should show the effects of acquisitions and disposals indicating:

(a)   how much of the consideration comprised cash and cash equivalents;
(b)   the amounts of cash and cash equivalents transferred within the subsidiary.

Where a subsidiary joins or leaves the group during the year, cash flows for the subsidiary should be brought into the cash flow statement for the same period as profit from the subsidiary is brought into the group profit and loss account. In the year the acquisition or disposal occurs the effect on amounts under each standard heading in the cash flow statement of the subsidiary acquired or disposed of should be shown.

Major non-cash transactions

Some material transactions do not result in cash flows. If necessary for an understanding of the underlying transactions, these should be disclosed in the notes to the cash flow statement.

Balance sheet reconciliations

The notes to the cash flow statement should show explanations of:

(a)   How the movements in cash and cash equivalents relate to changes between the opening and closing balance sheet cash amounts.
(b)   How financing cash flows relate to changes between the opening and closing balance sheet finance items.

These reconciliations should disclose separately movements from cash flows, differences from foreign currency translation, and other movements. Where several balance sheet amounts have to be combined to form the reconciliation there must be sufficient detail to enable the movements to be understood. Possible formats are discussed below.

Comparative figures

These must be given for the cash flow statement and related notes.

Preparation of the statement – exam technique

There are two routes to the preparation of the cash flow statement:

(a)   analysis of the cash books and records;
(b)   adjustment of balance sheet movements by elimination of non-cash movements and their analysis under the five cash flow statement headings.

The first approach gives easy access to the data needed to show operating cash flow on a 'gross' basis, but needs detailed analysis of transactions, is more complex in compilation of the reconciliation notes, and may be costly to apply. The second approach risks oversight of relevant adjustments but is easier to prepare, automatically provides a reconciliation between operating profit and operating cash flow, and is more familiar to those accustomed to preparing funds flow statements.

Given two different approaches to preparing the cash flow statement, examiners have a variety of ways in which they can present a cash flow statement. No one computational approach can embrace all of these. The well prepared candidate will:

(a)   be familiar with the format of the cash flow statement so as to be aware of the data which will need to be extracted from the question;
(b)   be alert to the range of differences between accrual and cash flow accounting so as to make appropriate adjustments.

Cash flow statement for the year ended . . .

Net cash inflow from operating activities
Returns on investment and servicing of finance

Net cash out/inflow from returns on investments and
   servicing of finance

Taxation

Investing activities

Net cash in/outflow from investing activities

Net cash in/outflow before financing

Financing

Net cash out/inflow from financing

In/decrease in cash and cash equivalents

Fig. 2.1 Outline cash flow statement.

Figure 2.1 shows an outline of a cash flow statement in compliance with FRS 1. This needs to be supported by a minimum of four notes:

1.   a reconciliation of operating profit to operating cash flows;
2.   an analysis of changes in cash and cash equivalents in the year;
3.   an analysis of the balance in cash and cash equivalents as shown in the balance sheet;
4.   an analysis of changes in financing during the year.

When preparing the cash flow statement by the indirect method a possible sequence is:

(a)   Prepare an outline of the statement itself and the four supporting notes. Preparation of the notes both provides a comprehensive answer and serves as a form of working schedule supporting the statement itself.

(b)   Work through each balance sheet heading analysing each movement in the year into its cash flow components, using supporting working notes when the analysis is too complex to show on the face of the solution. Areas of complexity traditionally include:

(i)   *Fixed assets.* The net balance can change for four reasons:
1.   Additions, shown as investing cash outflows.
2.   Depreciation, which is an expense in the profit and loss account which has not involved any cash flow and is therefore shown as an item added back to operating profit in computing operating cash flows.
3.   Disposals, where the sale proceeds are shown as an investing cash inflow and the profit and loss on disposal constitutes a final revision to the depreciation charge on the asset disposed of and accordingly is reflected in the adjustments to arrive at operating cash flows.
4.   Revaluations, which do not involve any cash flow and are simply cancelled out against related changes in the revaluation reserve.

(ii)   *Working capital items* such as stock, debtors, and creditors. Normally balance sheet movements in these items are part of the adjustments to reconcile operating profit to operating cash flow. However, where opening or closing balances include non-trading items such as liabilities for outstanding plant purchases or interest obligations then these should be adjusted in arriving at the related cash flow in the statement.

(iii)   *Share capital movements* can arise because of:
1.   Bonus issues, involving no cash flows, where the balance sheet movement is cancelled out against the related transfer from reserves.
2.   Issues for cash, where the cash inflow should be shown in the finance section of the statement inclusive of share premium.
3.   Issues in exchange for non-cash assets, such as shares exchanged for shares in another company. In this case no entry in the cash flow statement arises, except in so far as acquisition of a subsidiary brings cash or cash equivalent balances into the group balance sheet.

(iv)   *Reserve movements* arise for a variety of reasons. Changes in retained profits link back to the profit and loss accounts and relate back to operating profit, cash flows arising from returns on investments and servicing of finance such as dividends and interest, and taxation.

Worked example

The accounts and associated notes for Lorrequer Ltd are provided below. From these we will illustrate how a cash flow statement may be drawn up.

Lorrequer Ltd – balance sheet as at 31 March 19X2

	Notes	31 March 19X2 £000	31 March 19X2 £000	31 March 19X1 £000	31 March 19X1 £000
Fixed assets	(1)		3000		2800
Current assets:					
Stock		2250		1900	
Trade debtors		1180		860	
Other debtors	(2)	90		—	
Prepayments	(3)	30		40	
Cash at bank		—		340	
		3550		3140	
Current liabilities:					
Trade creditors		1340		1250	
Accruals	(3)	110		100	
Proposed dividends		150		200	
Taxation		410		390	
Overdraft		200		—	
		2210		1940	
Net current assets			1340		1200
			4340		4000
8% loan stock					
(repayable 31.12.X7)			1500		1500
			2840		2500
Ordinary shares of £1			1600		1200
Share premium			300		500
Retained profits			940		800
			2840		2500

Lorrequer Ltd – profit and loss account for the year to 31 March 19X2

	£000	£000
Turnover		4000
Cost of sales		1800
Gross profit		2200
Administration	445	
Distribution	820	
		1265
Operating profit		935
Interest receivable	(5)	
Interest payable	140	
		135
Profit before tax		800
Taxation		410
Profit after tax		390
Dividends:		
Interim	100	
Final	150	
		250
Retained profit for year		140

Note 1: Fixed assets

	Freehold property £000	Plant £000	Total £000
Cost 1.4.X1	1100	2800	3900
Additions at cost	320	590	910
Disposals at cost	(220)	—	(220)
Cost 31.3.X2	1200	3390	4590
Depreciation 1.4.X1	100	1000	1100
Charge for year	20	475	495
Depreciation on disposal	(5)		(5)
Depreciation 31.3.X2	115	1475	1590
NBV 31.3.X2	1085	1915	3000

During the year freehold property was sold for £390 000.

Note 2
'Other debtors' represents an amount receivable in relation to the sale of property.

Note 3
'Prepayments' and 'accruals' relate to the following items:

	Prepayments		Accruals	
	19X2	19X1	19X2	19X1
	£000	£000	£000	£000
PAYE			20	15
Other expenses	30	40	90	85
	30	40	110	100

Note 4
On 30 June 19X1 the share premium was reduced by a 1 for 4 bonus issue. On 1 January 19X2 100 000 new shares were issued for cash £2 per share.

Note 5
Stock and cost of sales relate entirely to bought-in goods. Admininstration and distribution costs consist of:

	Administration	Distribution
	£000	£000
Depreciation	105	390
Wages and salaries	415	200
Other expenses	100	230
Profit on property sale	(175)	
	445	820

Applying this procedure to the example Lorrequer Ltd we would first draw up an outline of the cash flow statement as shown above. We then work through the balance sheet as follows:

(a) The movement in fixed assets is analysed in the question:
  (i) Additions at cost represent an investing cash outflow for the year, since there is no evidence of an opening or closing creditor for these.
  (ii) The depreciation charge has been recorded in the profit and loss account as an expense but does not involve any cashflow. Accordingly this is added back to operating profit in order to compute cash flow from operations.
  (iii) The sale of property may be summarised as follows:

	£000
Cost	220
Depreciation	5
	215
Profit on sale	175
Sale price	390

The 'profit on sale' is the result of an investing activity, and accordingly must be deducted from the operating profit. The sale price of £390 000 has apparently not been received in full, since Note 2 tells us that £90 000 'other debtors' relates to this sale. Accordingly only cash received (£390 000 – £90 000 = £300 000) is shown under investing activities.

(b) Stock has increased by £350 000. To this extent operating profit has not resulted in cash flow, instead being tied up in increased working capital. Accordingly this amount is deducted from operating profit.

(c) The increase in trade debtors of £320 000, as with the increase in stock, must be deducted from operating profit.

(d) The increase in other debtors has already been accounted for in considering the related sale of property.

(e) Like stock and debtors, the change in prepayments (in this case a reduction) is reflected in the adjustments to operating profit.

(f) The decrease in the bank balance forms part of the change in the net cash balance, and is shown in Note 3 to the statement.

(g) The increase in trade creditors is added to operating profit to find operating cash flow.

(h) The increase in accruals is added to operating profit to find operating cash flow.

(i) To find the cash outflow on dividends a simple schedule is prepared:

	£000
Proposed dividend b/fwd	200
+ P&L appropriation for year	250
− Proposed dividend c/fwd	(150)
= Cash paid in year	300

The cash outflow is then recorded on the face of the cash flow statement as part of servicing of finance.

(j) A similar schedule to that prepared above identifies the cash outflow related to tax:

	£000
Liability b/fwd	390
+ P&L change	410
− Liability c/fwd	(410)
= Cash paid	390

(k) The increase in the overdraft forms part of the cash change, and again is included in Note 3.

(l) The changes in share capital and share premium are normally best taken together. In this case the net increase of £200 000 clearly represents the proceeds of the share issue and should be shown in the financing section of the cash flow statement.

(m) The movement of retained profits is explained by the profit and loss account. Taking the items shown:

(i) Operating profit is shown at the head of Note 1 on operating cash flows.

(ii) In the absence of information to the contrary, interest receivable and payable is assumed to represent cash flows and accordingly are shown as 'return on investment' and 'servicing of finance'.

The cash flow statement as prepared above is shown in full opposite.

Lorrequer Ltd – cash flow statement for the year ending 31 March 19X2

	£000	£000
Net cash inflow from operating activities (Note 1)		695
Returns on investments and servicing of finance:		
Interest received	5 (m)	
Interest paid	(140)(m)	
Dividends paid	(300) (i)	
Net cash outflow from returns on investments and servicing of finance		(435)
Taxation:		
Corporation tax paid		(390)
Investing activities:		
Payment to acquire property	(320) (a)	
Payment to acquire plant	(590) (a)	
Receipt from sale of property	300 (a)	
		(610)
Net cash outflow before financing		(740)
Financing:		
Issue of ordinary share capital		200 (l)
Decrease in cash ((340)(f) + (200)(k))		(540)

Notes to cash flow statement

1. Reconciliation of operating cash flows to operating profit

	£000	£000
Operating profit		935 (m)
Depreciation charge	495 (a)	
Profit on property sale	(175)(a)	
Stock increase	(350)(b)	
Debtor increase	(320)(c)	
Prepayment decrease	10 (e)	
Trade creditor increase	90 (g)	
Accrual increase	10 (h)	
		(240)
Net cash inflow from operating activities		695

2. Analysis of changes in cash and cash equivalents during the year

	£000
Balance at 1.4.X1	340
Net cash outflow in year	(540)
Balance at 31.3.X2	(200)

3. Analysis of the balance in cash and cash equivalents as shown in the balance sheet

	31.3.X2 £000	31.2.X1 £000	Change £000
Cash at bank	—	340	(340)
Overdraft	(200)	—	(200)
	(200)	340	(540)

4. Analysis of changes in financing during the year

	Share capital and premium £000
Balance at 1.4.X1	1700
Net cash inflow in year	200
Balance at 31.3.X2	1900

Controversy over the statement

Funds flow or cash flow?

As we have seen above, FRS 1 with its requirement to present a cash flow statement replaces SSAP 10 with its requirement to present a funds flow statement. In an 'explanation' accompanying FRS 1 the ASB offers the following arguments in support of this change:

(a)   Where a funds flow statement focuses on working capital this may obscure cash movements.
(b)   Cash flow is a clearer concept than changes in working capital.
(c)   Cash flow relates directly to a business valuation model.
(d)   The cash flow statement and related notes as required by FRS 1 introduces data not shown in a funds flow statement.

SSAP 10 was criticised not only for the inherent limitations of 'funds flow' as opposed to 'cash flow' but also because of the failure to define 'funds' and to provide firm guidance on formats. As a result, companies adopted a range of approaches that meant that funds flow statements were not easily compared.

Internationally there is a trend, particularly in the English speaking world, to move from funds flow statements to cash flow statements. Countries making this move have included the USA (1987), New Zealand (1987) and Australia (1992).

Formats

FRS 1 offers a range of illustrative formats:

(a) a simple single company arrangement, as shown above;
(b) a group cash flow statement;
(c) an investment property company;
(d) an investment company;
(e) a bank;
(f) an insurance company.

This comprehensive guidance responds to one of the criticisms made of SSAP 10.

The form of presentation chosen by FRS 1 contrasts with that in Australia, New Zealand and the USA, by having five major headings rather than three. Table 2.1 shows the differences between the four countries. During 1992 New Zealand revised their first cash flow statement, 'SSAP 10' to a new statement, FRS 10. It is interesting to note that in the light of experience New Zealand accountants moved in line with the US and Australian formats. By contrast the UK has chosen to adopt a distinctly different format, thereby making international comparison more difficult.

Table 2.1 Main components of cash flow statement

USA FAS 95	UK FRS 1	Australia AASB 1026	New Zealand SSAP 10	New Zealand FRS 10
Operating activities (includes taxation, dividends received, interest received and paid)	Operating activities	Operating activities (illustration includes taxation, returns on investments, and interest paid)	Operating activities (includes taxation)	Operating activities (includes taxation, dividends received, interest received and paid)
	Returns on investments and servicing finance			
	Taxation			
Investing activities	Investing activities	Investing activities	Investing activities (includes returns on investments)	Investing activities
Financing (includes dividends paid)	Financing	Financing (includes dividends paid)	Financing (includes servicing of finance)	Financing (includes dividends paid)

Gross method vs. net method

By requiring a note to the funds statement to show the reconciliation between operating profit and operating cash flows FRS 1 effectively requires that the 'net method' be shown. FRS 1 also permits, but does not require, disclosure of the cash flow that constitutes the 'gross' method. In the USA a similar choice is permitted, with the vast majority of companies opting for the 'net' method. This is not surprising, given that this is simpler and less costly. However, US analysts have criticised this approach on the grounds that there is a problem of comparability. In both Australia and New Zealand the 'gross' method is prescribed. When the requirement was reviewed in New Zealand 47 respondents supported its continuance, compared with 6 against.

The 'objectivity' of cash flow

One benefit argued in favour of the cash flow statement is that 'cash flow' is an objective fact not subject to the manipulation that can arise with accrual accounting. While the opportunity for such manipulation is less, in practice it still exists. For example, a short-term investment with less than three months to maturity at the time of purchase is a 'cash equivalent', while where there is more than three months to maturity then an 'investment' arises. Judicious manipulation of such investments can, therefore, change the apparent position on cash flow.

Using the cash flow statement

The cash flow statement gives a useful picture of how the overall liquidity of a business has increased or diminished. For example, a glance at the example of Lorrequer Ltd above shows how:

(a)   increases in stock and debtors have absorbed a major part of operating cash flow;
(b)   substantial new long-term investments have not been supported by long-term finance.

A range of ratios can also be computed. Broadly speaking these are identified in two ways:

(a)   The ratios used to relate the components of accruals-based accounts can be adapted to relate the equivalent components of cash flow. For example, the relationship between operating cash flows gives an insight into gearing.
(b)   Ratios can be computed relating cash flows to accruals-based data. For example, the ratio of cash inflows from customers to accruals-based turnover gives insight into the control of trade credit, and avoids the problem of using balance sheet debtor figures that might be distorted by the year-end date. Another example is the ratio of operating cash flow to total assets, which gives a picture of the liquidity generated from asset utilisation.

A commonly quoted ratio is that of operating cash flow to operating profit, often referred to as 'quality of earnings'.

Conclusion

The cash flow statement commands widespread support as a stronger guide to a company's liquidity position than the funds flow statement. The formats used in FRS 1 are somewhat different from those used in other countries, and some aspects, such as the definition of cash equivalents, are open to question.

EXAMINATION PRACTICE

2.1 Forecast cash flow statement

The balance sheet of Chiron Ltd as at 31 March 19X6 together with its projected balance sheet as at 31 March 19X7 and profit and loss account for the year ending on that date is as follows:

Chiron Ltd – Balance sheets as at:

	31 March 19X6		31 March 19X7	
	£000	£000	£000	£000
Ordinary share capital in £1 shares fully paid		200		250
Capital reserve:				
Share premium a/c				25
Profit and loss a/c		70		108
		270		383
Represented by:				
Fixed assets:				
Freehold premises – cost		60		90
Plant and machinery at cost less depreciation		48		125
		108		215
Current assets:				
Stock	140		170	
Debtors	100		120	
Cash	1		2	
	241		292	
Less: Current liabilities:				
Trade creditors	40		64	
Accrued expenses	1		2	
Corporation tax	16		26	
Proposed dividends	16		20	
Bank overdraft	6		12	
	79	162	124	168
		270		383

Budgeted profit and loss account for the year ended 31 March 19X7

	£000	£000
Sales		300
Cost of sales (including plant depreciation £28 000)		180
Gross profit		120
Distribution	15	
Administration	19	
		34
Operating profit		86
Bank interest		2
Profit before tax		84
Tax		26
Profit after tax		58
Proposed dividend		20
Retained profit for the year		38

You are required to prepare a predicted cash flow statement for the year to 31 March 19X7 with supporting notes as required by FRS 1.

2.2   Preparation of cash flow statement
The balance sheets of Beatem Ltd as at 31 March 19X8 (with comparative figures as at 31 March 19X7), together with other pertinent information, are given below:

	31 March 19X8		31 March 19X7	
Balance sheet as at:	£000	£000	£000	£000
Share capital – ordinary shares of £1 each fully paid		1 200		1 000
Reserves:				
Share premium		550		600
Retained profits		3 725		3 500
		5 475		5 100
Debentures – 8% £1 Convertible		2 000		—
Current liabilities:				
Bank overdraft	1 750		1 500	
Creditors	1 450		1 550	
Taxation	820		1 150	
		4 020		4 200
		11 495		9 300

Fixed assets:			
Land and building at cost		3 500	1 800
Plant and machinery at cost	6 100		5 800
Less: Depreciation	3 900		3 850
		2 200	1 950
		5 700	3 750
Current assets:			
Stock and work in progress	3 435		3 150
Debtors	2 200		1 900
Cash and bank balance	160		500
		5 795	5 550
		11 495	9 300

Note 1

The profit for the year 19X8, after charging all expenses including the loss on the sale of the plant, but before interest depreciation and taxation, was £2 015 000. The corporation tax of £820 000 charged in the profit and loss account on the profits for the year was reduced by the over provision for corporation tax on the 19X7 profit, i.e. by £150 000. The ordinary dividend paid during the year and charged against the profit after tax was £180 000. Interest of £300 000 was made up of:

	£	
Debenture interest	160 000	(£80 000 accrual included in creditors)
Overdraft interest	140 000	(all paid in year)

Note 2

During the year, plant and machinery which had cost £1 200 000 and in respect of which depreciation of £590 000 had been provided was sold for £565 000. There had been a rights issue of ordinary shares at the rate of 1 for 10 at a price of £1.50 per share payable in full on 1 April 19X7. Subsequently, a scrip (bonus) issue of 1 for 11 had been made utilising the share premium account. The convertible debentures had been issued at par on 1 April 19X7, payable in full. The conversion terms exercisable on 31 March 19Y1 are 1 ordinary share for every 4 £1 debentures. Agreed corporation tax of £1 million on the 19X7 profits had been paid on the due date.

You are required to:
Prepare a cash flow statement for the year ended 31 March 19X8 bearing in mind the requirements of FRS 1.

2.3   Treatment of items in the cash flow statement

The Directors of Vienne Ltd wish to prepare a consolidated cash flow statement in line with FRS 1: Cash Flow Statements. They are uncertain how to deal with a number of items which are listed below.

1. Consolidated creditors decreased by £70 000.
2. Vienne Ltd declared and distributed a 50% scrip issue on the share capital of £10 million, in fully-paid ordinary shares of £1 each.

3. The minority interest in a cash dividend declared and paid by a consolidated subsidiary was £10 000.
4. Equipment costing £90 000 was purchased from outside the group.
5. Following the year-end date, the directors declared a final dividend of £400 000.
6. On 30 October 19X2 £48 000 had been spent on 4% loan stock with a nominal value of £50 000 maturing on 15 February 19X3.
7. Vienne Ltd's share of the profits of an associated company were £52 000 for the year. No dividend was received from the associate in the year.
8. Loan stock of £100 000 was redeemed at par during the year.
9. Plant with a net book value of £40 000 was scrapped during the year with no proceeds arising from the disposal.
10. On 30 November 19X2 damages for defective workmanship at £400 000 were awarded against the company. The court agreed that no payment need be made pending an appeal to be heard in April 19X3.

In order to identify the appropriate treatment of these items the Directors have specified the following symbols:

AO   Add to operating profit in determining cash flow from operating activities.
DO   Deduct from operating profit in determining cash flow from operating activities.
R   Include in returns on investments and servicing of finance.
T   Include in taxation.
I   Include in investing activities.
F   Include in financing.
A   Include in analysis of cash and cash equivalents.
N   No effect on the cash flow statement.

You are required to indicate now each of the items 1–10 listed above should be disclosed in the consolidated cash flow statement of Vienne Ltd, making use of the symbols specified by the directors.

You are *not* required to rewrite the question. Merely list the items in sequence and opposite each item record the symbol you think appropriate.

3 | FRS 2: Accounting for Subsidiary Undertakings

Introduction

Evolution of group accounts

The holding company originated in the USA, the first recorded instance arising in 1832. Accountants soon came to appreciate the weakness of a holding company's own accounts showing only its own income and balance sheet position. The concept of presenting group accounts to the shareholders of the holding company in order to overcome these weaknesses developed in the USA earlier than in the UK. For example, Dicksee's *Auditing* first mentions the desirability of consolidated accounts in the 1908 American edition, but the subject is only included in the English edition from 1924 onwards. The first consolidated balance sheet presented in the UK was at the AGM of Nobel Industries Ltd, in September 1922, while in 1923 Sir Gilbert Garnsey published his *Holding Companies and Their Published Accounts*. In 1939 the London Stock Exchange introduced rules concerning consolidated accounts and the Companies Act 1947 (later consolidated into the Companies Act 1948) introduced a legal requirement to present group accounts. While company law defined the general nature of group accounts together with certain specific requirements relating to their production and content, experience has revealed a number of areas of controversy and variation in practice. SSAP 14, issued in September 1978, narrowed some of these areas of difference.

In the light of the Companies Act 1989 a new standard was required and FRS2 fills this need.

Scope of the chapter

It would clearly be unreasonable to attempt to cover the whole topic of group accounts in one chapter; at the same time it is not practical to consider FRS 2 in isolation from a knowledge and understanding of consolidation procedures. Such a knowledge will therefore be assumed in this chapter, although for the sake of clarity some requirements of the accounting standard will be compared with the related requirements of the Companies Acts.

Summary of the statement

Definitions

FRS 2 identifies the legislation governing consolidated accounts as 'The Act' being the 'Companies Act 1985 as amended by the Companies Act 1989'. The term 'undertaking' is defined as:

> A body corporate, a partnership or an unincorporated association carrying on a trade or business with or without a view to profit.

This reflects the broader responsibility to consolidate which, previously, referred only to corporate bodies.

The definition of the situation where a 'parent undertaking' has a 'subsidiary undertaking' identifies the following circumstances:

(a) Where

> It holds a majority of the voting rights in the undertaking.

The key term here is 'voting rights in an undertaking' defined as:

> Rights conferred on shareholders in respect of their shares or, in the case of an undertaking not having a share capital, on members; to vote at general meetings of the undertaking on all, or substantially all, matters. Schedule 10A deals with the attribution of voting rights in certain circumstances.

(b) Where

> It is a member of the undertaking and has the right to appoint or remove directors holding a majority of the voting rights at meetings of the board on all, or substantially all, matters.

(c) Where

> It has the right to exercise a dominant influence over the undertaking:

> (i) by virtue of provisions contained in the undertaking's memorandum or articles; or
> (ii) by virtue of a control contract. The control contract must be in writing and be of a kind authorised by the memorandum or articles of the controlled undertaking. It must also be permitted by the law under which that undertaking is established.

The key term 'dominant influence' is defined:

> Influence that can be exercised to achieve the operating and financial policies desired by the holder of the influence of any other party.

> (a) The right to exercise a dominant influence means that the holder has a right to give directions with respect to the operating and financial policies of another undertaking with which its directors are obliged to comply, whether or not they are for the benefit of that undertaking.

> (b) The actual exercise of dominant influence is the exercise of an influence that achieves the result that the operating and financial policies of the undertaking influenced are set in accordance with the wishes of the holder of the influence and for the holder's benefit whether or not those wishes are explicit. The actual exercise of dominant influence is identified by its effect in practice rather than by the way in which it is exercised.

And 'control' is defined:

> The ability of an undertaking to direct the financial and operating policies of another undertaking with a view to gaining economic benefits from its activities.

(d) Where

> It is a member of the undertaking and controls alone, pursuant to an agreement with other shareholders or members, a majority of the voting rights in the undertaking.

(e) Where

> It has a participating interest in the undertaking and:
>
> (i) it actually exercises a dominant influence over the undertaking; or
> (ii) it and the undertaking are managed on a unified basis.

The key term 'managed on a unified basis' is defined:

> Two or more undertakings are managed on a unified basis if the whole of the operations of the undertakings are integrated and they are managed as a single unit. Unified management does not arise solely because one undertaking manages another.

And the key term 'participating interest':

> An interest held by an undertaking in the shares of another undertaking which it holds on a long-term basis for the purpose of securing a contribution to its activities by the exercise of control or influence arising from or related to that interest [from s.260].
>
> (a) A holding of 20% or more of the shares of an undertaking shall be presumed to be a participating interest unless the contrary is shown.
> (b) An interest in shares includes an interest which is convertible into an interest in shares, and includes an option to acquire shares or any interest which is convertible into shares.
> (c) An interest held on behalf of an undertaking shall be treated as held by that undertaking.

Consolidation is defined as:

> The process of adjusting and combining financial information from the individual financial statements of a parent undertaking and its subsidiary undertakings to prepare consolidated financial statements that present financial information for the group as a single economic entity.

Key terms in deciding whether or not consolidation should apply are:

(i) Interest on a long-term basis:

> An interest which is held other than exclusively with a view to subsequent resale.

(ii) Interest held exclusively with a view to subsequent resale:

> (a) An interest for which a purchaser has been sought, and which is reasonably expected to be disposed of within approximately one year of its date of acquisition; or
> (b) an interest that was acquired as a result of the enforcement of a security, unless the interest has become part of the continuing activities of the group or the holder acts as if it intends the interest to become so.

While some subsidiaries excluded from consolidation are subject to the 'equity method' defined as:

A method of accounting for an investment that brings into the consolidated profit and loss account the investor's share of the investment undertaking's results and that records the investment in the consolidated balance sheet at the investor's share of the investment undertaking's net assets including any goodwill arising to the extent that it has not previously been written off.

The equity method is discussed in detail in Chapter 5 below on SSAP 1.

Scope and exemptions

The situations where a parent undertaking is excluded from an obligation to present consolidated accounts are explained in detail in company law and falls under two broad headings:

(a)   A size exemption embracing most small and medium sized companies.
(b)   An exemption where the parent is itself a subsidiary of another EC company. The detailed conditions for this exemption to apply are specified in company law.

FRS 2 provides that a parent undertaking should disclose the grounds for exemption.

Exclusion of subsidiaries from consolidation

There are a number of circumstances where company law permits or requires the exclusion of subsidiaries from the consolidated accounts. FRS 2 defines these situations more closely, working on a broad principle that: 'The FRS requires the circumstances in which subsidiary undertakings are to be excluded from consolidation to be interpreted strictly.' The company law provisions for permitting exclusion are:

(a)   Inclusion of the subsidiary in the consolidated accounts would not be material. Two or more subsidiaries may only be excluded where taken together they are not material.
(b)   The information necessary to prepare consolidated accounts cannot be obtained without disproportionate expense or undue delay. FRS 2 effectively tightens up this provision by stating that it cannot be applied unless the subsidiaries to be excluded are not individually or collectively material to the group, i.e. the first exemption above applies in any case.
(c)   Severe long-term restrictions substantially hinder the exercise of the parents' rights over the assets or management of the undertaking. Where this situation arises FRS 2 *requires* exclusion, as opposed to company law which merely *permits* exclusion.
(d)   The parent's interest in the undertaking is acquired and held exclusively with a view to subsequent sale. Again, whereas company law *permits*, FRS 2 *requires* exclusion in this case.
(e)   Company law *requires* exclusion where the activities of one or more subsidiaries are so different from those of the other undertakings included in the consolidated accounts that their inclusion would be incompatible with the obligation to give a true and fair view. FRS 2 seeks to minimise the application of this exemption by:
    (i)   citing the clause in the Companies Act that exclusion on these grounds does not apply 'merely because some of the undertakings are industrial,

some commercial and some provide services, or because they carry on industrial or commercial activities involving different products or provide different services';

(ii) adding the observation that 'it is exceptional for such circumstances to arise and it is not possible to identify any particular contrast of activities where the necessary incompatibility with the true and fair view generally occurs';

(iii) also suggesting that where the activities of different undertakings contrast then a true and fair view may be achieved by supporting the consolidated accounts with appropriate segmental information.

FRS 2 reaffirms the provision of company law that the names of any subsidiaries excluded from consolidation must be shown, with the reasons for exclusion.

Accounting for excluded subsidiaries

The way in which excluded subsidiaries should be accounted for in the consolidated accounts depends on the reasons for exclusion:

(a) Where severe long-term restrictions hinder the exercise of the rights of the parent undertaking then the treatment depends on the date at which the restrictions came into force. If the restrictions were in force at the acquisition date then the subsidiary will be carried at cost from the start. If restrictions come into force at a later date then the subsidiary will cease to be consolidated at that date and will instead by recorded as an investment at an amount based on the equity method, i.e. associated company treatment. While the restrictions are in force no further accruals should be made for the profits or losses of the subsidiary unless there is a significant degree of influence, despite the restrictions, to justify treatment as an associated company. Both the carrying value of such investments and intra-group amounts due from them should be reviewed each year and written down for any permanent diminution in value.

(b) Where an investment in a subsidiary is held exclusively with a view to subsequent resale then it should be recorded as a current asset at the lower of cost and net realisable value.

(c) Where exclusion is on the grounds of different activities then, as required by company law, the equity method (i.e. associated company treatment) should be used.

A number of special disclosure requirements for subsidiaries excluded from consolidation are provided in FRS 2:

(a) Particulars of balances between the excluded subsidiaries and the rest of the group.

(b) The nature and extent of transactions of the excluded subsidiaries with the rest of the group.

(c) Where the equity method is not applied to the excluded subsidiary any amounts included in the consolidated accounts for:

(i) dividends received and receivable from the subsidiary.

(ii) any write down of the investment in or amounts due from the subsidiary.

(d) Where a subsidiary is excluded because of different activities, separate accounts for the subsidiary. Summarised information may be provided for subsidiaries that, individually or in combination with similar operations, do not account for more than 20 per cent of any of operating profits, turnover or net assets of the whole group (including excluded subsidiaries).

Disclosure requirements for excluded subsidiaries must apply to the individual subsidiary if it accounts for more than 20 per cent of any of the operating profits, turnover or net assets of the whole group. For other subsidiaries disclosure may be made on an aggregate basis for sub-units of subsidiaries which together fall under one of the grounds for exclusion from consolidation.

Minority interests

The balance sheet should show the minority's share of capital and reserves under the heading 'minority interests' while the profit and loss account should similarly show separately the aggregate of profit or loss on ordinary items attributable to 'minority interest', with the minority share in any extraordinary items shown separately. The minority share of losses in a subsidiary are attributable in principle even where this results in the interest being in a net liability rather than an asset; however, in this case the group will need to make a provision to the extent that there is a commercial or legal obligation, whether formal or implied, to finance any such deficit that cannot be recovered from the minority.

Where, on consolidation, adjustments are made to the values attributed to the assets or liabilities of a subsidiary, then the appropriate adjustment should be made to the minority interest. However, no acquisition goodwill should be allocated to the minority.

Profits or losses on transactions between group companies must be eliminated in full on consolidation, irrespective of whether the subsidiary concerned is included within the consolidation or not. The appropriate part of the consolidation adjustment must be allocated to the minority interests. In this respect FRS 2 is less flexible than company law, which permits the alternative treatment of restricting the elimination of profits or losses on intra-group transactions to the portion attributable to the controlling entity.

Consolidation accounting policies

Common account policies should be used in preparing the consolidated accounts with adjustments being made to the accounts of subsidiaries with different accounting policies. In exceptional cases where different accounting policies are used on consolidation then disclosure of the particulars, including details of the different accounting policies used, must be made.

In preparing the consolidated accounts the accounts of the subsidiaries should all cover the same period and run to the same date as the parent. If this is impracticable then:

(a)   If possible, interim accounts should be prepared to a common accounting date.
(b)   Failing the above, accounts of the subsidiary for its last financial year should be used, provided that these are prepared to a date within three months of the

parent undertaking's year end. In this case any material changes in the intervening period must be taken into account as consolidation adjustments. For any subsidiary where the year end or accounting period does not coincide with that of the parent the following must be disclosed:

(i)   the name of the subsidiary;
(ii)   the accounting date or period of the subsidiary;
(iii) the reason for the difference.

Changes in the group

FRS 2 addresses a number of issues that arise at the time when a subsidiary becomes or ceases to be a subsidiary, or the holding in the subsidiary changes.

The date for commencing to account for a subsidiary is the day when acquisition or merger takes place. The date for ceasing to account for a subsidiary is that when the parent relinquishes control.

In the year an undertaking ceases to be a subsidiary the consolidated results will include both the appropriate share of the subsidiary's results up to the date of cessation and any gain or loss on cessation, calculated as the difference between:

(a)   the amount at which the net assets of the subsidiary, including goodwill, are carried in the accounts, and
(b)   any proceeds of disposal plus the amount at which any interest in the undertaking continues to be carried in the accounts.

The consolidated accounts should give the name of any material undertaking that has ceased to be a subsidiary, showing any ownership interest retained. If cessation is not attributable to a disposal then the circumstances should be explained. Similarly, where an undertaking has become or ceased to be a subsidiary other than by a purchase or share exchange then the circumstances should be explained.

Where a subsidiary is acquired in stages then the deemed date of acquisition is the date on which the part of the investment that causes the undertaking to become a subsidiary is acquired. Thus it is on that date that the fair value of all the identifiable assets and liabilities of the subsidiary must be computed, with the consequent quantification of consolidation goodwill. If a further interest in an existing subsidiary is acquired then a further valuation of identifiable assets and liabilities to compute acquisition goodwill in relation to the further interest will be required, if material.

Where there is a reduction in the interest held in an undertaking that continues to be a subsidiary then:

(a)   a profit and loss on disposal will be computed as the difference between:
    (i)   the disposal proceeds, and
    (ii)   the reduction in the carrying amount of the subsidiary including goodwill;
(b)   the portion of identifiable net assets, but not goodwill, removed from the parent share in consolidated accounts will be attributed to the minority interest.

Other disclosures

Where there are significant restrictions on dividend payments by subsidiaries, thereby limiting the parent's access to their retained profits, then the nature and extent of the restrictions should be disclosed. Where there is a possibility of tax arising on the remittance of accumulated reserves of overseas subsidiaries:

(a)   the extent of any related deferred tax provision must be disclosed;
(b)   the reason for not making any provision in full must be disclosed.

Conclusion

FRS 2 is unusual as an accounting standard in covering an area where company law already provides a range of highly detailed prescription. It is interesting that in that context the ASB have chosen explicitly to restrict further the limited range of choice permitted by legislation. Since these matters have recently been ruled on by Parliament in the Companies Act 1989 the ASB might be open to criticism for seeking to deny companies areas of choice that the legislation explicitly allows them.

The flow chart in Fig. 3.1 provides a summary of FRS 2's rules on exemptions from consolidation.

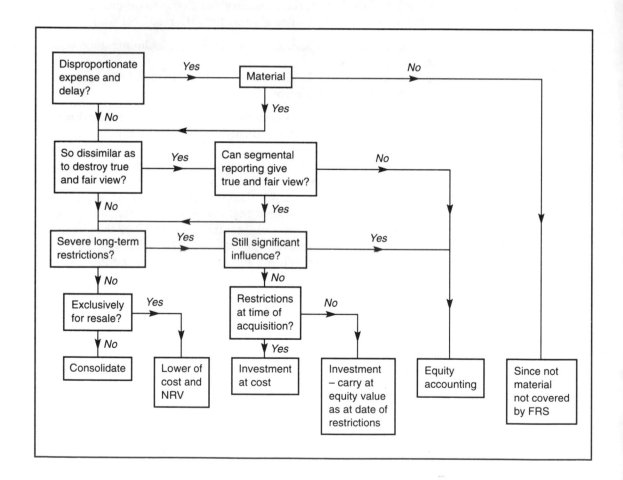

Fig. 3.1   How to account for a subsidiary.

FRS 2 should also be considered in conjunction with a number of other standards:

(a) FRS 3 amplifies the treatment of acquired and discontinued operations.
(b) SSAP 1 deals with equity accounting.
(c) SSAP 20 deals with the translation of subsidiary accounts in a foreign currency.
(d) SSAP 22 deals with consolidation goodwill.
(e) SSAP 23 deals with acquisitions and mergers.
(f) SSAP 25 deals with the segmental reporting rules that might help solve the 'dissimilar activities' problem.

EXAMINATION PRACTICE

3.1 Exclusion from consolidation

Prepare a note on the circumstances in which UK company law and FRS 2: Accounting for Subsidiary Undertakings allow a subsidiary to be excluded from consolidation, and explain how excluded subsidiaries should be accounted for in the consolidated accounts.

4 FRS 3: Reporting Financial Performance

Introduction

Accountants have to decide to what extent gains or losses should be included within their definition of profit for the year, how to analyse and present that figure of profit in a meaningful way, and how to disclose other gains or losses in the accounts. In 1974 the ASC issued SSAP 6: Extraordinary Items and Prior Year Adjustments to address this issue. As we shall see below, this was a difficult standard to formulate and enforce. FRS 3, issued in October 1992, replaced SSAP 6. It is the first standard to be based on an exposure draft issued by the ASB, FRED 1, since both FRS 1 and FRS 2 were based on exposure drafts issued by the old ASC.

The basic issue

There are two broad approaches to the presentation of the profit and loss account. One, the 'current operating income' approach, involves disclosing on the face of the profit and loss account only those items relating to the normal recurring activities of the company. Advocates of this approach argue that this profit figure provides a more meaningful guide to profits and gives a useful indication of management's achievement in running the business. The approach is also referred to as 'reserve accounting', on the grounds that other gains and losses are recorded as reserve movements.

The alternative is the 'all-inclusive' concept of profit, that the profit and loss account should include not only the results of ordinary activities but also all other profits and losses for the year. Arguments in support of this approach are:

(a) With disclosure rules requiring separate identification of items outside the normal course of trading, the profit or loss on normal recurring items can still be identified.
(b) Exclusion of certain items is necessarily subjective, and could lead to loss of comparability between companies.
(c) Exclusion of certain items may also result in items being overlooked in any consideration of results over a number of years.

Both SSAP 6 and FRS 3 have been based, in principle, on the 'all-inclusive' approach. The main difference between them is that SSAP 6 provided for separate identification of 'extraordinary items' in such a way that these could be regarded as falling outside normal profit. This separate identification was taken up by the

European Community in the Fourth Directive and consequently enshrined in UK company law. It appears that, in formulating FRS 3, the ASB would have liked to abolish the category 'extraordinary item'. They felt unable to do this because the term is established in law, but have sought to achieve their objective by defining the term so restrictively that it is unlikely to be used in practice.

Summary of the statement

Definitions

The definitions provided in FRS 3 reflect the ASB's intention to restrict the exclusion of items from the reporting of normal activities.

Ordinary activities are defined as:

Any activities which are undertaken by a reporting entity as part of its business and such related activities in which the reporting entity engages in furtherance of, incidental to, or arising from, these activities. Ordinary activities include the effects on the reporting entity of any event in the various environments in which it operates, including the political, regulatory, economic and geographical environments, irrespective of the frequency or unusual nature of the events.

This is a more comprehesive definition than that previously provided in SSAP 6, particularly in its reference to the inclusion within ordinary activities of all events within the various environments in which the business operates.

Acquisitions are defined in a straightforward way as:

Operations of the reporting entity that are acquired in the period.

Discontinued operations are defined in some detail as:

Operations of the reporting entity that are sold or terminated and that satisfy all of the following conditions:

(a) The sale or termination is completed either in the period or before the earlier of three months after the commencement of the subsequent period and the date on which the financial statements are approved.
(b) If a termination, the former activities have ceased permanently.
(c) The sale or termination has a material effect on the nature and focus of the reporting entity's operations and represents a material reduction in its operating facilities resulting either from its withdrawal from a particular market (whether class of business or geographical) or from a material reduction in turnover in the reporting entity's continuing markets.
(d) The assets, liabilities, results of operations are clearly distinguishable, physically, operationally and for financial reporting purposes.

Operations not satisfying all these conditions are classified as continuing.

Exceptional items, which fall within the results of ordinary activities while calling for extra disclosure, are defined as:

Material items which derive from events or transactions that fall within the ordinary activities of the reporting entity and which individually or, if of a similar type, in aggregate need to be disclosed by virtue of their size or incidence if the financial statements are to give a true and fair view.

In contrast to the above definition, which is a broad one, the definition of an *extraordinary item* is tightly drawn:

Material items possessing a high degree of abnormality which arise from events or transactions that fall outside the ordinary activities of the reporting entity and which are not expected to recur. They do not include exceptional items nor do they include prior period items merely because they relate to a prior period.

The term *prior period adjustments* is defined as:

Material adjustments applicable to prior periods arising from changes in accounting policies or from the correction of fundamental errors. They do not include exceptional items nor do they include prior period items merely because they relate to a prior period.

This is the same definition as that previously used in SSAP 6 except that 'period' has been used in place of 'year', presumably on the grounds that the accounting period is not necessarily of exactly one year, e.g. where there is a change of accounting date.

A new term introduced in FRS 3 is *total recognised gains and losses* defined as:

The total of all gains and losses of the reporting entity that are recognised in a period and are attributable to shareholders.

The face of the profit and loss account

FRS 3 is supported by a number of illustrative examples. The following are shown below by way of illustration:

(a)   'Example 1', offering the minimum information to be shown on the face of the profit and loss account where the 'functional format' is chosen.
(b)   The necessary supporting note where the minimum disclosure has been shown on the face of the profit and loss account.
(c)   An example of a 'statement of total recognised gains and losses' with a 'note on historical cost profits and losses'.
(d)   A reconciliation of profit for the year to the movement in shareholders' funds.

Profit and loss account example 1

	1993	1993	1992 as restated
	£m	£m	£m
Turnover:			
Continuing operations	550		500
Acquisitions	50		
	600		
Discontinued operations	175		190
		775	690
Cost of sales		(620)	(555)
Gross profit		155	135
Net operating expenses		(104)	(83)

	1993	1993	1992 as restated
	£m	£m	£m
Operating profit:			
Continuing operations	50		40
Acquisitions	6		
	56		
Discontinued operations	(15)		12
Less 1992 provision	10		
		51	52
Profit on sales of properties in continuing operations		9	6
Provision for loss on operations to be discontinued			(30)
Loss on disposal of discontinued operations	(17)		
Less 1992 provision	20		
		3	
Profit on ordinary activities before interest		63	28
Interest payable		(18)	(15)
Profit on ordinary activities before taxation		45	13
Tax on profit on ordinary activities		(14)	(4)
Profit on ordinary activities after taxation		31	9
Minority interests		(2)	(2)
[Profit before extraordinary items]		29	7
[Extraordinary items] (included only to show positioning)		—	—
Profit for the financial year		29	7
Dividends		(8)	(1)
Retained profit for the financial year		21	6
Earnings per share		**39p**	**10p**
Adjustments [to be itemised and an adequate description to be given]		*x*p	*x*p
Adjusted earnings per share		*y*p	*y*p

[Reason for calculating the adjusted earnings per share to be given.]

Note required in respect of profit and loss account example 1

	1993 Continuing £m	1993 Discontinuing £m	1993 Total £m	1992 (as restated) Continuing £m	1992 (as restated) Discontinuing £m	1992 (as restated) Total £m
Cost of sales	455	165	620	385	170	555
Net operating expenses:						
Distribution costs	56	13	69	46	5	51
Administrative expenses	41	12	53	34	3	37
Other operating income	(8)	0	(8)	(5)	0	(5)
	89	25	114	75	8	83
Less 1992 provision	0	(10)	(10)			
	89	15	104			

The total figures for continuing operations in 1993 include the following amounts relating to acquisitions: cost of sales £40m and net operating expenses £4m (namely distribution costs £3m, administrative expenses £3m and other operating income £2m).

Statement of total recognised gains and losses

	1993 £m	1992 as restated £m
Profit for the financial year	29	7
Unrealised surplus on revaluation of properties	4	6
Unrealised (loss)/gain on trade investment	(3)	7
	30	20
Currency translation differences on foreign currency net investments	(2)	5
Total recognised gains and losses relating to the year	28	25
Prior year adjustment (as explained in note *x*)	(10)	
Total gains and losses recognised since last annual report	18	

Note of historical cost profits and losses

	1993 £m	1992 as restated £m
Reported profit on ordinary activities before taxation	45	13
Realisation of property revaluation gains of previous years	9	10

	1993	1992 as restated
	£m	£m
Difference between a historical cost depreciation charge and the actual charge of the year calculated on the revalued amount	5	4
Historical cost profit on ordinary activities before taxation	59	27
Historical cost profit for the year retained after taxation, minority interests, extraordinary items and dividends	35	20

Reconciliation of movements in shareholders' funds

	1993	1992 as restated
	£m	£m
Profit for the financial year	29	7
Dividends	(8)	(1)
	21	6
Other recognised gains and losses relating to the year (net)	(1)	18
New share capital subscribed	(20)	
Goodwill written off	(25)	
Net addition to shareholders' funds	15	25
Opening shareholders' funds (originally £375m before deducting prior year adjustment of £10m)	365	340
Closing shareholders' funds	380	365

A basic rule in FRS 3 is that all recognised gains and losses must appear on the face of the profit and loss account unless specifically permitted or required to be taken direct to reserves by law or by accounting standards. To reinforce this application of the 'all-inclusive' concept a statement of total recognised gains and losses must also appear as a 'primary statement' showing the components of total recognised gains and losses attributable to shareholders. The illustrative example of such a statement is shown above. A further requirement is that there should be a note explaining any material difference between the results as disclosed and the results on an unmodified historical cost basis; this note should reconcile the two figures both for profit on ordinary activities and for retained profit. The note should follow either the profit and loss account or, as in the example above, the statement of total recognised gains and losses. In addition, a note reconciling the opening and closing totals of shareholders' funds should be shown, as illustrated above.

As shown in the example profit and loss account above the aggregate results of each of:

(a)　continuing operations
(b)　acquisitions (unless they have also been discontinued during the period)
(c)　discontinued operations

must be disclosed separately. As a minimum, this analysis must be shown for both turnover and operating profit on the face of the profit and loss account. A similar analysis for other expense items must be shown either on the face of the profit and loss account or, as in the example above, by way of note. If interest charges are allocated between continuing and discontinued operations then the basis for the allocation must be explained.

Certain types of exceptional item must be shown on the face of the profit and loss account after operating profit and before interest. These are:

(a)　profits or losses on the sale or termination of an operation;
(b)　costs of a fundamental reorganisation or restructuring which has a material effect on the nature and focus of the reporting entity's operations;
(c)　profits or losses on the disposal of fixed assets.

The notes to the accounts should explain the impact of these items on taxation and minority interests.

Other exceptional items should be included under the statutory format headings in arriving at the results of ordinary activities, being attributed to continuing or discontinued activities as appropriate. Individual items, or categories of items, should be disclosed and explained in the notes to the accounts. Where 'necessary in order to give a true and fair view', exceptional items must be shown on the face of the profit and loss account.

The example provided in FRS 1 shows, as can be seen above, two examples of exceptional items shown immediately above the interest charge.

The taxation charge should include, with separate disclosure, the effects of any fundamental change in the basis of taxation. Any 'special circumstances' affecting the tax change should be disclosed by way of note.

'Extraordinary items' are shown after the profit on ordinary activities after tax and after minority interests but before appropriations. They are shown net of related taxation. Related taxation is computed by:

(a)　calculating the overall tax position for the period;
(b)　calculating the tax position as though the extraordinary item had not arisen;
(c)　related taxation is the difference between the two figures.

A note to the accounts should describe each extraordinary item.

Acquisition and discontinuance

When a business operation is acquired then there may be practical problems in determining the part of profits for the accounting period that are attributable to the part of that period after acquisition. In that case, an indication of the contribution of the acquisition to turnover and operating profit should be made. If this cannot be given, the fact and the reason must be explained.

Only directly related income and costs should be reported under the heading 'discontinued operations'. Costs such as those of reorganising or restructuring continuing operations in response to the discontinuance should be treated as part of continuing operations.

Where a decision has been made to sell or terminate an operation then it will be necessary to make a provision to the extent that obligations arise from that decision that will not be covered by future profits of the operation or the disposal. To justify this provision the reporting entity must be able to demonstrate either:

(a) a binding sale agreement, or
(b) a detailed formal plan for termination from which withdrawal is realistically impractical.

The provision should only cover:

(a) the direct costs of the sale or termination;
(b) operating losses of the operation up to the date of termination.

In both cases, the aggregate gains expected from future operating profits or related asset disposals should be set off against the provision.

The example profit and loss account above shows how such a provision should be shown. In the year of provision, 1992, a total provision of £30m appears in arriving at profit on ordinary activities. In 1993, the year of discontinuance, the provision is shown on the face of the profit and loss account as an abatement of related costs, i.e.

(a) £10m set against the operating loss of the discontinued operations;
(b) £20m set against the exceptional item loss on disposal.

If an acquisition or discontinuance has a major impact on a business segment this must be disclosed.

Asset disposals

The old SSAP 6 failed to address the problem of how to account for the disposal of a revalued fixed asset. Two approaches are possible:

(a) Profit or loss is computed as the difference between disposal proceeds and the revalued amount. This is the requirement of FRS 3.
(b) Profit and loss is computed as the difference between the disposal proceeds and the historical cost, the revaluation difference being transferred from the revaluation reserve. The logic underlying this approach is that the revaluation surplus has not previously appeared in the profit and loss account and, at the time of disposal, becomes a realised profit. FRS 3 does not allow this approach but does identify the revaluation surplus as realised in the note of historical cost profits and losses, as can be seen in the example above.

Prior period adjustments

These are accounted for by:

(a) restating the comparative figures for the preceding period in the accounts;
(b) adjusting the opening balance of reserves for the cumulative effect;

(c)   noting the cumulative effect of the adjustments at the foot of the current year's statement of total recognised gains and losses, as illustrated in the example above;

(d)   disclosing the effect of prior period adjustments on the results for the preceding period where practical.

Comparative figures

These should be given for all items required by FRS 3. The profit and loss account comparative figures for continuing operations should include in the continuing category only those operations treated as continuing in the current period.

Investment companies

Investment companies as defined in company law should only include profits available for distribution in the profit and loss account.

Background

Extraordinary items

SSAP 6, the predecessor to FRS 3, defined extraordinary items as:

> Material items which derive from events or transactions that fall outside the ordinary activities of the company and which are therefore expected not to recur frequently or regularly. They do not include exceptional items nor do they include prior year items merely because they relate to a prior year [1986 revised version].

This was widely criticised as a broad definition that allowed company directors to exclude unwelcome items from the main profit figure. Abuse of SSAP 6 was seen as a major factor in 'creative accounting'. This was particularly significant because under SSAP 3: Earnings per Share, this key ratio was computed on the basis of profit *excluding* extraordinary items. FRS 3 has amended SSAP 3 to include extraordinary items in the earnings per share computation, thereby playing down the significance of the 'extraordinary item' classification. FRS 3 has also tightened up the definition of an extraordinary item, requiring 'a high degree of abnormality' and that the 'item is not expected to recur'. The definition of 'ordinary activities' has been written so widely that it is difficult to imagine what might fall outside it. A range of activities traditionally classified as extraordinary, such as losses on discontinued activities, are explicitly identified as falling within ordinary activities by FRS 3. Finally, in their example, the ASB have left a space for extraordinary items but have chosen to take the view that a specific example should not be given. Overall, FRS 3 gives a clear message that while space for extraordinary items has been retained in line with company law in practice such items should not arise. To illustrate this, Table 4.1 considers how the examples of extraordinary items in SSAP 6 would be considered under FRS 3.

Table 4.1 Comparative treatment of 'extraordinary items'

Examples of extraordinary items in SSAP 6	Treatment in FRS 3
1. Discontinuance of a business segment.	Exceptional item, shown after operating profit and before interest.
2. Sale of an investment not acquired with the intention of resale.	Exceptional item, treated as 1 above.
3. Provision made for permanent diminution in value of a fixed asset because of extraordinary events in period.	Since ordinary activities include '*any* event in the various environments in which it operates . . . irrespective of . . . frequency . . . or nature' then it would appear that no such thing as an 'extraordinary event' now exists.
4. The expropriation of assets.	This is an event, as in 3 above, that now falls under ordinary activities.
5. A change in the basis of taxation, or a significant change in governmental policy.	As in 3 above, this event, of a 'political' or 'regulatory' environmental change, is within 'ordinary' activities, subject to separate disclosure.

Prior period adjustments

FRS 3 emphasises that most items relating to prior periods arise because of corrections to and adjustments of estimates inherent in preparing accounts periodically. These should be included in the accounts of the year in which they are identified. Items which justify a prior period adjustment 'are rare' arising either from changes in accounting policy or from the correction of fundamental errors.

Under the consistency concept changes in accounting policy should not normally arise. Such changes arise from making a choice between two or more accounting methods. They are only justified where the new policy gives a fairer presentation of the accounts. One example of a circumstance that might justify such a rule is a change in an FRS. Where accounting methods are varied in the light of a change in the nature of transactions this does not constitute a change of policy.

A 'fundamental error' is one that should have been detected at the time it was made. The term does not embrace revision of estimates made in the light of subsequent events or experience.

International accounting standards

FRS 3 is consistent with IAS 5: Information to Be Disclosed in Financial Statement, IAS 8: Unusual and Prior Period Items and Changes in Accounting Policies, and with the proposed revision to IAS 8 issues in July 1992.

EXAMINATION PRACTICE

4.1   FRS 3 – allocation of items

A manufacturing company, Peel Ltd, has a turnover of £6 million and pre-tax trading profits of £1 000 000 before taking account of the following items:

(a)   costs of £750 000 incurred in terminating production at one of the company's factories;

(b)   provision for an abnormally large bad debt of £500 000, arising in a trading contract;

(c)   profits of £150 000 on sale of plant and machinery written off in a previous year when production of the particular product ceased.

You are required to indicate whether these items should be treated as exceptional, extraordinary or normal trading transactions within the terms of FRS 3, giving your reasons.

4.2   FRS 3 – presentation

Bellamy Ltd is a company in the furniture retailing trade with 324 shops, a turnover of £79 million and pre-tax profits of £8 million in the year to 31 December 19X1, tax on profit being computed at £4 million, before taking into account the following items:

(a)   As part of a programme of updating and improving shop premises thirteen shop sites were disposed of during the year at a profit of £320 000 subject to capital gains tax of £104 000.

(b)   During the course of audit of the accounts for the year to 31 December 19X1 it is discovered that an error was made in the previous year's accounts whereby the closing stock of £8.7 million was brought into the accounts at £7.8 million.

(c)   During the year it was discovered that certain beds imported and distributed by the company were liable, in certain circumstances, to collapse, due to a fundamental design fault. Fortunately, the company received no claims for personal injury arising from this problem, but it was necessary to recall for checking and repair all of the beds sold. The cost of this was £300 000 relating to beds sold in 19X1, £500 000 relating to beds sold in 19X0, and £180 000 relating to beds sold in previous years.

(d)   During the year the directors made a decision to sell all the company's investments on the Stock Exchange and in doing so realised a profit of £2 million. These investments had been shown as fixed assets.

You are required to explain the appropriate treatment for each of the above items in the accounts of Bellamy Ltd for the year ended 31 December 19X1.

4.3   FRS 3 – conceptual basis

Discuss the merits of *both* the 'all-inclusive' income and the 'current operating' income concepts. (*Note:* The current operating income approach is sometimes referred to as reserve accounting.)

5 | SSAP 1: Accounting for the Results of Associated Companies

Background

Until the late 1960s income from investments where less than 50 per cent of the equity had been held was normally only included in the accounts of the investing company to the extent that dividends were receivable, ignoring the profits earned but not distributed by the company invested in, on the grounds that the companies concerned were separate legal entities and that income should not be taken to the profit and loss account until received or receivable. This principle can, however, lead to distortion of the results of a company that conducts an important part of its business through the medium of other companies; for this reason the Companies Act 1948 had required the presentation of group accounts. In the late 1960s there was considerable growth in the practice of companies conducting an important part of their business through companies where they held a substantial but not a controlling interest, often through consortia or joint venture companies; also, investors came to attach more importance to the reported profit figure through price/earnings ratios and earnings per share figures, rather than dividend yield information. In response, a number of companies developed the 'associated company' method of bringing into the consolidated accounts the group share of associated companies' profits or losses.

Accounting for the results of associated companies was the subject of ED 1 issued in June 1970 and SSAP 1 issued in January 1971. At first sight it may seem surprising that the ASC should have chosen a rather technical and narrow subject as its first topic. The reason appears to have been that the ASC wished to lay down standard practice in this area before too many variations developed and, as one commentator put it 'before the arteries harden'. It was also something of a boost to the battered morale of the UK accounting profession to produce a firm statement on a topic where new practices had only developed recently and which no other body of accountants, 'even the Americans', had then tackled. In April 1982 a revised SSAP 1 was issued.

Summary of the statement

Definitions

A company is an associate of another where it is not a subsidiary and either:

(a)   the interest in the company is effectively that of a partner in a joint venture or consortium, and the investing group or company is in a position to exercise a significant influence over the company in which the investment is made; or

(b)   the investment in the company is long term, substantial and the investing group or company is able to exercise a significant influence over the company, bearing in mind the disposition of the other shareholdings.

The key term in this definition is 'significant influence'. SSAP 1 defines significant influence as participation in, but not necessarily control of, the financial and operating policy decisions of that company. Representation on the board of directors may indicate such participation but does not constitute proof. SSAP 1 lays down an assumption that the investing company can exercise significant influence when the equity holding is 20 per cent or greater; this assumption applies unless the contrary can be clearly demonstrated. Similarly, where the equity holding is less than 20 per cent there is an assumption that the investing company cannot exercise significant influence unless the company can demonstrate otherwise and the associate company itself concurs.

Accounts of the investing company

Normal practice in the case of income receivable from an investment would be to bring dividends into the profit and loss account for the period in which they are received; however, in the case of an investment in an associated company, proposed dividends receivable should also be brought into the investing company's accounts provided that they relate to an accounting period ending on or before its own accounting date and are declared prior to the completion of the investing company's own accounts.

Consolidated profit and loss account

The consolidated accounts should include the group's share of the results of associated companies on the following basis:

(a)   Profit before tax should include and identify separately the aggregate of the group's share of pre-tax profits and losses of associated companies.
(b)   The taxation charge should include and identify separately tax attributed to the group's share of the associated companies' results.
(c)   Extraordinary items should include the group's share of associated company extraordinary items provided that these fall within the definition of an extraordinary item, as laid down in FRS 3, from the perspective of the group. These should be separately identified if material.
(d)   The group's share of associated company retained profits should be shown separately.

The investing group should not show its attributable share of other items requiring disclosure, such as turnover and depreciation, as part of the aggregate of those items in the accounts. Where the results of associated companies are of such significance as to make more detailed information material to the furnishing of a true and fair view, then separate disclosure should be made of the total turnover, total depreciation charges and the total profits less losses before taxation of associated companies. In judging materiality both the profit and the scale of operations of the associate should be considered.

Consolidated balance sheet

In the consolidated balance sheet the investment in each associated company will be shown as the original cost of the investment, less any amounts written off, plus the group share of post-acquisition retained profits and reserves. This should be analysed into:

(a)   the group's share of the net assets of the associate other than goodwill;
(b)   the group's share of the associate's goodwill;
(c)   the premium paid (or discount) on the acquisition of the interest in the associate.

Items (b) and (c) may be combined. Where any goodwill is impaired in value an appropriate write down must be made.

Loans to or from associated companies must be separately identified, as must any material trading balances.

Where materially relevant, information regarding associated companies' tangible and intangible assets and liabilities should be given.

The accumulated reserves of the group should identify separately profits retained in associated companies. It will also be necessary to take into account and disclose movements on other reserves in associated companies, such as revaluation surpluses on fixed assets.

A further requirement is that if retained profits of overseas companies would be subject to further taxation on distribution this should be disclosed.

Consideration should be given to making an appropriate provision for any deficiency of net assets in the associate which the investing company may have to make good.

Consolidated accounts not prepared

Where an investing company does not itself present group accounts it should show the required information about the associate as follows:

(a)   Profit and loss information either by inclusion in supplementary form in its own profit and loss account, in such a way as not to treat its share of the associate's retained profit as a realised profit, or in a separate profit and loss account.
(b)   Balance sheet information can be shown either as a note to the accounts or by preparation of a separate balance sheet.

Accounts to be used

The accounts used for the purpose of including associated companies' results should be made up to the investing company's own accounting date, or to a date not more than six months before, or 'shortly after', that date. Where an associated company is listed on the Stock Exchange, then only published financial information should be used. Before incorporating information in the group accounts from associated company accounts made up to an earlier accounting date care should be taken to ensure that later information is correct. Where the accounts are not made up to the same date as the investing company or are unaudited, then the facts and dates used should be disclosed, if the effect is material. As with consolidated accounts it may be necessary to make adjustments to exclude inter-company profits and to achieve consistency of accounting policies for the group.

Loss of status as an associated company

A problem arises when an investment in an associated company loses that status and is considered as an ordinary investment. SSAP 1 requires that the amount at which the associate is stated in the accounts at that point in time be carried forward as the cost of investment, subject to provision against any impairment in value and adjustment for dividends paid out of profits earned prior to the change of status.

Technical points

SSAP 1 includes a number of minor technical points including:

(a)   The effective date of acquisition or disposal of an interest in an associate is to be taken as the earlier of the date on which consideration passes and the date on which an offer becomes unconditional.

(b)   The extent of any restrictions on the ability of an associate to distribute its retained profits must be indicated.

(c)   If the investment in an associate is held by a subsidiary which has minority interests then in the consolidated accounts the total minority interest should include the minority's interest in the associate.

(d)   Where an associate is itself a holding company then the investing group should use the associate's group accounts for consolidation.

Current cost accounts

Where the investing group prepares current cost accounts then current cost figures for the associate, based on estimates if necessary, should be used.

Disclosure

The accounts should disclose the names of the principal associated companies showing for each:

(a)   the proportion of issued shares of each class held by the investing group;

(b)   an indication of the nature of the business.

Legal requirements

The account formats of the Companies Act 1985 include the term 'related company' which is defined rather more broadly than the SSAP 1 definition of an associate.

Where all related companies are also associates, then the term 'related company' does not have to be used in the accounts, although a note should explain this position.

Worked example

To illustrate the preparation and presentation of associated company information the following example is given.

Hampden Ltd, a company with subsidiaries, acquired a 30 per cent investment in Pym Ltd on 1 January 19X1. The accounts of the Hampden group and of Pym Ltd for the year to 31 December 19X1, before consolidating the results of the associate, were as follows:

Balance sheets	*Hampden Group* £000	*Pym Ltd* £000
Fixed assets	500	200
Investment in associate	100	
Net current assets	200	120
	800	320
Share capital	400	200
Retained profits	400	120
	800	320

Profit and loss accounts	*Hampden Group* £000	*Pym Ltd* £000
Turnover	1200	400
Profit before taxation	284	120
Taxation	144	60
Profit after taxation	140	60
Extraordinary items	25	10
Profit attributable to the members	115	50
Dividends	55	30
Net profit retained	60*	20
*By Hampden Ltd	25	
By subsidiaries	35	
	60	

Dividends of £9000 receivable from Pym Ltd, an overseas company, are included in the profit before tax of the Hampden Group.

The accounts of the Hampden Group will have to be adjusted to incorporate the results of the associate as follows:

(a)   Turnover will not be adjusted since the turnover of the associated company is not incorporated in the group accounts.

(b) The operating profit of the group must be adjusted to exclude the dividend from the associate, while the group's share of the pre-tax profit of the associate will be brought into the accounts and shown separately.

(c) In this example no adjustment to group taxation is required. If Pym Ltd were a UK company then, as we shall see in Chapter 8 on SSAP 10, the dividend receivable would carry a related tax credit, the gross amount being included in profit before taxation and the related ACT in the taxation charge: in that case it would have been necessary to eliminate the gross dividend from profit before tax and the related ACT from the taxation charge. The group's share of the associated company's tax charge is brought into the group profit and loss account and shown separately.

(d) The group's share of the associate's extraordinary items is added to the total of the group's own extraordinary items; to comply with FRS 3 it will be necessary to identify the size and nature of all extraordinary items in the notes to the accounts.

(e) SSAP 1 specifically requires that profit for the year retained in the associated companies be specifically identified.

(f) The group reserves must identify that portion of the reserves retained in the associated company.

(g) The identifiable assets of Pym Ltd at the acquisition date were:

	£000
As at 31 December 19X1	320
Less retained profit for 19X1	20
As at 1 January 19X1	300

The group share of these assets was:

$$30\% \times 300 = 90$$

So that the premium on acquisition must have been:

	£000
Cost	100
Share of net assets	90
Premium	10

The group share of the associate's net assets at 31 December 19X1 is:

$$£320\,000 \times 30\% = £96\,000$$

Hampden Ltd – Consolidated Profit and Loss Account for the year ended 31 December 19X1

	£000	£000
Turnover (a)		1200
Operating profit (284 − 9) (b)		275
Share of profit associated company (30% × 120) (b)		36
Profit before taxation		311

	£000	£000
Taxation: Hampden Ltd and subsidiaries	144	
Associated company (c) (30% × 60)	18	162
Profit after taxation and before extraordinary items		149
Extraordinary items (25 + 30% × 10) (d)		28
Profit attributable to members of which £80 000 is dealt with in the accounts of Hampden Ltd		121
Dividends		55
Net profit retained (e)		66*

*Analysis of retained profit

By Hampden Ltd	25
By subsidiaries	35
In associated company	6
	66

Hampden Ltd – Consolidated balance sheet at 31 December 19X1

	£000	£000
Fixed assets		500
Investment in associate (f)		
Share of net assets	96	
Premium on acquisition	10	106
Net current assets		200
		806
Share capital		400
Retained profits (g)		
Hampden Ltd	220	
Subsidiary companies	180	
Associated company	6	406
		806

Development of the statement – response

Perhaps because SSAP 1 was issued at a time when the concept of any form of 'equity accounting' for associated companies was a new one, the statement did not stir a great deal of controversy. A number of accountants objected in principle to the concept of equity accounting for any minority interest on grounds of prudence, but the majority of the profession accepted SSAP 1. Some controversy has arisen, however, over the definition of an associated company and there were several well publicised cases of companies with substantial shareholdings of slightly less than 20 per cent of the equity treating those investments as associated companies.

Thus the main purpose for issuing a revised SSAP 1 in 1982 was to define an associate more precisely.

SSAP 1 and the examiner

Questions on SSAP 1 can take the following form:

(a) Written questions, with special reference to the definition of an associated company.
(b) Questions involving specific SSAP 1 computations, often involving comparison with alternative treatments.
(c) Inclusion in a consolidated accounts question.

EXAMINATION PRACTICE

5.1   Definition of associated company
Explain how, under SSAP 1, an 'associated company' would be defined.

5.2   Consolidating an associate's results
The draft consolidated profit and loss account for the year of Crust Ltd and its subsidiaries, before including the results of its associated company, together with the results of the group's 40 per cent owned associated company Pie Ltd, for the year ended 31 December 19X0 were as follows:

Profit and loss account		*Crust Ltd*	*Pie Ltd*
		£	£
Turnover		6 800 000	3 200 000
Operating profit		702 000	420 000
Dividend receivable		56 400	—
		758 400	420 000
Tax on profit for the year	282 000		170 000
Tax on franked investment	18 800	300 800	
Income		457 600	250 000
Proposed dividends		264 000	94 000
Retained profit		193 600*	156 000
*Crust Ltd	123 600		
Subsidiaries	70 000		
	193 600		

You are required to prepare a consolidated profit and loss account incorporating the results of the associate.

6 | *SSAP 2:*
Disclosure of Accounting Policies

Introduction

One of the methods by which the 'Statement of Intent' on accounting standards in the 1970s proposed to advance accounting standards was by recommending disclosure of accounting bases used in arriving at the amount attributed to significant items depending on judgements of value or estimates of future events. SSAP 2 issued in November 1971 can be seen as an attempt to ensure such disclosure.

The terminology of SSAP 2 is frequently used in other accounting standards.

Summary of the statement

Definitions

A number of terms, such as accounting 'principles', 'practices', 'rules', 'conventions', 'methods' and 'procedures' have in the past been treated as interchangeable. For the purposes of SSAP 2 a distinction has been made between three terms:

(a) *Fundamental accounting concepts* are 'the broad basic assumptions which underlie the periodic financial accounts of business enterprises'.

(b) *Accounting bases* are 'the methods developed for applying fundamental accounting concepts to financial transactions and items, for the purpose of financial accounts. Such methods are necessary:
   (i)   to decide in which periods revenue and expenditure should be brought into the profit and loss account;
   (ii) to decide the amounts at which material items should be shown in the balance sheet.

(c) *Accounting policies* are 'the specific accounting bases selected and consistently followed by a business enterprise'. Management should select those accounting policies which are believed to be appropriate to the circumstances of the business and best suited to present fairly the results and financial position.

The statement specifically identifies four fundamental accounting concepts as having 'general acceptability'. These are defined as follows:

(a) *The going concern concept*, that 'the enterprise will continue in operational existence for the foreseeable future. This means in particular that the profit and loss account and balance sheet assume no intention or necessity to liquidate or curtail significantly the scale of operation'.

(b)   *The accruals concept*, that 'revenue and costs are accrued (that is, recognised as they are earned or incurred, not as money is received or paid), matched with one another so far as their relationship can be established or justifiably assumed, and dealt with in the profit and loss account of the period to which they relate; the accruals concept implies revenue and profit dealt with in the profit and loss account will be matched with related costs and expenses where these are material and identifiable'.

(c)   *The consistency concept*, that 'there is consistency of accounting treatment of like items within each accounting period and from one period to the next'.

(d)   *The prudence concept*, that 'revenue and profits are not anticipated, but are recognised by inclusion in the profit and loss account only when realised in the form either of cash or of other assets the ultimate cash realisation of which can be assessed with reasonable certainty; provision is made for all known liabilities (expenses and losses) whether the amount of these is known with certainty or is a best estimate in the light of the information available'.

While the statement says that the relative importance of these four concepts will 'vary according to the circumstances of the particular case', it is made clear that where the accruals concept is inconsistent with the prudence concept the latter should prevail.

Required practice and disclosure

The basic requirement laid down in SSAP 2 is that there should be disclosure in the accounts of the accounting policies followed for dealing with items 'judged material or critical in determining profit or loss for the year and in stating the financial position'. The explanations given should be 'clear, fair, and as brief as possible'. There is also a requirement that where the accounts are based on assumptions which depart from the four fundamental concepts the facts should be explained. It follows that, unless there is a clear statement to the contrary, there is a presumption that the four fundamental concepts have been observed.

The fundamental concepts

SSAP 2 does not claim to lay down a conceptual foundation on which to erect the accounting standards programme. The statement lays down that:

> It is not the purpose of this statement to develop a basic theory of accounting. An exhaustive theoretical approach would take an entirely different form and would include, for instance, many more propositions than the four fundamental concepts referred to here. It is, however, expedient to recognise them as working assumptions having general acceptance at the present time.

Altogether academic writers on accountancy have contrived to list more than 150 accounting concepts. The list given in SSAP 2 is only a selection of particularly important concepts which it can be assumed will always apply. However, the treatment decided on in SSAPs is often explained and justified by reference to SSAP 2; for example, the first paragraph of SSAP 13: Accounting for Research and Development discusses the application of the 'accruals' and 'prudence' concepts to the subject matter of the statement.

Accounting policies

SSAP 2 requires that explanations of accounting policies should be 'clear, fair, and as brief as possible'. There is no specific requirement in the statement that information on accounting policies should be disclosed as one note to the accounts rather than in individual notes under the relevant headings, but in practice most companies show an 'accounting policies' statement attached, or as a note, to the accounts. SSAP 2 lists a number of topics for which different accounting bases are recognised as follows:

> Depreciation
> Treatment of intangibles such as research and development, patents and trade marks
> Stocks and work in progress
> Long-term contracts
> Deferred taxation
> Hire purchase, leasing, and rental transactions
> Conversion of foreign currencies
> Repairs and renewals
> Consolidation policies
> Property development transactions
> Warranties for products or services.

Most of these are now covered by individual FRSs or SSAPs or exposure drafts. Clearly the list is not exhaustive.

There are a number of disclosure requirements laid down by the Companies Acts which are now normally complied with by inclusion in the statement of accounting policies, such as the method of calculating turnover and the basis of the computation of tax liability.

IAS 1: Disclosure of Accounting Policies (issued January 1975)

This Statement covers much the same ground as SSAP 2 in the UK, but with some differences in terminology and emphasis.

Definitions

Fundamental accounting assumptions underlie the preparation of financial statements. They are usually not specifically stated because their acceptance and use are assumed. Disclosure is necessary if they are not followed. IAS 1 recognises three fundamental accounting assumptions:

(a) Going concern, that the enterprise is viewed as continuing in operation for the foreseeable future.
(b) Consistency, that accounting policies are consistent from one period to another.
(c) Accrual, that revenue and costs are recognised as they are earned or incurred and recorded in the accounts of the periods to which they relate.

Accounting policies are defined as encompassing 'the principles, bases, conventions, rules, and procedures adopted by managements in preparing and presenting financial statements'. Because there are many different accounting policies that may be applied even to the same subject, it is necessary for management to exercise judgement in selecting and applying appropriate accounting policies. IAS 1 defines three considerations which should govern the selection of accounting policies:

(a) *Prudence.* Because of the uncertainties that surround many transactions it is necessary to exercise prudence in the preparation of accounts but it is emphasised that this does not justify the creation of secret or hidden reserves.
(b) *Substance over form.* The substance and financial reality of transactions should govern their treatment in the accounts rather than legal form.
(c) *Materiality.* All items which are sufficiently material to affect evaluations or decisions should be disclosed.

Required practice and disclosure

The requirements of IAS 1 can be compared with requirements in the UK as follows:

(a) IAS 1 requires disclosure and explanation of any departure from the three fundamental accounting assumptions. IAS 1 requires clear and concise disclosure of all 'significant' accounting policies. SSAP 2 contains similar provisions.
(b) IAS 1 requires that accounts should show corresponding figures for the previous period. Such a requirement is laid down in the UK by the Companies Act 1985.
(c) IAS 1 requires disclosure of the nature and effect of, and reason for, any change in accounting policy. This topic is dealt with in detail in the UK in FRS 3.
(d) IAS 1 defines the considerations of prudence, substance over form, and materiality which should govern the selection of accounting policies. There is also a requirement in IAS 1 that accounting policies 'should normally be disclosed in one place'. There are no equivalent requirements in the UK.

While SSAP 2 has been an important SSAP in affirming the principle of disclosure of accounting policies, it has been necessary in subsequent SSAPs to spell out in detail the disclosure necessary on specific areas. For example, prior to the issue of SSAP 12 on depreciation, many companies would disclose an accounting policy in such terms as 'Fixed assets are depreciated by such methods and at such rates as will write off cost over the period of expected use'. As we shall see, SSAP 12 lays down specific disclosure requirements ensuring that the accounting policies note on depreciation will be considerably more informative than this!

EXAMINATION PRACTICE

6.1 Defining the terms
Define the terms:

(a) fundamental accounting concepts;
(b) accounting bases;
(c) accounting policies.

6.2   Understanding the concepts

List and define the four fundamental accounting concepts, and explain in what order of priority they rank.

6.3   Accounting bases

List four significant matters for which different accounting bases are recognised, and give two examples of a different accounting base for each.

6.4   Accounting policies

Draft an 'accounting policies' note for a limited company covering five different items.

7 SSAP 3: Earnings per Share

Introduction

As we have already seen, during the 1960s investors became more interested in earnings rather than dividend yield measures of company performance, the most common ratios used being earnings per share and the related price/earnings ratio. In fact, since the price/earnings ratio came to be commonly quoted in the financial press, it is likely that the earnings per share figure has become the most significant item in the published accounts. It was, therefore, important that the accountancy profession should give a lead in establishing a consistent basis for presenting this key information. In 1971 the ASC issued ED 4 on earnings per share, followed in 1972 by SSAP 3. In 1974, as a result of the introduction of the imputation system of taxation, it was necessary to revise the statement. In 1992 FRS 3 revised the definition of earnings.

When ED 4 was issued it was observed in *Accountancy* that this 'first venture into the field of investment ratios is likely to encourage investors and investment analysts . . . to ask . . . for the publication of other key ratios and statistics'. In fact the same need for guidance on the presentation of other ratios has not arisen. One problem in laying down a standard in the early 1970s was that at that early stage in the accounting standards programme it was not possible to predict exactly how the concept of earnings would develop, and the SSAP issued in 1972 actually forecast that future amendment might therefore be necessary.

Summary of the statement

Definitions

The term 'earnings per share' is defined as the profit in pence attributable to each equity share; the figure is calculated by taking the consolidated profit of the period after tax and after deducting minority interests, preference dividends and extraordinary items, divided by the number of equity shares in issue and ranking for dividend in respect of the period.

There are two bases for calculating the charge for taxation; the 'net' basis includes in the taxation charge irrecoverable ACT and unrelieved overseas taxation arising from dividend payments while the 'nil' basis excludes these items from the tax charge except in so far as they arise from the payment of preference dividends.

Required practice and disclosure

SSAP 3 applies only to Stock Exchange listed companies; such companies are required to show on the face of the profit and loss account earnings per share calculated on the 'net' basis for both the current and the previous period. There is a strong recommendation in the statement that the earnings per share figure calculated on the 'nil' basis should also be disclosed where it is materially different from that calculated on the net basis.

A possibility of future dilution of earnings may arise in the following circumstances:

(a) where the company has issued a separate class of equity shares which do not rank for dividend in the period under review but will do so in the future;

(b) where the company has issued loans or preference shares convertible into equity of the company;

(c) where options to subscribe for equity shares have been granted.

Where the possible dilution exceeds 5 per cent of the basic earnings per share then the company is required to disclose the figure of diluted earnings per share, giving it equal prominence with the basic earnings per share figure. The figure of diluted earnings per share for the previous period should only be given where the assumptions on which it is based still apply.

The notes to the accounts should disclose the basis of calculating both the basic and the fully diluted earnings per share, in particular showing the amount of earnings and the number of equity shares used in the calculation.

Practical guidance

SSAP 3 is accompanied by an appendix giving detailed practical guidance on the determination of the earnings per share figure. Although the appendix does not form part of the statement it does provide a useful source of advice on technical difficulties, including the following.

Calculation of earnings
The amount earned for the equity will consist of the consolidated profit after tax and extraordinary items, including the earnings of associated companies, less minority interests and preference dividends. If preference dividends are cumulative then the dividend for the period should be taken into account whether or not it is to be paid, while arrears of preference dividend paid during the year should be ignored; non-cumulative dividends should only be taken into account in so far as they are paid or proposed. Where the amount earned for equity is a negative figure the earnings per share should still be calculated and shown as a loss per share.

Computing the number of shares
SSAP 3 specifically states that the earnings per share calculation should be based on the number of shares in issue and ranking for dividend in respect of the period. Where there have been any changes in the equity share capital during the period then the computation of the number of shares will depend on the nature of the share issue.

(a)   Where there is a bonus issue there will be no change in the earning capacity of the company and the only effect will be to spread the earnings over a greater number of shares; therefore we calculate earnings per share on the basis of the number of shares ranking for dividend after the bonus issue and adjust the corresponding figures of earnings per share for earlier periods on the same basis.

(b)   Where there is an issue of shares at full market price then the earning capacity of the company should have been raised as a result of the new resources injected into the business, while these increased earnings will be spread over a greater number of shares; therefore we calculate the earnings per share on the basis of the average number of shares in issue during the year weighted on a time basis. Where shares have been issued as consideration for shares acquired in a subsidiary we take the date of issue as being the same as the date from which the earnings of the subsidiary have been brought into the consolidated accounts.

(c)   A rights issue of shares at less than the full market price combines the characteristics of both the types of share issue we have already considered, in that the earning capacity of the company will be increased as a result of the injection of new resources but, to the extent that the shares are issued at a discount on their market value, part of the increase in the share capital is similar to a bonus issue in character. We separate these two elements by computing a 'theoretical ex rights price' immediately after the rights issue and compare this with the 'actual cum rights price' of the shares immediately before the rights issue. The theoretical ex rights price can be calculated in three stages:

   (i)   *Stage 1.* Multiplying the actual cum rights price of the shares immediately before the rights issue by the total number of shares in issue at that time, thus ascertaining the total market value of the equity.

   (ii)   *Stage 2.* Multiplying the issue price of the shares to be issued by the number of shares to be issued to ascertain the expected proceeds of the rights issue.

   (iii)   *Stage 3.* Dividing the sum of the total market value of the equity prior to the issue and the expected proceeds of the rights issue by the total number of shares in issue following the rights issue.

Having devised a mechanism to identify the separate 'full price' and 'bonus issue' elements of our rights issue, we now need to compute our earnings per share figure accordingly. To the extent that the rights issue equates to a 'full price issue' we must calculate the average number of shares on a time basis. To the extent that the issue equates to a bonus issue we must adjust the comparative earnings per share figure and also adjust the number of shares in the whole of the current period. We achieve this objective by applying to the comparative figure of earnings per share the factor:

$$\frac{\text{Theoretical ex rights price}}{\text{Actual cum rights price}}$$

Also, in computing the weighted average share capital for the current period we apply to the proportion of shares in issue before the rights issue the factor:

$$\frac{\text{Actual cum rights price}}{\text{Theoretical ex rights price}}$$

in order to include the bonus element of the rights issue in the calculation of total share capital in issue in the year, while making no adjustment to the proportion in issue after the rights issue.

Dilution

Where a company has an existing obligation to issue new shares then those who hold the option to acquire those shares have a potential claim on the earning capacity of the company with a consequent possibility of diluting the earnings per share figure. Where another class of equity share not yet ranking for dividend has already been issued then the diluted EPS figure can be calculated by including these shares in the calculation of the total number of shares as though they had ranked for dividend from the date of issue.

Where the possibility of dilution arises from the existence of some form of option to subscribe for new equity shares in the future then in order to compute the diluted EPS it is necessary to estimate the prospective effect of such an issue both on the earnings and on the number of shares in issue. The method of calculation of the effect on earnings will depend on the nature of the option:

(a)   Where the option consists of a right to convert loan stock or preference shares for equity shares then there should be added back to the earnings figure the prospective saving of interest (net of tax) or preference dividend.

(b)   Where the option consists of a right to subscribe cash for new shares then the prospective earnings of the funds to be raised should be estimated as though these would be invested in 2½ per cent consolidated stock purchased at the price ruling at the end of the day prior to the commencement of the accounting period. In either case the diluted EPS is calculated as though the option had been exercised on the first day of the accounting period under review.

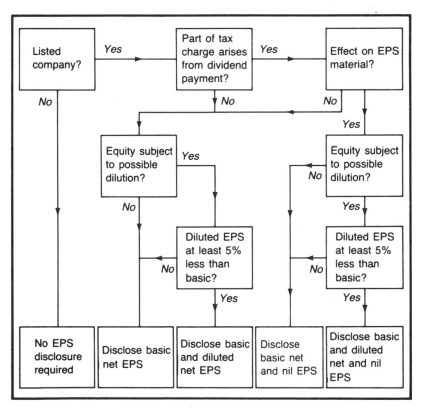

Fig. 7.1 Earnings per share: required disclosure.

The appendix to SSAP 3 advises that where the diluted EPS figure shows an increase over the basic EPS figure then it is not appropriate to show the diluted figure, since it is unlikely that any option will be exercised under such circumstances.

Practical problems of application

Required disclosure

Figure 7.1 summarises the information required by SSAP 3.

Calculations

The calculation of the earnings per share figure will be illustrated by the following example. The consolidated profit and loss account of Carlisle Ltd for the year to 31 December 19X0 was as follows:

	£000	£000
Turnover		32 000
Group profit for the year		5 120
Share of profits of associated companies		230
		5 350
Taxation:		
The group	2 570	
Associated companies	120	2 690
		2 660
Minority interest		170
		2 490
Extraordinary item		410
		2 900
Dividends: Preference shares	100	
Ordinary shares	500	600
Retained profit		2 300
Group taxation is made up as follows:		
UK tax at 50%	2 300	
Irrecoverable ACT	270	
	2 570	

Share capital has moved during the year as follows:

	£1 10% preference shares £	£1 ordinary shares £
B/fwd 1.1.X0	1 000 000	4 000 000
Bonus issue 31.3.X0		1 000 000
Issue at full market price 30.6.X0		1 000 000
1:4 rights issue price £1.20 at 30.9.X0		1 500 000
C/fwd 31.12.X0	1 000 000	7 500 000

The market price of shares immediately prior to the rights issue was £1.80.

We will also consider three different possible forms of dilution:

(a)   That at 31 December 19X0 there was in issue an extra 1 500 000 ordinary shares issued on 1 January 19X0 and due to rank for dividend as from 1 June 19X1.

(b)   That during the year there had been issued £3 000 000 of 10 per cent loan stock convertible on 31 December 19X3 to ordinary shares at £1.20 per share.

(c)   That during the year there had been issued options to subscribe for 1 000 000 ordinary shares at a price of £1.50.

The closing price of 2½ per cent consolidated stock on 31 December of the previous year was £25, and the corporation tax rate during the year was 50 per cent. All calculations should be made to the nearest month.

Our first step in calculating the earnings per share will be to compute the earnings attributable to ordinary shareholders. Since the taxation charge includes irrecoverable ACT it will also be necessary to add this figure back in order to compute earnings on the 'nil' basis:

	£000
Profit after taxation, minority interest and extraordinary items	2900
Less: Preference dividend	100
Earnings attributable to ordinary shareholders on the 'net' basis	2800
Irrecoverable ACT	270
Earnings attributable to ordinary shareholders on the 'nil' basis	3070

The next step is to compute the number of ordinary shares in issue and ranking for dividend during the year. For this purpose we need to calculate the theoretical ex rights price of the shares following the rights issue:

	Number of shares	£000
Market capitalisation prior to rights issue	6 000 000 × £1.8	10 800
Cash raised by rights issue	1 500 000 × £1.2	1 800
	7 500 000	12 600

$$\text{Theoretical ex rights price} = \frac{£12\ 600\ 000}{7\ 500\ 000} = £1.68$$

The next step is to calculate the number of shares in issue during the year.

Portion of period	Fraction of period	Shares in issue	Rights factor	Number of shares
1.1.X0 to 30.6.X0	$\frac{6}{12}$	× 5 000 000	× $\frac{1.80}{1.68}$	= 2 678 571
1.7.X0 to 30.9.X0	$\frac{3}{12}$	× 6 000 000	× $\frac{1.8}{1.68}$	= 1 607 143
1.10.X0 to 31.10.X0	$\frac{3}{12}$	× 7 500 000		= 1 875 000
				6 160 714

We can now compute the basic earnings per share:

On the net basis $\quad \dfrac{2\ 800\ 000}{6\ 160\ 714} = 45.4\ p$

On the nil basis $\quad \dfrac{3\ 070\ 000}{6\ 160\ 714} = 49.8\ p$

Since earnings per share computed on the nil basis are 11 per cent greater than on the net basis we would disclose both figures. The diluted earnings per share would be calculated as follows:

(a)   On the assumption that there are already shares in issue which do not yet rank for dividend, to calculate the diluted earnings per share we need only change our computation of the number of shares in issue:

	£
Basic share calculation	6 160 714
Shares, issued and not ranking for dividend	1 500 000
	7 660 714

Diluted 'net' earnings per share $= \dfrac{2\ 800\ 000}{7\ 660\ 714} = 36.6p$

Diluted 'nil' earnings per share $= \dfrac{3\ 070\ 000}{7\ 660\ 714} = 40.1p$

(b)   Where there is convertible loan stock in issue we have to compute the effects of conversion both on earnings and the number of shares.

Earnings will be increased	£
£3 000 000 × 10%	300 000
Less: Tax @ 50%	150 000
	£150 000

Giving revised earnings:	*Net*	*Nil*
	£000	£000
Basic earnings	2800	3070
Increase if loan stock converted	150	150
	2950	3220

The number of shares will be increased by:

$$\frac{\text{Nominal value of convertible loan stock}}{\text{Price at which shares are to be converted}}$$

i.e. $\dfrac{3\ 000\ 000}{1.20} = 2\ 500\ 000$

Giving total shares in issue:	£
Basic share calculation	6 160 714
Prospective dilution	2 500 000
	8 660 714

Diluted 'net' earnings per share $= \dfrac{2\ 950\ 000}{8\ 660\ 714} = 34.1\text{p}$

Diluted 'nil' earnings per share $= \dfrac{3\ 220\ 000}{8\ 660\ 714} = 37.2\text{p}$

(c) Where there are options to subscribe cash for new shares we compute the prospective effect on earnings thus:

Cash to be raised: 1 000 000 × £1.50 = £1 500 000
Closing price of 2½ per cent consolidated stock on 31 December of the previous year = £25

Therefore prospective earnings:	£
$\dfrac{1\ 500\ 000 \times £2.50}{25}$	= 150 000
Less: Tax @ 50%	= 75 000
	75 000

	Net	*Nil*
	£000	£000
Basic earnings	2800	3070
Increase if option exercised	75	75
	2875	3145

The number of shares will be increased:

	£
Basic share calculation	6 160 714
Prospective dilution	1 000 000
	7 160 714

$$\text{Diluted 'net' earnings per share} = \frac{2\ 875\ 000}{7\ 160\ 714} = 40.1\text{p}$$

$$\text{Diluted 'nil' earnings per share} = \frac{3\ 145\ 000}{7\ 160\ 714} = 43.9\text{p}$$

EXAMINATION PRACTICE

7.1 Net and nil EPS

Explain the difference between the 'net' basis and 'nil' basis of computing earnings per share.

7.2 Dilution of EPS

Explain what is meant by 'dilution' of earnings per share and the circumstances in which this may arise.

7.3 Computation of EPS

The consolidated profit and loss account of Camborne Ltd for the year ended 31 December 19X1 was as follows:

	£000	£000
Turnover		89 000
Profit for the year of Camborne Ltd and its subsidiaries		10 226
Share of associated company profit		580
		10 806
Taxation:		
Camborne Ltd and subsidiaries	4 618	
Associated companies	280	4 898
Profit after taxation		5 908
Profit attributable to minority shareholders		618
Profit attributable to shareholders		5 290
Dividends paid and proposed:		
Preference shares	84	
Ordinary shares	1 940	2 024
		3 266

The group taxation charge includes a correction of an overprovision in the previous year of £548 000 and irrecoverable ACT of £112 000.

The issued share capital of Camborne Ltd was as follows:

	31 December 19X1	*31 December 19X0*
	£	£
2 000 000 4.2% cumulative preference shares	2 000 000	2 000 000
Ordinary shares of 50p each	15 316 100	11 750 000

Changes in the ordinary share capital during the year were:

(i)   On 5 May, 816 000 shares were issued at a premium of 40p on the acquisition of Redruth Ltd.

(ii) On 14 June the company made a rights issue of one share for every four held at a price of 70p per share.

(iii) On 11 November 237 200 shares were issued at a premium of 70p in part consideration for the acquisition of Bodmin Ltd.

Options to subscribe for 730 000 shares were granted to directors and senior executives on 1 January 19X0. These options will be exercisable at £1.20 per share between 1 January 19X6 and 31 December 19X0. The market price immediately before the rights issue was 90p per share. The closing price of 2½ per cent consolidated stock at the close of business on 31 December 19X0 was £20. Assume a corporation tax rate of 50 per cent.

You are required:

(a)   To calculate the figures for basic and fully diluted earnings per share on the net basis and the nil basis.

(b)   To outline any adjustments required to earnings per share of previous years in the comparative figures in the accounts.

7.4   Computation of two years' EPS

The profit and loss accounts of Gnome Ltd for the year to 31 December 19X6 and 31 December 19X7 were as follows:

	19X7	*19X6*
	£000	£000
Turnover	6 500	6 700
Profit before taxation	450	460
Taxation	250	240
Profit after taxation	200	220
Dividends	50	45
Profit for the year retained	150	175

The share capital of the company is divided into ordinary shares of 10p each; the nominal value of the share capital in the two years to 31 December 19X7 has been as follows:

		£
B/fwd	1.1.X6	280 000
Rights issue	31.3.X7	70 000
C/fwd	31.12.X7	350 000

The rights issue was for cash 40p per share; the cum rights market price immediately before the rights issue was 60p. At 31 December 19X2 the company had established an executive share option scheme allowing certain executives to subscribe for up to 600 000 shares at 10p each. The market value of 2½ per cent consolidated stock at 31 December 19X5 was £25 and at 31 December 19X6 was £20. Assume a corporation tax rate of 50 per cent.

You are required:

(a)   To calculate the earnings per share figures to be disclosed in the accounts for the year to 31 December 19X6.

(b)   To calculate the earnings per share figures to be disclosed in the accounts for the year to 31 December 19X7.

7.5   EPS

Answer the following questions in accordance with SSAP 3: Earnings per Share (EPS).

(a)   Why is it considered important to measure EPS and what figure for earnings should you use when calculating EPS for a group of companies with ordinary and preference shares?

(b)   Explain the difference between the nil distribution basis and the net basis for calculating EPS and give the advantage of each method.

(c)   How should you deal with the following situations when calculating EPS?

    (i)   The issue of a separate class of equity shares which do not rank for any dividend in the period under review, but which will do so in the future.

    (ii)   A scrip (or bonus) issue of shares during the year.

    (iii)   Shares issued during the period as consideration for shares in a new subsidiary.

(d)   On 1 January 19X3 a company had 3 million ordinary shares of £1 each in issue. On 1 July 19X3 the company made a rights issue of 1 for 2 at a price of £1.50. The market price of the existing shares immediately before the rights issue was £2.00. The earnings of the company for the year ended 31 December 19X3 were £750 000.

    Calculate the EPS for the year ended 31 December 19X3.

8 SSAP 4: The Accounting Treatment of Government Grants

Introduction

Successive governments have produced a variety of different grant schemes to encourage specific aspects of industrial activity. The appropriate accounting treatment has not always been obvious – in the late 1960s the English and Scottish Institutes contrived to publish opposing recommendations on the topic. Following the Industry Act 1972 this was an obvious area for the ASC to tackle.

SSAP 4 was issued in April 1974. A revised version was issued in July 1990 to allow for changes in types of grant and in company law.

Summary of the statement

Definitions

Government grants are 'assistance by government in the form of cash or transfers of assets to an enterprise in return for past or future compliance with certain conditions relating to the operating activities of the enterprise'. Government includes government and inter-governmental agencies and similar bodies whether local, national or international.

The original SSAP 4 divided government grants between 'revenue-based' grants linked to revenue expenditure and 'capital-based' grants linked to capital expenditure. The revised SSAP 4 drops this distinction, preferring a more flexible statement that 'in the absence of persuasive evidence to the contrary, government grants should be assumed to contribute towards the expenditure that is the basis for their payment'.

Required practice

The key issue to be addressed is that of when government grants should be credited to profit and loss. A grant should not be recognised until:

(a) conditions for its receipt have been complied with;
(b) there is reasonable assurance that the grant will be received.

Once these conditions are met then grants should be credited to profit and loss so as to match them with related expenditure.

Thus:

(a) Grants made to reimburse costs previously incurred, or to give immediate assistance to the business, are recognised as income in the year when they become receivable.

(b) Grants made to finance the general activities of the enterprise over a specific period should be credited to profit in that same period.

(c) Where grants are made to contribute towards specific expenditure on fixed assets they should be credited to profit and loss over the expected useful lives of the related assets.

In principle SSAP 4 recognises two ways of achieving the objective of crediting grants to profit over the life of the related asset as in (c) above:

(a) The objective can be met by setting off the amount of the grant against the cost of the acquisition of the asset. The effect of this method is that the depreciation charge in each year will be based on the net cost of the asset and the grant will effectively be credited to profit and loss over the period that the asset is depreciated.

   While recognising this method 'in principle', SSAP 4 points out that counsel's opinion argues that this is not acceptable under the Companies Act 1985.

(b) The objective can also be met by treating the amount of the grant as a deferred credit and transferring a portion to revenue in each period of the asset's expected useful life. In this case the amount of the deferred credit should be shown separately in the balance sheet if material and must not be shown as part of the shareholders' funds.

Potential liabilities to repay grants in specified circumstances should only be provided for if repayment is 'probable'. Such potential liabilities may require disclosure in line with SSAP 18: Accounting for Contingencies (see Chapter 17).

Disclosure

Disclosure should include:

(a) the accounting policy adopted for grants;

(b) the effects of government grants on the accounts;

(c) where the enterprise receives material government assistance in a form other than grants the nature of the assistance should be disclosed, with an estimate of the financial effects if possible.

Practical application

Recording in the accounts

SSAP 4 considers bookkeeping methods for crediting a capital-based grant to revenue over the life of an asset. The two methods will be illustrated with the simple example of a company buying a machine costing £5000 on 1 April 19X3 on which a grant of 20 per cent is received. Assuming that the plant is written off evenly over a period of four years and that the company makes up its accounts to 31 March the machine will be recorded in the books as follows:

(a) If the company's accounting policy is to reduce the cost of acquisition of the asset by the amount of the grant:

Plant Account

	£			£
1.4.X3 Bank (cost of machine)	5 000	1.4.X3 Bank (grant rec'd)		1 000
31.3.X4 Depreciation c/f	1 000	31.3.X4 Profit and loss (depreciation)		1 000
		31.3.X4 Cost c/f		4 000
	6 000			6 000
1.4.X4 Cost b/f	4 000	1.4.X4 Depreciation b/f		1 000
31.3.X5 Depreciation c/f	2 000	31.3.X5 Profit and loss (depreciation)		1 000
		31.3.X5 Cost c/f		4 000
	6 000			6 000
1.4.X5 Cost b/f	4 000	1.4.X5 Depreciation b/f		2 000
31.3.X6 Depreciation c/f	3 000	31.3.X6 Profit and loss (depreciation)		1 000
		31.3.X6 Cost c/f		4 000
	7 000			7 000
1.4.X6 Cost b/f	4 000	1.4.X6 Depreciation b/f		3 000
31.3.X7 Depreciation c/f	4 000	31.3.X7 Profit and loss (depreciation)		1 000
		31.3.X7 Cost c/f		4 000
	8 000			8 000

Balance sheet extracts

Fixed assets	*31.3.X4*	*31.3.X5*	*31.3.X6*	*31.3.X7*
Plant:				
Cost	4 000	4 000	4 000	4 000
Depreciation	1 000	2 000	3 000	4 000
Written down value	3 000	2 000	1 000	—

(b)   If the company's accounting policy is to treat the amount of the grant as a deferred credit, a portion being transferred to revenue annually:

Plant Account

		£			£
1.4.X3	Bank (cost of machine)	5 000	31.3.X4	Profit and loss (depreciation)	1 250
31.3.X4	Depreciation c/f	1 250	31.3.X4	Cost c/f	5 000
		6 250			6 250
1.4.X4	Cost c/f	5 000	1.4.X4	Depreciation b/f	1 250
			31.3.X5	Profit and loss (depreciation)	1 250
31.3.X5	Depreciation c/f	2 500	31.3.X5	Cost c/f	5 000
		7 500			7 500
1.4.X5	Cost b/f	5 000	1.4.X5	Depreciation b/f	2 500
			31.3.X6	Profit and loss (depreciation)	1 250
31.3.X6	Depreciation c/f	3 750	31.3.X6	Cost c/f	5 000
		8 750			8 750
1.4.X6	Cost b/f	5 000	1.4.X6	Depreciation b/f	3 750
			31.3.X7	Profit and loss (depreciation)	1 250
31.3.X7	Depreciation c/f	5 000	31.3.X7	Cost c/f	5 000
		10 000			10 000

Investment Grant Account

		£			£
31.3.X4	Profit and loss	250	1.4.X3	Bank (grant received)	1 000
31.3.X4	C/f	750			
		1 000			1 000
31.3.X5	Profit and loss	250	1.4.X4	B/f	750
31.3.X5	C/f	500			
		750			750
31.3.X6	Profit and loss	250	1.4.X5	B/f	500
31.3.X6	C/f	250			
		500			500
31.3.X7	Profit and loss	250	1.4.X6	B/f	250

Balance sheet extracts:

Fixed assets	*31.3.X4*	*31.3.X5*	*31.3.X6*	*31.3.X7*
Plant:				
Cost	5 000	5 000	5 000	5 000
Depreciation	1 250	2 500	3 750	5 000
Written down value	3 750	2 500	1 250	—
Deferred liabilities:				
Investment grant				
deferred credit	750	500	250	—

The original exposure draft on the accounting treatment of government grants, ED 9, would have required the second of these two methods, crediting the grant to a deferred credit account, to be used. Arguments in favour of this approach include:

(a)   Assets acquired at different times and locations are recorded on a uniform basis, leading to greater comparability.

(b)   Accounting controls on the ordering, construction and maintenance of assets will be based on the gross value.

(c)   Where an estimate of grant receivable made in one year requires an amendment on receipt of the grant in a subsequent year the necessary adjustment can be made more easily.

The principal argument in favour of the alternative approach, of crediting the amount of the grant to the relevant asset account, is its simplicity, in that by means of the reduced depreciation charge the grant is automatically credited to revenue over the life of the asset.

The legal position

The Companies Act 1985 includes provisions that:

(a)   the amount to be included in the balance sheet in respect of any fixed asset shall be its purchase price or production cost (Sch. 4, para. 17);

(b)   the purchase price of an asset shall be determined by adding to the actual price paid any expenses incidental to its acquisition (Sch. 4, para. 26.1).

The CCAB has received counsel's opinion that the combined effect of these provisions is to rule out the setting off of a grant against the cost of a fixed asset. However, this method does continue to be acceptable for any enterprise not covered by company law.

IAS 20: Accounting for Government Grants and Disclosure of Government Assistance

SSAP 4 is closely in line with the above international standard.

EXAMINATION PRACTICE

8.1   Accounting for grants

On 1 January 19X4 Labrador Ltd purchased an item of plant costing £100 000 with an estimated useful life of five years and no residual value. An investment grant of £20 000 was received relating to this asset on 31 January 19X4. Labrador Ltd makes up its accounts to 31 December.

(a)   You are required to show, for the year ended 31 December 19X4, the entries in the books of account and the entries in the balance sheet relating to this item of plant under both methods considered by SSAP 4.

(b)   Discuss the relative merits of the two methods and explain, with reasons, which method is not permitted under company law.

9

SSAP 5: Accounting for Value Added Tax

Introduction

Background

Value added tax (VAT) was introduced in the UK on 1 April 1973. The main implications for the accountant related to adaptations to the bookkeeping system needed in order to meet the requirements of the Customs and Excise and to enable registered businesses to complete their quarterly VAT returns. Indeed because the VAT system obliged small businesses to maintain detailed and up-to-date records of their transactions one benefit was to make the life of the small practitioner specialising in incomplete records considerably easier! The appropriate accounting treatment of VAT is generally self-evident from an understanding of the principles and workings of the system. SSAP 5, therefore, is not a controversial or complex statement. The ASC issued SSAP 5 in April 1974 with application to accounting periods starting on or after 1 January 1974, and so contrived to establish standard practice at an early stage.

Nature of VAT

The decision to introduce value added tax into the UK was taken at the time of the UK's application to join the then EEC, and brought the UK into line with other member states of the EEC. A proportion of VAT receipts is set aside as part of the income of the Community, and the principles of coverage (but not the rate of tax) have been harmonised throughout the EC.

If we imagine a transaction in a standard rated product, assuming a VAT rate of 15 per cent:

	Selling price £	VAT £	Paid to Customs and Excise £
A Ltd, a producer of raw materials, sells £100 worth to B Ltd, a manufacturer	100	15.00	
A Ltd pays over output tax			15.00
B Ltd, the manufacturer, produces a widget with the raw materials and sells it to C Ltd, a wholesaler	200	30.00	

	Selling price £	VAT £	Paid to Customs and Excise £
A Ltd pays output tax – input tax (30 – 15)			15.00
C Ltd sells the widget to D Ltd, a retailer	250	37.50	
C Ltd pays output tax – input tax (37.50 – 30)			7.50
D Ltd sells the widget to John Smith, an accountancy student who has heard a lot about widgets and has always wanted to own one	300	45.00	
D Ltd pays output tax – input tax (45 – 37.50)			7.50
Total VAT paid			45.00

John Smith, the individual customer, pays £345 for his widget to D Ltd; of this £300 is the purchase consideration due to D Ltd and £45 is value added tax collected by D Ltd and paid over to the Customs and Excise. Customs and Excise have collected their £45 in four stages, on each occasion when the product has changed hands. Each of the four companies involved has acted as a collector of the tax, paying over to the Customs and Excise tax they have collected (output tax) after deducting tax they have borne themselves.

There are currently two rates of VAT, 'zero rate' of 0 per cent and 'standard rate' of 17.5 per cent. The total amount of tax collected by the Customs and Excise will depend on the rate applicable to the transaction entered into with the final customer; a registered business will be able to recover input tax relating to its purchases even if its sales are 'zero-rated' so that an amount is repaid to the business by the Customs and Excise. A registered business cannot reclaim input tax on motor cars used in the business or expenditure on business entertainment (other than of overseas customers) so that the burden of this 'non-deductible' input tax falls on the business itself.

Certain types of supply are 'exempt', in that the business is not required to charge VAT on goods and services it supplies but is not able to recover input tax on its own purchases; thus in this case the business itself is the final consumer and VAT on purchases is part of their cost. A complication arises in relation to businesses whose trade is part taxable and part exempt; such 'partially exempt' businesses may only recover a part of their input tax.

Summary of the statement

General principles

SSAP 5 is based on the view that the accounting treatment of VAT should reflect the role of the business as a *collector* of tax, VAT being, as we have already seen, 'a tax on the supply of goods and services which is eventually borne by the final consumer but collected at each stage of the production and distribution chain'. Thus VAT will not be included in income and expenditure except where the business itself bears the tax. The provisions of SSAP 5 cover two areas:

(a)   accounting for the normal situation where the business acts as a collector of VAT;

(b)   accounting for the position where the business bears the cost of VAT.

The collection of VAT

SSAP 5 provides that turnover shown in the profit and loss account should exclude the related VAT. If the company wishes to show gross turnover as well, the related VAT should be shown as a deduction in arriving at turnover exclusive of VAT.

The net amount due to or from the Customs and Excise in respect of VAT should be shown as part of debtors or creditors and will not normally require separate disclosure.

SSAP 5 provided guidance on disclosure appropriate during the transitional period, when comparative figures for sales in the accounts covering the period prior to the introduction of VAT might include purchase tax. The statement suggested that to provide comparability both the net and the gross figures be shown for each period.

VAT borne by the business

Where VAT paid on goods and services acquired by the business is not recoverable, either because the business is 'exempt' or because input tax on those specific goods and services is 'non-deductible', then VAT forms part of the cost of those goods and services and should be accounted for accordingly. Specifically irrecoverable VAT allocable to fixed assets and to other items separately identified in the published accounts should be included in cost where 'practicable and material'.

A practical problem does arise in the case of the partially exempt business where, normally, the proportion of input tax disallowed will be equal to the proportion of sales which are exempt. Where the financial and VAT accounting periods do not coincide it may be necessary to make an estimate of irrecoverable VAT for the year. Having found the proportion of input tax which is irrecoverable that amount should be allocated over the cost of the related goods and services, if material.

SSAP 5 and the examiner

It is difficult to envisage a situation where a question on accounting would be totally devoted to VAT. The subject is only likely to arise as part of a 'published accounts' or 'tax in accounts' question, when it is important to remember the principles of SSAP 5.

EXAMINATION PRACTICE

9.1   VAT and turnover
Should the turnover figure shown in a set of published accounts include VAT?

9.2   VAT and fixed assets
Should the amount at which additions to fixed assets is stated in a limited company's published accounts include or exclude VAT?

10

SSAP 8:
The Treatment of Taxation under the Imputation System in the Accounts of Companies

Taxation of companies – an overview

For the purposes of taxation, company profits can be approached from two viewpoints. The company trades as a distinct legal personality in its own right, and can be regarded as liable to taxation on the profits of its trade. The company's shareholders draw profits out of the business in the form of dividends, and profits withdrawn in this way can be regarded as income of the individual investors and, again, be liable to taxation in their hands. Prior to 1965, companies were assessed to income tax on their profits in the same way as sole traders and partnerships. The tax paid by the company covered the income tax liability of shareholders on dividends paid to them. Companies were not liable to surtax, but shareholders were liable to surtax on dividends received by them. In the latter years of this system, companies were also liable to pay profits tax.

The 1965 Finance Act introduced a completely new system whereby corporation tax was levied on the profits of the company. Dividends paid by the company were treated as taxable income in the hands of the recipient. Thus company profits were subject to corporation tax, and when distributed as dividends were again subject to tax as income of the shareholder, so that the total tax taken from profits distributed as dividends was higher than that taken from retained profits. Under this system companies had an obligation to deduct basic rate tax from dividends distributed and pay this over to the Inland Revenue, in exactly the same way as tax is deducted from such items as loan interest and royalty payments.

The imputation system, adopted in the United Kingdom in 1973, is intended to ensure that company profits are only subject to taxation once, by allowing shareholders to treat a proportion of the corporation tax on the profits of the company as a credit against their own income tax liability. In very brief outline the system, as amended by subsequent legislation, works as follows:

(a) Corporation tax is levied on the profits of the company. This liability is payable on a date nine months after the end of an accounting period.

(b) When in an accounting period a company makes a distribution to shareholders, it is required to make an advance payment of corporation tax (ACT) equivalent to:

$$\frac{\text{Current ACT rate}}{100 - \text{Current ACT rate}} \times \text{The amount of the distribution}$$

In practice, the ACT rate will be equal to the basic rate of income tax.

(c)   The shareholder receiving the dividend is liable to tax on an amount equal to the total of the dividend plus the related tax credit. The tax credit can be set off against the shareholder's own tax liability.

(d)   Distributions received by a company from another UK resident company are called 'franked investment income'. The tax credit on such income can be set off against a company's liabilities to pay ACT on its own distributions; where the payment of ACT on a distribution precedes receipt of franked investment income in the same period, the tax credit on the income received may be reclaimed up to the amount of ACT paid. Where franked investment income in a period exceeds franked payments, the excess tax credit may be set off against any ACT liability arising in a future period.

(e)   ACT paid in a period can be set off against the liability to corporation tax on the profits of the period up to a maximum of:

$$\frac{\text{Current ACT rate}}{100} \times \text{Taxable profit for year}$$

Unrelieved ACT can be carried back six years or can be carried forward indefinitely. The liability to corporation tax after set off of ACT is known as the 'mainstream' liability.

The problem of accounting for taxation

The imputation system of taxation posed a number of problems to accountants. These included:

How to show dividends paid and proposed

The benefit of a dividend to a UK resident shareholder consists of the cash amount plus the related tax credit, and therefore it could be argued that the amount of dividend for the year should be shown including ACT, and that only the 'mainstream' tax liability should be shown as the corporation tax charge. Such a treatment would make dividend figures comparable with previous years. On the other hand, as far as the company is concerned, the amount it pays to its members is the actual dividend declared, while the payment of related ACT normally only affects the date at which corporation tax is paid. The effect of 'grossing up' dividends and correspondingly reducing the tax charge for the year by the amount of ACT would be to make the amount of the tax charge, and consequently the figure for after-tax profit, dependent on the company's dividend policy. SSAP 8, therefore, requires that dividends paid and proposed be shown without including related ACT.

Determining whether ACT is recoverable

Where ACT cannot be set off against corporation tax on the profits of the period in which it is paid or be carried back six years, then it is necessary to predict whether the ACT will be recoverable against tax on the profits of future periods. If the company has a deferred taxation account, then it is reasonable to forecast that ACT will be recoverable up to the amount of:

$$\frac{\text{Current ACT rate}}{100} \times \text{Amount on which deferred tax account has been calculated}$$

To the extent that ACT cannot be set off against the deferred tax balance, then it will be necessary to predict future profit and dividend levels. SSAP 8 recommends that such predictions should not normally be made more than one year ahead.

Treatment of irrecoverable ACT in the profit and loss account

While there is no doubt that irrecoverable ACT should be written off to the profit and loss account, there are two differing views on the appropriate presentation. One view is that irrecoverable ACT is an expense arising from the payment of dividends, and should be treated as an appropriation in the same way as the dividend itself. The alternative view is that irrecoverable ACT should be regarded as part of the tax charge for the year deducted in arriving at profits after tax. SSAP 8 takes the second view but also requires that the amount of irrecoverable ACT should be disclosed separately if material so that readers of accounts may adjust the figures for their own purposes if they wish. As we have already seen, SSAP 3 on Earnings per Share was amended at the time of the introduction of the imputation system to deal with the problem of irrecoverable ACT.

Similar problems may arise in respect of overseas tax unrelieved because of dividend payments.

Accounting for tax relating to franked investment income

The company is not liable to corporation tax on such income but cannot reclaim the related tax credit. The effect is that the dividend, representing income earned and distributed by another company which will already have been subject to corporation tax, will not be subject to further taxation. The right to reduce ACT paid by a company by the amount of the tax credit on its franked investment income ensures that no problem of irrecoverable ACT will arise as a result. A discussion paper issued by the ICAEW in 1972 considered two methods:

(a) grossing up the net amount of the franked investment income at the full corporation tax rate, including the gross amount in profit before tax, and including the taxation element in the tax charge;

(b) bringing net franked investment income into the profit and loss account at the 'profit after tax' stage.

The discussion paper favoured the first approach. The exposure draft on the imputation system of taxation proposed that companies be allowed a choice of treatment, either:

(a) bringing franked investment income into the profit and loss account at the cash amount received; or

(b) bringing franked investment income into the profit and loss account grossed up to include related ACT, and showing the related ACT as part of the tax charge.

SSAP 8, in fact, does not allow any choice of treatment and requires that method (b) should always be followed.

It is interesting to observe the change in approach between 1972 and 1974. The discussion paper expressed a preference for a method not even considered in the exposure draft; the exposure draft gave a choice between a method considered suitable in the discussion paper and one which had been rejected as unsuitable in the discussion paper; while the SSAP finally issued required use of the method rejected in the discussion paper as 'not considered appropriate because it ignores the mainstream corporation tax additionally payable in respect of the underlying profits from which the dividends are derived'.

Disclosure in the balance sheet

A company may find itself with either one mainstream liability disclosed in the balance sheet, representing tax on the profit of the year, or two mainstream liabilities representing tax on the profits of the previous year payable within the year following the balance sheet date and tax on the profits of the year under review payable more than twelve months after the balance sheet date. Thus it is necessary to decide whether tax liabilities should be disclosed as current or deferred, and where a liability is not current, SSAP 8 requires disclosure of the date for payment.

Where a dividend is proposed at the balance sheet date, ACT in respect of the proposed dividend, if regarded as recoverable, will be both an asset and a liability. However, the amount of ACT will become payable within three months of the payment of the dividend, so that it will constitute a current liability, while the ACT will only be recoverable against tax due on the profits of the year in which the dividend is paid, i.e. 21 months from the balance sheet date, so that the ACT recoverable will be a deferred asset.

The change to the imputation system in 1973

This created a problem in relation to dividend percentages, in that a dividend percentage expressed under the old system referred to dividend before deduction of tax, while a dividend percentage under the new system referred to the net dividend exclusive of related ACT. The Finance Act 1972 reduced dividend rights on preference shares to seven-tenths of their former amount, the ACT rate then being 30 per cent, so as to maintain the same benefit for preference shareholders. Subsequent changes in the ACT rate have no effect on this once-for-all reduction in yield, so that in years when the ACT rate exceeds 30 per cent, the preference shareholder is better off as a result of this change, and in a year when the ACT rate is lower than 30 per cent, the preference shareholder is worse off. Where, therefore, preference shares in issue prior to 6 April 1973 are described by the old gross rate, SSAP 8 requires that the new rate must also be disclosed.

Definition and summary of requirements

SSAP 8 defines the following terms.

(a) *Recoverable ACT* is 'that amount of the ACT paid or payable on outgoing dividends paid and proposed which can be:
   (i)   set off against a corporation tax liability on the profits of the period under review or of previous periods; or
   (ii) properly set off against a credit balance on deferred tax account; or
   (iii) expected to be recoverable taking into account expected profits and dividends — normally those of the next accounting period only'.
(b) *Irrecoverable ACT* is 'ACT paid or payable on outgoing dividends paid or proposed other than recoverable ACT'.

Profit and loss account

SSAP 8 requires that the following should be included in the taxation charge and separately disclosed where material:

(a) The amount of the UK corporation tax charge specifying:
   (i)   charge to tax on income for the year, separately identifying the deferred tax movement;
   (ii) tax on franked investment income;
   (iii) ACT considered irrecoverable;
   (iv) Relief for overseas taxation.
(b) Total overseas taxation, relieved and unrelieved, specifying that part of overseas taxation arising from payment of dividends. The statement also lays down:
   (i)   that outgoing dividends should be shown at the net cash amount excluding related ACT;
   (ii) incoming dividends should be shown at the amount of cash received plus the related tax credit;
   (iii) That the tax rate used in computing the tax charge for the year should be disclosed, and that where the rate applicable to the period is not known, the latest known rate should be used.

Balance sheet

SSAP 8 lays down the following requirements:

(a) Proposed dividends should be included as current liabilities excluding related ACT. The ACT on proposed dividends should be shown as a current tax liability.
(b) Where ACT on proposed dividends is regarded as recoverable, it should be deducted from the deferred tax account; where a deferred tax account is not available for this purpose ACT recoverable should be shown as a deferred asset.
(c) Where the title of preference shares issued prior to 6 April 1973 includes a fixed rate of dividend, the new rate of dividend should be included in the description of the shares in the balance sheet.

Worked example

Examination questions involving an understanding of SSAP 8 normally fall into one of two categories:

(a) Questions on the presentation of published accounts requiring the student to make the final adjustments for such items as ACT on the proposed dividend and to make full and accurate disclosure in accordance with SSAP 8.

(b) Questions requiring the student to draw up the ledger accounts relating to taxation and to show extracts from the published profit and loss account and balance sheet relating to taxation. Such questions may require the student to show the ability to handle the double entry problems of accounting for situations where the company acts as a *collector* of tax, e.g. PAYE, VAT, and deductions from payments made, as well as being able to account for the company's corporation tax liabilities.

The following question on Horace Ltd is of the second kind taken from an old ACCA paper.

As the accountant of Horace Ltd, a public limited company, you are responsible for the preparation of its accounts for publication. You have been presented with an agreed trial balance at the year ended 30 September 19X6, including the following accounts, which whilst balanced, are incomplete due to the omission of the entries reflecting taxation.

Dividends Received

Dr		£	Cr			£
19X6 30 Sep	Balance c/f	442	19X6 4 Mar	Bank		442
			19X6 30 Sep	Balance b/f		442

Royalties Receivable

Dr		£	Cr			£
19X6 30 Sep	Balance c/f	871	19X5 30 Nov	Bank		403
			19X6 31 Aug	Bank		468
		871				871
			19X6 30 Sep	Balance b/f		871

Debenture Interest Payable

Dr		£	Cr			£
19X6 31 Jan	Bank	1 950	19X5 1 Oct	Balance b/f		1 000
19X6 31 Jul	Bank	1 950	19X6 30 Sep	Balance c/f		2 900
		3 900				3 900
19X6 30 Sep	Balance b/f	2 900				

Taxation Account

Dr			£	Cr			£
19X5	1 Oct	Balance b/f	3 058	19X5	1 Oct	Balance b/f	35 547
19X5	31 Dec	Bank	3 058				
19X6	1 Jan	Bank	15 489				
19X6	31 Mar	Bank	833				
19X6	30 Sep	Bank	798				
19X6	30 Sep	Balance c/f	12 311				
			35 547				35 547
				19X6	30 Sep	Balance b/f	12 311

The following information is relevant:

(i) Dividends received. These arise from a 5 per cent equity shareholding in a UK-registered company quoted on the London Stock Exchange. The associated tax credit amounts to £238.

(ii) Royalties receivable. These were received under deduction of tax.

(iii) Debenture interest payable. The payments made are the half-yearly instalments in respect of £80 000 7½ per cent mortgage debentures made on the due dates under deduction of tax.

(iv) Taxation account. Only payments to the Inland Revenue have been dealt with. The opening debit balance represents advance corporation tax recoverable. The opening credit balance comprises the agreed corporation tax liability of £15 489, based on the accounting year ended 30 September 19X4; £17 000, the estimated liability for corporation tax based on the accounting year ended 30 September 19X5; and advance corporation tax liability of £3058.

(v) The basic rate of income tax is to be taken as 35 per cent.

(vi) You need to deal with a proposal to provide for a dividend of £6500 for 19X6. The 19X5 dividend was paid on 20 December 19X5, and associated ACT of £3058 on 31 December 19X5.

(vii) The corporation tax liability based on the accounting year ended 30 September 19X6 is estimated to be £18 000, while the corporation tax liability based on the year ended 30 September 19X5 had been agreed at £15 844.

(*Note:* Although recent legislation eliminates the 15-month payment time implied in this example, no change has been made in order to illustrate how to account for two years' liabilities.)

You are required, using the information available:

(a) to continue and to complete the accounts by making the necessary entries; and

(b) to show, by way of extracts therefrom, how the resultant figures would be revealed in the published profit and loss account and balance sheet, conforming with contemporary legal and accounting standards.

We would work through this question as follows:

(1) The dividend received is shown as the net cash amount. To comply with SSAP 8 we must show the gross dividend received as part of the profit for the year

and the related ACT as part of the tax charge, so we make the following journal entry (a):

Dr	Taxation	£238
Cr	Dividends received	£238

(2)   Royalties receivable and debenture interest payable are shown under deduction of tax. The related tax will be:

Royalty received 30 Nov	$£403 \times \dfrac{35}{65} = £217$
Royalty received 31 Aug	$£468 \times \dfrac{35}{65} = £252$
Interest paid 31 Jan	$£1950 \times \dfrac{35}{65} = £1050$
Interest paid 31 Jul	$£1950 \times \dfrac{35}{65} = £1050$

So that the following journal entry (b) will be required:

		£	£
Dr	Debenture interest	2100	
Cr	Taxation		2100
Cr	Royalties receivable		469
Dr	Taxation	469	
		2569	2569

(3)   The balance of £12 311 on the taxation account has been made up as follows:

		£
19X4 liability b/f		15 489
19X5 liability b/f		17 000
ACT payable		3 058
		35 547
Less: ACT recoverable b/f		3 058
		32 489
Less: Cash payments:		
ACT paid	3 058	
19X4 liability paid	15 489	
Tax deducted at source paid	1 631	20 178
		£12 311

The 19X4 liability brought forward has been paid. The 19X5 liability of £17 000 has now been agreed at £15 844, so that an adjustment (c) is required:

Taxation	£1156	
Profit and loss		£1156

It is important to remember that FRS 3 requires that such items must *not* be shown as prior year adjustments.

The ACT payable brought forward has been paid during the year and the ACT recoverable brought forward can therefore be set off against the tax liability on profits for the year. Having provided for tax on profits for the year by adjustment (d):

Dr	Profit and loss	£18 000	
Cr	Taxation		£18 000

we carry forward the mainstream liability for 19X6 less the ACT recoverable against it, i.e. £18 000 − £3058 = £14 942.

Finally, it is necessary to work out the ACT payable and recoverable on the proposed dividend of £6500. ACT on the dividend would amount to:

$$£6500 \times \frac{35}{65} = £3500$$

from which should be deducted the ACT on franked investment income of £238 to give a current liability and deferred asset of £3262.

These accounts will then appear as follows:

Dividends Received

		£			£
19X6 30 Sep	Profit and loss	680	19X6 30 Sep	Balance b/f	442
			19X6 30 Sep	Taxation account	
				(a)	238
		680			680

Royalties Receivable

		£			£
19X6 30 Sep	Profit and loss	1 340	19X6 30 Sep	Balance b/f	871
		1 340	19X6 30 Sep	Taxation (b)	469
					1 340

Debenture Interest Payable

		£			£
19X6 30 Sep	Balance b/f	2 900	19X6 30 Sep	Profit and loss	6 000
19X6 30 Sep	Taxation (b)	2 100			
19X6 30 Sep	Balance c/f				
	(2/12 × 6 000)	1 000			
		6 000			6 000

Proposed Dividends

		£			£
19X6 30 Sep	C/f	6 500	19X6 30 Sep	Profit and loss	6 500
		6 500			6 500

Taxation Account

			£			£
19X6 30 Sep	Dividends received (a)		238	19X6 30 Sep	Balance b/f	12 311
19X6 30 Sep	Tax deducted (b)		469	19X6 30 Sep	Tax deducted at source (b)	2 100
19X6 30 Sep	Profit and loss (c)		1 156	19X6 30 Sep	Profit and loss (d)	18 000
19X6 30 Sep	Balance c/f:			19X6 30 Sep	Profit and loss – Tax on FII	238
	19X5 Tax	15 844		19X6 30 Sep	ACT recoverable c/f	3 262
	19X6 Tax	14 942				
	ACT payable	3 262				
			34 048			
			35 911			35 911

Horace Limited
Profit and loss account for year to 30 September 19X6

	£	£
Profit for year		x
After charging:		
Debenture interest	6 000	
and crediting:		
Quoted investment income	680	
Profit before tax		x
Corporation tax		
(i.e. 18 000 – 1 156)	16 844	
ACT on franked investment income	238	
		17 082

Profit after tax	x
Less: Proposed dividends	6 500
Profit taken to reserves	x

Balance sheet extracts

Current liabilities

Current taxation	15 844
Proposed dividend	6 500
ACT payable	3 262

Deferred liabilities

Taxation payable 1 Jan 19X8	14 942

Deferred assets

ACT recoverable	3 262

Note that in this example a single taxation account was used to embrace entries relating to corporation tax, ACT and tax deducted from interest payments. It is equally acceptable to use separate accounts for these items.

Of the two questions that follow the first, Chatham Ltd, is extracted from a published accounts question set in a professional examination, while the second, Pitt Ltd, requires an ability to prepare the ledger accounts. In answering these questions, some knowledge of the principles of deferred taxation (covered in Chapter 14) is required.

EXAMINATION PRACTICE

10.1   Tax in published accounts

The accounts of Chatham Ltd at 30 November 19X0 included the following balances:

	Dr £	Cr £
Interim dividend	9600	
Advance corporation tax	4945	
Corporation tax payable 1 January 19X1		32 000
Deferred taxation		52 720

The following additional information is available:

(i)   Corporation tax payable on the adjusted profits for the year is estimated at £17 000 and the liability for the previous year has now been agreed at £31 752.

(ii)   The balance of the deferred taxation account comprises transfers in respect of accelerated capital allowances of £58 902 less recoverable ACT on the previous years' dividend £6182 (no interim dividend had been paid in the previous year). A further £50 600 is to be transferred to the account this year in respect of accelerated capital allowances.

(iii)   A final dividend totalling £14 400 is proposed.

(iv)   The ACT rate is 34 per cent and the corporation tax rate is 52 per cent.

You are required to prepare the extracts from the published profit and loss account and balance sheet relating to taxation. *(Extracted from ACCA question)*

10.2 Tax in the ledger

Pitt Ltd has an issued capital of £330 000 in fully paid 50p ordinary shares. At 31 December 19X6 the following balances were included in the company's balance sheet:

	£
Agreed corporation tax liability on 19X5 profits	16 300
Estimated corporation tax liability on 19X6 profits	5 000
Deferred taxation account	29 400
Profit and loss account (credit)	43 000

(No dividends had been paid or proposed in respect of 19X6)

The following information relates to the year ended 31 December 19X7:

Corporation tax liability for 19X5 settled (January)
Interim dividend of 2p per share paid (August)
Advance corporation tax on interim dividend paid (October)
Corporation tax liability for 19X6 agreed at £3800 (December)
Net profit for 19X7 before tax calculated at £88 800
Corporation tax based on the 19X7 profits estimated at £36 000
Directors proposed a final dividend of 5p per share

A transfer to the deferred taxation account of £7000 for 19X7 is to be made in respect of capital allowances in excess of depreciation charges.

Required:

(a) Make all relevant entries in the ledger accounts (except cash and share capital) and complete the profit and loss account for 19X7. Show how the final balances would be included in the balance sheet at 31 December 19X7. (Assume that the basic rate of income tax is 34 per cent.)

(b) A holder of 3300 shares has asked you about his own position. He is not sure whether the dividend declared is gross or net. Briefly explain. *(ACCA)*

10.3 Definitions

How should you treat the following items when preparing financial statements in accordance with statements of standard accounting practice:

(i) franked investment income;
(ii) proposed dividends and the related advance corporation tax;
(iii) recoverable advance corporation tax;
(iv) irrecoverable advance corporation tax;
(v) value added output tax on turnover for a VAT registered trader;
(vi) irrecoverable value added input tax on a fixed asset, purchased by a VAT registered trader;
(vii) the receipt and payment of VAT to the Customs and Excise? *(CACA)*

11 SSAP 9: Stocks and Long-term Contracts

Introduction

In practice no area of accounting has produced wider differences than the valuation put on stock and work in progress in the financial accounts. SSAP 9 was issued with the following objectives:

(a)   to narrow the areas of difference and variation in accounting practice on stock and work in progress;

(b)   to ensure adequate disclosure in the accounts.

The problems involved in laying down a coherent set of rules which will cover the practical problems of stock valuation in all kinds of trading activity, and in all kinds of accounting systems, are very considerable. SSAP 9 is made up of a fairly brief set of principles laying down a wide ranging set of requirements relating to accounting practice and disclosure, together with extensive guidance given in the explanatory notes and appendices relating to the practical problems of complying with the standard.

Summary of the statement

Definitions

The definition of terms in SSAP 9 is particularly important because of the technical detail they contain; many companies had to change their accounting policies in order to come into line with these definitions.

The term 'stocks and work in progress' is defined in terms of its component parts, these being listed as goods purchased for resale, consumable stores, materials purchased for manufacture into products for sale, products and services in the course of completion, and finished goods. The following terms are important in valuing stock:

(a)   *Cost* is defined as the expenditure 'incurred in the normal course of business in bringing the product or service to its present location and condition'. The statement specifically lays down that this expenditure includes both the 'cost of purchase', defined as the purchase price including such items as import duties and handling costs and deducting such items as trade discounts and rebates, and the 'cost of conversion', defined as comprising direct costs, 'production overheads', and any other attributable overheads. 'Production overheads' are defined as those incurred in respect of materials, labour and services for production, based on the normal level of activity. It is therefore necessary to classify each overhead as to function, such as production, selling or administration, so as to include in the cost of stock all overheads relating to production, including depreciation.

(b) *Net realisable value* is defined as estimated selling price less all costs to completion and all costs relating to sale of the product.

The following terms are important in valuing long-term contract work in progress:

(a) *Long-term contract:* a contract entered into for the design, manufacture or construction of a single substantial asset or the provision of a service (or of a combination of assets or services which together constitute a single project) where the time taken substantially to complete the contract is such that the contract activity falls into different accounting periods. A contract that is required to be accounted for as long term by this accounting standard will usually extend for a period exceeding one year. However, a duration exceeding one year is not an essential feature of a long-term contract. Some contracts with a shorter duration than one year should be accounted for as long-term contracts if they are sufficiently material to the activity of the period that not to record turnover and attributable profit would lead to a distortion of the period's turnover and results such that the financial statements would not give a true and fair view, provided that the policy is applied consistently within the reporting entity and from year to year.

(b) *Attributable profit:* that part of the total profit currently estimated to arise over the duration of the contract, after allowing for estimated remedial and maintenance costs and increases in costs so far as not recoverable under the terms of the contract, that fairly reflects the profit attributable to that part of the work performed at the accounting date. (There can be no attributable profit until the profitable outcome of the contract can be assessed with reasonable certainty.)

(c) *Foreseeable losses:* losses which are currently estimated to arise over the duration of the contract (after allowing for estimated remedial and maintenance costs and increases in costs so far as not recoverable under the terms of the contract). This estimate is required irrespective of:
    (i)   whether or not work has yet commenced on such contracts;
    (ii) the proportion of work carried out at the accounting date;
    (iii) the amount of profits expected to arise on other contracts.

(d) *Payments on account:* all amounts received and receivable at the accounting date in respect of contracts in progress.

Stock

SSAP 9 requires that stock and work in progress, other than long-term contract work in progress, should be valued at the total of the lower of the cost and the net realisable value of each individual item or, where this is impractical, of each group of individual items. The statement specifically rejects the idea of taking the lower of the total of cost and the total of net realisable value on the grounds that this could result in setting off foreseeable losses on items with a net realisable value lower than cost against unrealised profits on items where cost is less than net realisable value. A summary in the notes to the accounts should show the amounts of stock held in each of the main categories.

Long-term contracts

For long-term contracts an assessment must be made on a contract by contract basis. In the profit and loss account turnover and related costs relating to each contract should be recorded as the contract activity progresses. Where it is considered that the outcome of a long-term contract can be assessed with reasonable certainty before its conclusion, then 'attributable profit' should be recognised in the profit and loss account as the difference between the reported turnover and related costs for that contract.

The following balance sheet treatment of long-term contracts is required:

(a)   If recorded turnover is in excess of payments received on account then the excess is disclosed separately within debtors as 'amounts recoverable on contracts'.

(b)   If payments received on account exceed related turnover and related long-term contract balances the excess is disclosed separately within creditors as payments on account.

(c)   The long-term contract costs less:
  (i)   amounts transferred to cost of sales, and
  (ii) foreseeable losses and payments on account not matched with turnover, should be shown as 'stocks'.
  The balance sheet note should identify separately:
  (i)   net cost less foreseeable losses, and
  (ii) applicable payments on account.

(d)   If the provision or accrual for foreseeable losses exceeds the costs incurred (after transfer to cost of sales) the excess should be included within either provisions for liabilities and charges or creditors as appropriate.

Accounting policies

The accounting policies that have been applied to stock and long-term contracts should be stated and applied consistently. In particular the methods of ascertaining turnover and attributable profit must be disclosed.

Practical problems

Types of problem

The basic principles to be applied in placing a value on stock and work in progress are laid down by the SSAP and by the accompanying definitions of terms. While these principles are in themselves quite straightforward, there can be considerable practical difficulties in their application; many of these difficulties will arise from circumstances relevant to particular types of business or will depend on the nature of the company's accounting system. The practical difficulties of application are dealt with in some detail in the appendices to SSAP 9.

Ascertaining cost

As we have seen, the definition of 'cost' in SSAP 9 requires that an appropriate portion of related production overheads should be added to the direct costs of stock, in order to reflect the expense of bringing the product 'to its present location and condition'.

Where the company needs to exercise prudence in valuing stock and work in progress this should be taken into account in arriving at the net realisable value, not by excluding from cost selected overheads.

Overheads should be allocated on the basis of function (e.g. production, marketing or selling) rather than according to whether the overhead arises from usage or on a time basis; therefore it will be necessary to exercise judgement in allocating overhead expenses to specific units of production. General management expenses are not directly related to production and therefore should not be included in the cost of stock, but in a small organisation where management responsibility may cover a number of functions including production it may be necessary to allocate management costs accordingly. Where a business has service departments it will be necessary to allocate these costs in proportion to the use made of them by the main functions of the business. For example, the accounting department might serve the production function by paying production wages and salaries and operating the purchase ledger function, the marketing function by paying sales staff salaries and controlling the sales ledger, and the general administrative function by the preparation of annual accounts and financial information for management purposes – in such a case only the costs of servicing the production function will be included in the 'cost of conversion'.

There is an exception to the rule that only production overheads should be included in the 'cost of conversion': where there is a specific contract to supply goods and services then overheads relating to design and the selling expenses related to the contract may also be included, while in the case of a long-term contract interest payments on borrowings specifically related to financing the work may also be carried forward as part of the cost. These circumstances should be rare in practice, and where non-production overheads are carried forward in the stock figure the accounting policy should be disclosed and explained.

When including overheads in the cost of stock and work in progress, allocations should be made on the basis of the normal level of activity, and abnormal costs should be excluded. There are a number of reasons why a factory might, during a period, run at less than its full capacity. For example, there may be stoppages due to industrial action, or there may be reduced production during the starting up, closing down, or reorganisation of a production line. In these cases indirect production expenses will remain constant, and if allocated over the reduced quantity of production would result in increased costs being carried forward in the stock valuation. The rule is that the cost of unused capacity should be written off in the year incurred, and costs carried forward should be based on the normal level of production. For example, supposing a factory with a capacity for producing a million cork-screws a year only produces 500 000 during one year because of industrial action. There are direct costs of £1 per cork-screw and overheads of £400 000, and stock at the year end is 250 000 cork-screws. If the total costs of the year were evenly spread over actual production then stock would be valued as follows:

	£
250 000 × £1 direct costs	250 000
$\dfrac{250\ 000}{500\ 000}$ × £400 000 overheads	200 000
Cost including 'conversion cost'	£450 000

Whereas based on the normal level of activity:

	£
250 000 × £1 direct costs	250 000
$\dfrac{250\ 000}{1\ 000\ 000}$ × £400 000 overheads	100 000
Cost including 'conversion cost'	£350 000

If costs were allocated on the basis of actual production we would have carried forward in the stock valuation £100 000 of costs which in fact arose not from producing that stock but from the failure during the year to achieve normal production; clearly this is unacceptable.

The practical problems of actually allocating cost will depend on the company's own costing system. Where a standard costing system is in operation, the variance accounts should be examined and, where substantial variances are shown, it may be necessary to adjust the stock value accordingly. Where a marginal costing system is used it will be necessary to calculate the appropriate portion of production overheads to add on to the direct costs of stock for the purposes of the financial accounts.

Normally a number of identical items will have been purchased or manufactured over a period of time, and there will be a problem in relating cost to specific stock items. Methods used include FIFO, LIFO, base stock, average cost and replacement cost. The appendix to SSAP 9 rejects LIFO, base stock and replacement cost but makes no recommendation on which of the other methods should be applied. In practice LIFO is rarely used in the UK, except for companies with USA subsidiaries where, for tax reasons, LIFO is a commonly used method.

SSAP 9 refers to the method used by some companies, particularly retail stores, of estimating the cost of stock by deducting from the sales value the gross profit percentage. While acknowledging that in some circumstances this may be the only practical method of finding a cost figure, the statement advises that it is only acceptable where it can be demonstrated that this method does give a reasonable approximation to actual cost.

Net realisable value

The net realisable value of stock is the amount which will be realised from the disposal of stock less all costs to complete the product and costs of marketing, selling and distribution. The principal situations in which net realisable value may be lower than cost are:

(a) obsolescence of stock, through technical or marketing developments;
(b) physical deterioration of stock;
(c) excessive or overpriced stockholdings arising from errors in production or purchasing;
(d) a fall in the market price of stock;
(e) a deliberate management decision to sell goods at a loss for marketing purposes.

The first three items can be linked to such factors as age, movements in the past and forecast movements, and companies may have standard formulae for making provisions against stock values based on age and movement analysis of stock. While such formulae will be helpful in establishing a consistent policy, it is still necessary to review any provision in case other circumstances apply. Where stocks of spares are held for resale then it may be possible to predict obsolescence by reference to the number of units sold to which the spares are applicable. In forecasting net realisable value, events occurring between the balance sheet date and completion of the accounts need to be considered.

SSAP 9 specifically rejects reduction to estimated replacement cost when this is lower than cost and net realisable value, on the grounds that the object of a provision against cost is to achieve a breakeven position, not to create profits for the future. However, the statement acknowledges that in some circumstances replacement cost will constitute the best guide to realisable value.

Comparison of cost and net realisable value

The comparison of cost and net realisable value needs to be made in respect of each item of stock separately. Where this is impractical it may be necessary to take groups of similar items together. Thus supposing a garage has the following stocks:

	Cost	NRV	Lower of cost and NRV
	£	£	£
Used car ABC 1	500	600	500
Used car ABC 2	1200	1000	1000
Used car ABC 3	1400	1600	1400
Spare engines	1000	800	800
Other spares	900	1200	900
	£5000	£5200	£4600

The correct value to put on cost is £4600. If the lower of total cost or total net realisable value were taken then the result would be to set off foreseen losses against unrealised profits.

Long-term contracts

The basic principle of SSAP 9 is that where there is reasonable certainty that a profit will be made on a long-term contract then the attributable profit should be included in the profit and loss account. Where a loss is expected on the contract then the whole of the loss should be provided for immediately.

The standard included a simple example to illustrate this, reproduced here as Table 11.1. Letters of the alphabet to designate lines have been added to help explanation.

For each project the results of the most recent evaluation are shown. Line (a) shows the estimated value of work done and line (h) shows the related costs – the totals of both lines are shown in the profit and loss account.

Table 11.1 Example as given in SSAP 9

Line		*Project number* 1	2	3	4	5	*Balance sheet total*	*Profit and loss account*
(a)	Recorded as turnover – being value of work done	145	520	380	200	55		1 300
(b)	Cumulative payments on account	(100)	(600)	(400)	(150)	(80)		
(c)	*Classified as amounts recoverable on contracts*	45				50	95 DR	
(d)	Balance (excess) of payments on account		(80)	(20)		(25)		
(e)	Applied as an offset against long-term contract balances – see below		60	20		15		
(f)	*Residue classified as payments on account*		(20)	—		(10)	(30)CR	
(g)	Total costs incurred	110	510	450	250	100		
(h)	Transferred to cost of sales	(110)	(450)	(350)	(250)	(55)		(1 215)
(j)		—	60	100	—	45		
(k)	Provision/accrual for foreseeable losses charged to cost of sales				(40)	(30)		(70)
(l)			60	100		15		
(m)	*Classified as provision/accrual for losses*				(40)		(40)CR	
(n)	Balance (excess) of payments on account applied as offset against long-term contract balances		(60)	(20)		(15)		
(p)	*Classified as long-term contract balances*		—	80		—	80 DR	
	Gross profit on long-term contracts	35	70	30	(90)	(30)		15

Projects 1, 2 and 3 are running profitably. On the assumption that work is sufficiently advanced to predict the outcome with 'reasonable certainty' profits on these projects will be:

	Project 1	2	3
Sales	145	520	380
Cost of sales	110	450	350
	35	70	30

Projects 4 and 5 are not running profitably so that a provision for a foreseeable loss, as shown at line (k), is needed. The total required provision is added to cost of sales, giving a total loss of:

	Project	
	4	*5*
Sales	200	55
Cost of sales	(250)	(55)
Foreseeable loss	(40)	(30)
Total loss	90	30

We now turn to the balance sheet. Where payments received on account (line (f)) are less than the value of work done then the difference is shown as a debtor, as in the case of projects 1 and 4 (see line (c)). In the case of projects 2, 3 and 5, payments received exceed the value of work done to the extent identified on line (d). In all three of these projects there is a balance of costs incurred to date after deduction of cost of sales (see line (j)), and after deducting provisions for losses (see line (l)). In the case of projects 2 and 5 this balance can be offset in full against the balance of payments on account leaving a net balance (line (f)) to be shown as a creditor in the balance sheet. In the case of project 3 only £20 of the balance of £100 cost can be offset against the excess of payment on account. The remaining £80 is classified as a long-term contract balance as part of stock (see line (p)).

In the case of project 4 the provision for losses cannot be offset against the accumulated costs of the contract, so is shown as a provision in the balance sheet. In the cases of projects 2, 3 and 5 a note to the account should disclose separately the net cost and applicable payment on account:

	Project			
	2	*3*	*5*	*Total*
Net cost (line (l))	60	100	15	175
Applied payment on account (line (e))	60	20	15	95

Controversy over the statement

The first SSAP 9, issued in May 1975, had been preceded by ED 6 issued in May 1972. SSAP 9 adopted the substance of ED 6, reducing the extent of the disclosure requirements, and the reason for the delay in issuing SSAP 9 was to permit time for discussions with the taxation authorities. Following the issue of SSAP 9 the *Survey of Published Accounts* showed failure to comply with SSAP 9 as the single largest cause of qualification or comment in auditors' reports. A number of companies felt sufficiently strongly in disagreement with SSAP 9 to refuse to comply with the statement, while some companies felt unable to comply with the statement because of special circumstances of their trade.

The revised SSAP 9, as described in this chapter, is similar to the original except

that the required detail of information has been expanded substantially to avoid conflict with company law changes in the 1980s, particularly on 'set off' of balances.
Major areas of controversy have been as follows.

Prudence in defining cost and attributing profit

Both the requirement to include a proportion of overheads in stock and the requirement to include an appropriate portion of profit on incomplete long-term contracts have been rejected by a number of companies on grounds of prudence. Some companies have been reluctant to adopt the SSAP 9 principle of including a portion of estimated profit on long-term contracts because of the Revenue's insistence on taking the closing long-term work in progress of the last period of the old basis of accounting as the opening figure for the first period of the new basis of accounting.

Use of LIFO

Although LIFO, even prior to the issue of SSAP 9, was not widely used in the United Kingdom, it is a method of allocating cost to stock widely used in the USA, where it is accepted as a method of stock valuation by the tax authorities. Where a UK company has subsidiaries in the USA it may, therefore, find itself consolidating LIFO stock figures into the UK group accounts.

Crops valued at selling price

A number of plantation companies have a long-established policy of valuing crops harvested and held in stock at the year end on the basis of the realised selling price. This method, which is not mentioned in SSAP 9, goes against the traditional accounting convention of recognising income at the point of sale; however, it will probably continue to be used on the grounds that it provides the only fair way of stating the results in the position where cost is very difficult to quantify.

Dealers in investments and commodities

A case can be made against the 'lower of cost and net realisable value' rule when valuing stocks held by dealers in items such as investments and commodities where a well-organised market exists; it can be argued that carrying forward such stocks at their market value gives a fairer view. Dealers who follow the rules in SSAP 9 can manipulate their results by 'bed and breakfast' operations, selling stocks at the end of one day's trading and buying back the following morning so as to incorporate the profit on sale and the new cost of stock in the accounts.

Interest on long-term contracts

The appendix to SSAP 9 advises that where borrowings can be related to the financing of specific long-term contracts then it may be appropriate to include the interest on these borrowings in the cost of work in progress. This view has been challenged on the grounds that once funds have been borrowed then, whatever the purpose for or security given on the loan, the money borrowed becomes part of and indistinguishable from the total liquid funds of the business.

Disclosure

An example of how major 'categories' of stock might be reported in the notes to the accounts is:

Stocks and work in progress

Stocks and work in progress comprise:

	19X9		19X8	
	£000	£000	£000	£000
Engineering				
Raw materials	530		490	
Work in progress	1175		995	
Finished goods	625		720	
		2330		2205

While the requirement to disclose the component parts of stock is normally met by disclosing the split between raw materials, work in progress and finished goods, in the case of a company carrying on different trades it may be helpful to show the split between categories of business. In some businesses, such as a chain of retail food stores, it may be that only one category of stocks will be held and that therefore no further analysis will be necessary.

International standards

SSAP 9 is in line with the two international standards, IAS 2: Valuation and Presentation of Inventories in the Context of the Historical Cost System and IAS 11: Accounting for Construction Contracts.

EXAMINATION PRACTICE

11.1 SSAP 9

(a) Explain what is meant by the term *long-term contract*.
(b) A company has four long-term contracts as at the balance sheet date. All four are sufficiently advanced to predict the outcome with reasonable certainty. Compute the amounts to be included in the profit and loss account and balance sheet in respect of these contracts, showing any additional information to be given in the notes.

	Contract			
	1	*2*	*3*	*4*
Value of work done	500	350	700	220
Related costs	450	400	600	230
Total costs to date	600	400	720	280
Payments received on account	525	200	610	235
Foreseeable additional loss	—	60	—	10

11.2   SSAP 9 terminology

'The amount at which stocks and work in progress (other than long-term contract work in progress) is stated in periodic financial statements should be the total of the lower of cost and net realisable value of the separate items of stock and work in progress or of groups of similar items' – Statement of Standard Accounting Practice No. 9.

You are required in the context of that accounting standard:

(a)   to define the phrase 'net realisable value';
(b)   to say whether 'replacement cost' is acceptable as an alternative basis of valuation and if so in what circumstances;
(c)   to say whether overheads should be included in cost and if so to what extent;
(d)   to explain *briefly* the following methods of valuing stock and work in progress:
    (i)   adjusted (discounted) selling price;
    (ii)   first in first out;
    (iii)   last in first out;
    (iv)   base stock.

Note: You are not required to write on references to stock valuation in SSAP 16.

(ACCA)

12 SSAP 12: Accounting for Depreciation

The need for a statement

The depreciation of fixed assets is an area of accounting practice calling for the exercise of considerable judgement and offering a considerable variety of existing practice. The topic was, therefore, an essential one for inclusion in the accounting standards programme. The requirement of the statement that depreciation should be provided on freehold and long leasehold buildings has caused such considerable debate in the accounting profession, and indeed amongst the users of accounts generally, as to overshadow the rest of the requirements of the statement. As we shall see, SSAP 12 in fact contains a number of important requirements relating to accounting practices to be adopted and the detail to be disclosed relating to accounting policies.

Summary of the statement

Definitions

SSAP 12 includes the following:

(a) *Depreciation* is the measure of the wearing out, consumption or other reduction in the useful economic life of a fixed asset whether arising from use, effluxion of time or obsolescence through technological or market changes.

(b) *The useful economic life of an asset* is the period over which the present owner will derive economic benefits from its use.

(c) *Residual value* is the realisable value of the asset at the end of its useful economic life, based on prices prevailing at the date of acquisition or revaluation where this has taken place. Realisation costs should be deducted in arriving at the residual value.

(d) *Recoverable amount* is the greater of the net realisable value of an asset and, where appropriate, the amount recoverable from its further use.

Scope

The statement applies to all fixed assets other than:

(a) investment properties, which are dealt with in SSAP 19;

(b) goodwill, which is dealt with in SSAP 22;

(c)   development costs, which are dealt with in SSAP 13;

(d)   investments.

Requirement to provide depreciation

SSAP 12 requires that a provision be made for depreciation on all 'fixed assets having a finite useful economic life'. The depreciation charge should be arrived at by allocating the cost or revalued amount, less estimated residual value, of assets as fairly as possible to the periods expected to benefit from their use. The statement gives no guidance on the depreciation methods to be chosen, apart from a requirement that they be 'appropriate' to the types of asset.

The whole of the depreciation charge should be charged in the profit and loss account. This requirement effectively outlaws the practice, adopted by some companies, whereby depreciation on revalued assets is split between the part relating to historical cost, which is charged in the profit and loss account, and the part relating to the revaluation surplus, which is taken directly against the revaluation reserve.

Asset lives must be estimated on a realistic basis. Thus identical lives must be used in preparing both the historical cost and the current cost accounts. Asset lives must be subject to 'regular review', but the standard makes no reference to how frequently such reviews should take place.

Changes in depreciation

Where there is a change in the method of providing depreciation the unamortised cost of the asset should be written off over the remaining useful life on the new basis, commencing in the year of change; similarly when there is a revision of the estimated useful life of an asset the unamortised cost should normally be written off over the revised useful life. If future results would be distorted then an immediate adjustment to depreciation should be made. This will normally be an exceptional item, and will only be extraordinary if the change arises from an extraordinary event.

If at any time it appears that the unamortised cost of an asset cannot be recovered in full, then the asset should be written down immediately to the estimated recoverable amount which should then be depreciated over the remaining useful life. Such a write down should be written back if in later periods it proves to be unnecessary.

Where fixed assets are revalued in the financial accounts the depreciation provision must be based on the new valuation and on the revised estimate of the remaining useful life. Depreciation already provided should not be written back in the profit and loss account except in so far as it represents reversal of a previous special write down.

Land and buildings

Freehold land will not normally require a provision for depreciation, unless subject to depletion or to loss of value on other grounds; buildings, on the other hand, will have to be depreciated in the same way as other assets, having a limited life and being subject to loss of value in the same way.

to assets of a certain class will depend on use or location; it may be possible to solve the problem by dividing the major classes of asset into further categories according to estimated lives, but where this is impractical because of the volume of detailed disclosure involved it would seem reasonable to show the range of estimated useful lives or depreciation rates used for each major class of asset. SSAP 12 also fails to offer guidance on appropriate disclosure to use when depreciation is calculated on a usage rather than a time basis; a reasonable approach might be to express the estimated life of the asset in terms of usage or units of production, possibly linked to estimated average annual requirements or output.

In the past some groups might have had difficulty in complying with the disclosure requirements of SSAP 12 through inheriting different depreciation policies in different subsidiaries. FRS 2, as we have seen, now requires that group accounting policies be harmonised, either by adopting common policies in all group companies or by making adjustments on consolidation to achieve that purpose. It is in any case difficult to see how group accounts can be justified as 'true and fair' if fixed assets within the group are depreciated by different methods, purely according to the company in which they are held.

It is important to note that the overall objective of the disclosure requirements in SSAP 12 is to make companies disclose meaningful and relevant information in their accounting policies notes on depreciation; before SSAP 12 many companies confined their disclosure to such expressions as 'fixed assets are depreciated over their estimated useful lives'.

Controversy over the statement

Background

The present SSAP 12, issued in February 1987, is similar to the original SSAP 12 issued in December 1977, which followed closely the proposals put forward in ED 15 issued in January 1975. A leading article in *The Accountant* commented that ED 15 was a 'disappointing document' in its failure to narrow the areas of difference in financial reporting. It can be argued that the principal areas of variation in accounting practice are in the valuation of stock and work in progress and in the making of provision for depreciation; if compared with the detailed discussion of problems of stock valuation contained in SSAP 9 the failure of SSAP 12 to provide a detailed discussion and comparison of the effects of the various possible methods of providing for depreciation is surprising. Rather than seeking to narrow areas of difference in companies' accounting policies, SSAP 12 seems to settle for detailed disclosure requirements in respect of depreciation methods and asset lives chosen in respect of each major class of asset.

There is, however, one area in which SSAP 12 has stirred considerable controversy, to such an extent as perhaps to overshadow all other aspects of the statement: that is the requirement to provide for the depreciation of freehold and long leasehold buildings. Of 107 comments made to the ASC on ED 15, 24 came from property companies. Objections were made both to the principle of providing depreciation on buildings generally and to the specific problem of investment properties.

Depreciation of buildings

A number of arguments have been advanced against the requirement to provide for depreciation on buildings. Most of these are countered by points made in the explanatory note to SSAP 12.

The most common argument put forward is that since freehold properties tend to increase in value it is absurd to provide depreciation on them; one suggestion frequently made is that, as an alternative, properties should be subject to regular revaluation. As one company chairman expressed himself in a trenchant criticism 'I am more attracted to a professional valuer's opinion than that of a committee of accountants'. These criticisms miss the point made in SSAP 12 that depreciation is not simply a measure of overall loss of value, but is the measure of loss of value arising from certain specific causes, being 'use, effluxion of time or obsolescence through technology or market changes'. Most buildings do, eventually, wear out, while over a period of time, many buildings become obsolescent with changes in technology and market demands, an example being a canal-side warehouse. The only difference between a building and any other sort of fixed asset is that buildings have a comparatively long useful life so that each year the proportion of their value consumed by these causes will be extremely small. There may well be other causes having a substantial effect on the value of property expressed in monetary terms, in particular changes in the general purchasing power of money or in the relative value of property. If a company revalues its property and ignores the need to provide for depreciation, then effectively it will be setting off an expense consumed, depreciation, against an unrealised surplus on increases in value arising from other causes such as inflation.

The requirement to provide for depreciation in full on the revalued amount of property has been criticised on the grounds that companies wishing to minimise their depreciation charge will be encouraged to leave property stated at cost in the accounts rather than incorporating revaluations, with the result that shareholders will be deprived of information. However, it may be argued conversely that companies approaching SSAP 12 in a positive spirit will be encouraged to incorporate revaluations in their accounts so as to make the depreciation charge more meaningful. The Company's Act also requires that material differences between the figure shown in the accounts for land and buildings and their market value should be disclosed in the directors' report.

When ED 15 was issued a practical objection was raised relating to the practical difficulties of apportioning the cost or value of property between land and buildings and of estimating the expected useful life of a building. The ASC held meetings with representatives of the Royal Institute of Chartered Surveyors, as a result of which it was agreed that these problems could be solved, although there would be difficulties in making precise estimates if the useful life of a building exceeded 50 years. The RICS has in fact issued a practice note indicating how this apportionment can be made. There remain those who object to providing depreciation on the grounds that the estimates involved will be subject to such a high degree of error. In response to this argument it can be said that while the exact life of a building cannot be predicted, it is certain that no building will have an indefinite life. Thus it has been said that to provide depreciation on a building is to be approximately right rather than precisely wrong. The special case of investment property is covered in SSAP 19.

IAS 4: Depreciation Accounting

Compliance with SSAP 12 ensures compliance with the above-mentioned standard.

EXAMINATION PRACTICE

12.1 Depreciation policies
The following are extracts from the accounting policies section of two different sets of accounts:

Depreciation of fixed assets
Fixed assets are depreciated on a straight line basis at annual rates of 2% to 20% of cost, depending on the class of asset. Expenditure on tools, dies, jigs and moulds is written off to revenue. Investment and regional grants in respect of each year's capital expenditure are included with the reserves on the balance sheet and credited to profit and loss account over a period of 12 years.

Depreciation
No depreciation is provided on freehold properties or properties held on leases with fifty years and over to run at the balance sheet date. Properties held on leases of less than fifty years are amortised over the unexpired term. All other fixed assets are depreciated over their estimated useful lives.

You are required to:

(a)   Comment upon the two accounting policies quoted above.
(b)   Discuss the purpose(s) of the depreciation charge in the profit and loss account.
(c)   Explain the necessity for an accounting standard on the topic of depreciation.

12.2 Depreciation adjustments
Discuss the accounting treatment in respect of each of the following situations as advocated by the UK accounting standard on depreciation (SSAP 12):

(a)   revision of estimate of the useful life of a depreciable asset;
(b)   change in the basis of computing depreciation;
(c)   disposal of a depreciable asset, and
(d)   revaluation of a depreciable asset.   *(SCCA)*

13 SSAP 13: Accounting for Research and Development

The basic problem

For a number of companies research and development expenditure constitutes a substantial and essential part of their activity. Such expenditure, by its very nature, tends to be speculative in character, and this poses a serious problem to the accountant preparing annual financial reports. Following the accruals concept it would seem logical to carry forward research and development expenditure as an asset in the year it is incurred, and to write off the asset against future related revenue; this is known as the deferral method. On the other hand, bearing in mind the speculative nature of such expenditure, it may be held that its relationship with the revenue of a future period cannot be established with reasonable certainty, and so in accordance with the prudence concept research and development expenditure would be written off in the year that it is incurred: this is known as the write-off method.

The main arguments used to support the deferral method rather than the write-off method are:

(a) The method is more realistic in commercial terms. Companies invest large sums of money in research and development expenditure with the intention of earning future profits, not as an overhead expense necessary for current production.

(b) A write-off policy may lead to distortion of profit trends, artificially depressing profits in the years leading up to the introduction of a new product, and inflating profits in the years of commercial production. This may lead to a misleading impression being given of rising profitability.

(c) It is generally accepted that investment in research and development is socially desirable, but the write-off method may well deter management from such investment since, in the short term, it results in a reduction of reported profits.

In support of the write-off method, it is argued that:

(a) Since cash resources absorbed by research and development are only released when revenue is earned, a profit figure arrived at under a write-off policy is a better indication of funds available for dividends.

(b) The deferral method calls for the exercise of subjective judgement regarding future revenue, while the write-off method is quite straightforward.

(c) There may be considerable practical difficulties in relating research and development expenditure to specific future income.

In 1971 public attention was drawn to the problem of accounting for research and development expenditure with the financial collapse of the Rolls-Royce group; the balance sheet of the group included a large deferred asset account for development expenditure in respect of a project which could not be completed profitably. Thus the question of research and development was an early candidate for consideration by the ASC.

SSAP 13 was first issued in 1977. A revised standard was issued in 1989.

Summary of the statement

Overview

SSAP 13 draws a distinction between research expenditure aimed at gaining new scientific or technical knowledge, and development expenditure aimed at using scientific or technical knowledge for a specific commercial project. All research expenditure must be written off as it is incurred. For development expenditure companies are allowed to choose between a write-off policy and a deferral policy, but where the latter policy is chosen then deferral is only permitted to the extent that the related project can meet a number of stringent tests to assess viability.

SSAP 13 requires disclosure of accounting policies on R&D, and details of movements on any deferred development account. The revised SSAP 13 also requires large (as defined below) companies to disclose their total R&D charge for the year.

Definitions

SSAP 13 offers the following definition:

Research and development expenditure means expenditure falling into one or more of the following broad categories (except to the extent that it relates to locating or exploiting oil, gas or mineral deposits or is reimbursable by third parties either directly or under the terms of a firm contract to develop and manufacture at an agreed price calculated to reimburse both elements of expenditure):

(a) *pure (or basic) research:* experimental or theoretical work undertaken primarily to acquire new scientific or technical knowledge for its own sake rather than directed towards any specific aim or application;

(b) *applied research:* original or critical investigation undertaken in order to gain new scientific or technical knowledge and directed towards a specific practical aim or objective;

(c) *development:* use of scientific or technical knowledge in order to produce new or substantially improved materials, devices, products or services, to install new processes or systems prior to the commencement of commercial production or commercial applications, or to improving substantially those already produced or installed.

The distinction between pure and applied research on the one hand, and development on the other, is essential to the application of a deferral policy under SSAP 13. The introduction in the revised SSAP 13 of a requirement for certain companies to disclose total R&D expenditure has also made it necessary to consider what expenditure does, or does not, fall under the 'research and development' heading. As a broad principle the revised SSAP 13 states:

Research and development activity is distinguished from non-research based activity by the presence or absence of an appreciable element of innovation. If the activity departs from routine and breaks new ground it should normally be included; if it follows an established pattern it should normally be excluded.

To illustrate how this principle might be applied SSAP 13 offers the following examples of R&D activity:

(a)   experimental or theoretical work to discover new knowledge or advance existing knowledge;
(b)   searching for applications of knowledge;
(c)   formulation and design of possible applications of such work;
(d)   testing to search for, or evaluate, alternative products, processes or services;
(e)   work on pre-production prototypes;
(f)   design of products, processes or services involving new technology or substantial improvements;
(g)   construction and operation of pilot plants.

By contrast examples of items which would not normally be classified as R&D include:

(a)   tests and analyses for quality control or quantity control;
(b)   periodic alterations to existing products, processes or services;
(c)   operational research not tied to a specific R&D activity;
(d)   cost of corrective action for breakdowns in commercial production;
(e)   legal and administration costs for patents and related litigation;
(f)   costs of constructing facilities or equipment unless related to a specific R&D project;
(g)   market research.

Required practice

Expenditure on fixed assets to provide R&D facilities should be capitalised and depreciated in line with SSAP 12. All other research costs should be written off in the year of expenditure.

In the case of development expenditure companies must choose either a write-off or a deferral policy. Whichever policy is chosen must be applied consistently to all development expenditure.

Where a write-off policy is chosen all development costs should be written off in the year of expenditure.

Where a deferral policy is chosen then development expenditure is deferred to future periods if all of the following conditions can be met:

(a)   There must be a clearly defined project.
(b)   Related expenditure must be separately identifiable.
(c)   The outcome of the project must be assessed with reasonable certainty as to:
    (i)   technical feasibility;
    (ii)   commercial viability, covering factors such as market conditions (including competition), public opinion, and consumer or environmental legislation.
(d)   Future revenues from the project must be 'reasonably expected' to exceed the

total of deferred development costs, any further development costs and related costs of production, selling and administration.

(e)   Adequate resources must be available, or reasonably be expected to be available, to complete the project, bearing in mind working capital needs.

When development costs are deferred to future periods then as soon as commercial application is under way amortisation must be commenced. Amortisation should be over the expected period of commercial exploitation, on either a time or a usage basis. Each year deferred development expenditure must be reviewed on a project by project basis, and if future recovery is considered doubtful an appropriate write-down must be made.

SSAP 13 explicitly states that if a deferral policy is chosen then it must be applied consistently to all development projects. However, in practice management can apply a write-off policy to any project they choose simply by professing doubts about future viability.

Fixed assets

Where fixed assets are acquired or constructed in order to provide facilities for research or development work, such assets should be capitalised and written off over their estimated useful lives. Depreciation on such fixed assets will be included in the total depreciation charge disclosed in accordance with the Companies Act, and will also form part of any total of research or development expenditure disclosed.

Work under contract

If a company carries out development work under a firm contract on behalf of third parties on such terms that all related expenditure will be reimbursed, then any such expenditure not reimbursed at the balance sheet date should be included in work in progress.

Exceptions

Costs incurred in locating and exploiting oil, gas and mineral deposits do not fall within the scope of SSAP 13. However, developments of new surveying techniques and methods during the course of such activity do fall within the SSAP 13 definition of research and development.

Required disclosure

The accounting policy on research and development must be stated and explained.

Movements on deferred development expenditure, and the amounts carried forward at the beginning and end of the period, must be disclosed. Deferred development expenditure should be shown in the balance sheet as an intangible fixed asset.

The revised SSAP 13 includes a further requirement to disclose the total R&D expenditure charged in the profit and loss account. This should be analysed between the current year's expenditure and amounts amortised from deferred development expenditure. This new disclosure requirement does not apply if:

(a) the company is not a plc, a holding company with a subsidiary plc, or a 'special category' company; and

(b) the company satisfies the criteria, multiplied by 10, for definition as a medium-sized company under the Companies Act 1985.

Summary of SSAP 13

Figure 13.1 provides a summary of the main points covered by SSAP 13.

Background

The first SSAP 13 was preceded by two exposure drafts, ED 14 issued in January 1975 and ED 17 issued in April 1976. ED 14 defined pure research, applied research and development in terms similar to those finally adopted in SSAP 13, argued that pure and applied research could only be treated on a write-off basis, and, having listed the conditions required to be met in order to defer development expenditure prudently (these conditions were identical to those eventually listed in SSAP 13), concluded that for practical purposes the elements of uncertainty inherent in the conditions made the deferral method unacceptable, and required that all research and development expenditure be written off in the year incurred. ED 14 would also have required the disclosure of the total of research and development expenditure written off in the year. A leading article in *The Accountant*, describing ED 14 as a grasp at an awkward nettle, remarked that the requirement to follow a total write-off policy would have a significant effect on the reported results of a number of companies and might be regarded as an 'intrusion, without legislative authority, into the proper area of managerial discretion'. In fact, the proposals were vigorously attacked by companies in the aerospace and electronics industries, and since these areas accounted for over half of the total research and development activity in the UK, such criticism had to be taken seriously.

In the 1970s government contracts for development work on defence projects allowed an agreed profit percentage to be charged on capital employed in contracts by developers. The government would only allow development expenditure shown in the published balance sheet to be counted as part of such capital employed. Thus a write-off requirement would have materially reduced profits earned by defence contractors in the aerospace and electronics industries.

In April 1976, therefore, the ASC produced ED 17, a revised proposal for a statement on research and development. ED 17 listed the same conditions for deferral as had been laid down in ED 14, but concluded that in certain circumstances companies might be able to meet these requirements, and in that case laid down that development expenditure should be deferred against future revenue arising from the project. While ED 17 enjoyed a more favourable response than ED 14,

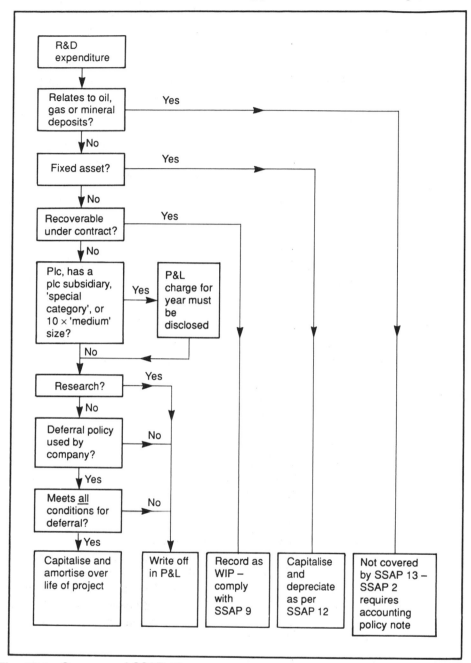

Fig. 13.1 Summary of SSAP 13.

there was some resistance to the idea of making deferral compulsory. Thus the element of choice allowed in SSAP 13 represents a compromise between the two exposure drafts.

The revised SSAP 13, issued in 1989, responds to the Companies Act 1985 and the European Community Fourth Directive with provisions for disclosure of the total R&D write-off in the year.

Choice of policy

We have already seen the arguments between a write-off approach and a deferral approach. Clearly company management will have in mind these arguments when choosing a company policy on research and development. Since SSAP 13 offers a choice between the two approaches the standard is presumably based on the assumption that conditions specific to the individual company may make one or the other approach more appropriate. Surprisingly, SSAP 13 offers no guidance on what relevant conditions might be expected to influence such a choice. Factors that might usefully be considered by management include:

(a)   The amount of development expenditure relative to the total scope of the company's activities. Operation of a deferral policy involves a time-consuming, and therefore costly, annual review of projects. This is only worthwhile if the impact on the accounts is going to be material.

(b)   The policies generally adopted by other companies in the same industry. Clearly it is useful to analysts if companies in the same industry adopt similar, and therefore comparable, accounting policies. From the company's point of view, failure to follow general industrial practice may cause analysts to query why the company feels reluctant to be portrayed in the same way as competitors.

(c)   For a company that is not in the SSAP 13 category for which disclosure of the R&D write-off for the year is required, a write-off policy may be attractive because it involves less disclosure than a deferral policy.

(d)   Any contractual restrictions on the company which are based on the reported balance sheet figures. For example, a company with tight borrowing power restrictions might welcome the opportunity to boost reported equity with a deferral policy. As we have already seen, some defence contractors find a deferral policy helps boost permitted profits under government contracts.

(e)   The company's competence and experience in handling budgeting and forecasting techniques. As we have seen, in order to apply a deferral approach a company needs to make a wide range of forecasts. These must be supported with convincing evidence for the auditors.

(f)   The company's sensitivity to 'income smoothing'. A write-off approach depresses profits in the years when a new project is developed. Conversely profits are artificially boosted in the years when commercial exploitation occurs because related development costs have already been written off. A deferral approach 'smooths' reported profits, and this may be important to a listed company sensitive to shareholder reaction.

Company law and international standards

The Companies Act 1985 provides that deferred development costs may only be included in the balance sheet in 'special circumstances'. Where such an amount is included then the notes to the accounts should include:

(a)   details of the write-off period for the deferred costs;

(b)   reasons for the capitalisation.

Where the unamortised costs are not treated as a realised loss in the computation of distributable reserves the notes to the accounts must state that fact, and explain the circumstances relied on by the directors to justify this treatment.

In practice, compliance with the stringent criteria for deferral laid down in SSAP 13 should offer sufficient justification.

SSAP 13 complies with the main requirements of IAS 9: Accounting for Research and Development Activities. The one exception is that IAS 9 requires *all* companies to disclose total R&D expenditure for the year.

Conclusion

SSAP 13 provides an interesting example of how the ASC dealt with an accounting problem on which accountants were divided, in that ED 14 prescribed a total write-off policy, ED 17 prescribed a deferral policy subject to a number of strict conditions being met, while SSAP 13 permits choice between two methods. While allowing this element of choice the statement, in laying down stringent conditions for deferral and providing detailed rules for amortisation, does in practice narrow considerably the range of possible treatment.

EXAMINATION PRACTICE

13.1 Allocation of R&D items

Current items charged to a research and development (R&D) suspense account in the books of Simple Limited, a company in the electronics industry, are analysed as follows:

		£
1.	Expenditure on applied research related to Project X (note 1)	500 000
2.	Contribution to University U for pure research related to the industry	50 000
3.	Expenditure on the development of Project Y (note 2)	100 000
4.	R&D expenditure relevant to a patent currently granted for Project Z, now being launched as Product Z (note 3)	125 000
5.	Cost of purchase of know-how of an efficient method of carrying out Process P	20 000

Note 1. Your enquiries show that the expenditure on Project X is the first annual instalment of the cost of the applied research which is likely to be repeated over the next two years. Management were cautiously optimistic about the successful development and sale of the resultant new product.

Note 2. Project Y is regarded enthusiastically by management and they believe they have sufficient evidence from pilot studies to support their view that there will be profitable returns from the new product launched in the near future.

Note 3. The £125 000 costs include £1000 fees paid to the Patent Office and to a patent agent.

You are required to advise management on the accounting treatment of each of the five items.

13.2 Treatment of R&D

During the course of a year Venture Ltd incurred expenditure on many research and development activities. Details of three of them are given below.

Project 3: To develop a new compound in view of the anticipated shortage of a raw material currently being used in one of the company's processes. Sufficient progress has been made to suggest that the new compound can be produced at a cost comparable to that of the existing raw material.

Project 4: To improve the yield of an important manufacturing operation of the company. At present, material input with a cost of £100 000 p.a. becomes contaminated in the operation and half is wasted. Sufficient progress has been made for the scientists to predict an improvement so that only 20 per cent will be wasted.

Project 5: To carry out work, as specified by a creditworthy client, in an attempt to bring a proposed aerospace product of that client into line with safety regulations.

Costs incurred during the year were:

Project	3	4	5
	£	£	£
Staff salaries	5 000	10 000	20 000
Overheads	6 000	12 000	24 000
Plant at cost (life 10 years)	10 000	20 000	5 000

You are required to:

(a) Define the following:
   (i) pure research expenditure,
   (ii) applied research expenditure, and
   (iii) development expenditure.
(b) State the circumstances in which it may be appropriate to carry forward research and development expenditure to future periods.
(c) Show how the expenditure on Projects 3, 4 and 5 would be dealt with in the balance sheet and profit and loss account in accordance with SSAP 13.

(ICAEW)

14 | SSAP 15: Accounting for Deferred Taxation

The need for a statement

The profit or loss of a company as calculated for the purposes of taxation is often substantially different from that reported in the financial accounts. This arises from two types of difference:

(a) Certain types of income or expenditure shown in the financial accounts may be non-taxable or non-allowable, for example, dividend income or entertainment expenditure relating to UK customers.

(b) Certain items of income or expenditure may be included in the computation of taxable profit in one period and in the financial accounts in another. These are known as 'timing differences' and we will be considering examples of these in some detail below.

Three approaches to accounting for the tax effects of these 'timing differences' have been put forward:

(a) The 'flow through' approach, whereby the tax charge is taken to be the tax assessment for the year and the question of timing differences is ignored.

(b) The 'full deferral' approach which, following the accruals concept, would charge to the profit and loss account the full tax effects of all timing differences.

(c) The 'partial deferral' approach whereby provision is made for the tax effect of timing differences except to the extent that it can be foreseen that the effect of these will continue indefinitely.

This became a particularly important topic during the 1970s with the introduction of 100 per cent first year allowances on plant and of stock appreciation relief since abolished. Moreover the basing of the calculation of earnings per share on the reported figure of profit after tax increased the significance of the company's approach to deferred taxation. The abolition of first year allowances in 1984 again changed the position.

Computation of deferred taxation

There are two main methods of computing a deferred tax balance, the liability method and the deferral method.

The liability method

Under this method the taxation effects of timing differences are regarded as liabilities for taxes payable in the future or as assets representing recoverable taxes. Thus the deferred taxation balances will be calculated on the basis of the current rate of tax on the grounds that the most recent rate of tax is the best available guide to the likely position when tax is actually paid or recovered. Whenever there is a change in the rate of taxation there will be a revision of the opening balance of deferred taxation; the effect of such a revision will normally be shown in the profit and loss account as part of the taxation charge.

The deferral method

This is a procedure whereby the taxation effects of timing differences are regarded as deferrals of taxation payable or recoverable to be allocated to future periods when the differences reverse. Balances on the deferred taxation account are regarded as deferred credits or deferred charges rather than as amounts payable or recoverable and are not revised on changes in the rate of taxation.

The deferral method can be applied in two ways:

(a) By accounting for each reversing timing difference in a year by the rate of tax applying in the year that difference originated. Originating timing differences will be accounted for by applying the current rate of tax.

(b) By using the 'net change' method whereby the net amount of all originating and reversing timing differences is calculated. If this produces a net 'originating' difference then the current tax rate will be applied, while if there is a net 'reversing' difference then either:

(i) a 'first in first out' basis is used, whereby the rate applying to the earlier timing differences making up the deferred tax account is used;

(ii) an 'average basis' is applied, a rate being arrived at by comparing the balance on the deferred taxation account at the beginning of the period with the total of related timing differences.

Example of the two methods

Consider the very simple example of a company with only one sort of timing difference arising from accelerated capital allowances.

Simplesoul Limited commenced business on 1 January 19X1 and trading in the four years to 31 December 19X4 was as follows:

	19X1	19X2	19X3	19X4
	£	£	£	£
Profit before depreciation	1 500 000	1 600 000	1 700 000	1 800 000
Depreciation	200 000	320 000	320 000	460 000
Profit before tax	1 300 000	1 280 000	1 380 000	1 340 000

	19X1 £	*19X2* £	*19X3* £	*19X4* £
Purchase of machines:				
A	1 000 000	—	—	—
B	—	600 000	—	—
C	—	—	—	700 000
Tax rates	50%	52%	54%	53%

Depreciation is provided at 20 per cent on a straight line basis and first year allowances of 100 per cent were available and used in each year. Taxation computations for the four years show:

	19X1 £	*19X2* £	*19X3* £	*19X4* £
Profit for the year	1 300 000	1 280 000	1 380 000	1 340 000
Add: Depreciation	200 000	320 000	320 000	460 000
Less: First year allowance	(1 000 000)	(600 000)	—	(700 000)
Taxable profit	500 000	1 000 000	1 700 000	1 100 000
Tax rate	50%	52%	54%	53%
Taxation	250 000	520 000	918 000	583 000

An extract from the company's fixed asset register reads as follows:

	Machines			
19X1	A £	B £	C £	*Total* £
Cost in year	1 000 000	—	—	1 000 000
Depreciation	(200 000)	—	—	(200 000)
NBV c/fwd	800 000	—	—	800 000
19X2				
NBV b/fwd	800 000	—	—	800 000
Cost in year	—	600 000	—	600 000
Depreciation	(200 000)	(120 000)	—	(320 000)
NBV c/fwd	600 000	480 000	—	1 080 000
19X3				
NBV b/fwd	600 000	480 000	—	1 080 000
Cost in year	—	—	—	—
Depreciation	(200 000)	(120 000)	—	(320 000)
NBV c/fwd	400 000	360 000	—	760 000
19X4				
NBV b/fwd	400 000	360 000	—	760 000
Cost in year	—	—	700 000	700 000
Depreciation	(200 000)	(120 000)	(140 000)	(460 000)
NBV c/fwd	200 000	240 000	560 000	1 000 000

Deferred taxation will now be computed using the liability and deferral methods.

The liability method

In 19X1 the company enjoyed first year allowances of £1 000 000 and charged depreciation of £200 000 giving us an originating timing difference of £800 000. At a tax of 50 per cent the deferred tax provision for the year will be £800 000 @ 50 per cent = £400 000 and this will be the amount carried forward.

In 19X2, because of the change in the tax rate, it will be necessary to revise the opening provision. During 19X2 the company has enjoyed first year allowance of £600 000 and charged depreciation of £320 000 giving a net timing difference of £280 000. (This is made up of an originating timing difference of £480 000 on Machine B less a reversing difference of £200 000 on Machine A.) Thus the provision to be made in 19X2 can be computed:

	£
Revision of opening balance (£800 000 × 2%)	16 000
Net timing difference in year (£280 000 × 52%)	145 600
Charge for year	161 600
Balance b/forward	400 000
Balance c/forward	561 600

In 19X3 it will again be necessary to revise the opening provision in the light of the change in the tax rate while, there being no capital allowances and a total depreciation charge of £320 000, there will be a net reversing timing difference of £320 000.

	£
Revision of opening balance (1 080 000 × 2%)	21 600
Net timing difference in year (320 000 × 54%)	(172 800)
Deferred tax written back in year	(151 200)
Balance b/forward	561 600
Balance c/forward	410 400

In 19X4, following the reduction in the tax rate, there will be another version of the opening balance together with a provision on the net timing difference in the year of £240 000 (£700 000 − £460 000).

	£
Revision of opening balance (£760 000 × 1%)	(7 600)
Net timing difference in year (240 000 × 53%)	127 200
Charge for year	119 600
Balance b/forward	410 400
Balance c/forward	530 000

Under the liability method it is possible to verify the balance on the deferred taxation account by comparing the balance sheet value of fixed assets with the tax value, i.e.

	19X1 £	*19X2* £	*19X3* £	*19X4* £
Balance sheet value of fixed assets	800 000	1 080 000	760 000	1 000 000
Tax written down value	—	—	—	—
	800 000	1 080 000	760 000	1 000 000
Tax rate	50%	52%	54%	53%
Deferred tax balance	400 000	561 600	410 400	530 000

Strict deferral method

Following the deferral method we have a deferral of a liability of £800 000 at 50 per cent in 19X1 on Machine A, a deferral of a liability of £480 000 at 52 per cent in 19X2 on Machine B, and a deferral of a liability of £560 000 at 53 per cent on Machine C in 19X4; each of these deferrals will be written back over the following four years.

	Machines A £	B £	C £	*Charge/ (write back) in year* £	*Total c/fwd* £
19X1					
Originating difference (800 000 @ 50%)	400 000	—	—	400 000	400 000
19X2					
Originating difference (480 000 @ 52%)	—	249 000	—		
Reversing difference	(100 000)	—	—	149 600	549 600
19X3					
Reversing difference	(100 000)	(62 400)	—	(162 400)	387 200

	Machines			Charge/ (write back) in year	Total c/fwd
	A	*B*	*C*		
	£	£	£	£	£
19X4					
Originating difference (560 000 @ 53%)	—	—	296 800		
Reversing difference	(100 000)	(62 400)	—	134 400	521 600

'Net change' deferral method

Under the 'net change' deferral method the computation of deferred tax is simplified by taking net timing differences and applying the appropriate rate; in the case of a net originating timing difference the appropriate rate will be that applying to the current year, while in the case of a net reversing difference the rate used will be either:

(a) that applied on the earlier portion of the originating timing differences accounting for the opening balance of deferred taxation (first in first out method); or

(b) the weighted average rate relating to the balance accumulated on the deferred taxation account.

Thus taking the figures in our example we would arrive at the results shown in Table 14.1.

Table 14.1 'Net change' deferral method

Year	Net difference	Tax rate	Charge to average (write back from) P & L	Balance c/forward	Charge to FIFO (write back from) P & L	Balance c/forward
	£		£	£	£	£
19X1	800 000	50%	400 000	400 000	400 000	400 000
19X2	280 000	52%	145 000	545 600	145 600	545 600
19X3	(320 000)	50.52%*	(161 664)	383 936		
		or 50%			160 000	385 600
19X4	240 000	53%	127 200	511 136	127 200	512 800

* $\dfrac{\text{Deferred tax balance b/forward}}{\text{Total related timing differences}} = \dfrac{£546\ 600}{£1\ 080\ 000} = 50.52\%$

In practice when the deferral method is used it would be far too time-consuming to use a 'strict deferral' approach and either the 'average' or 'FIFO' approach is used. As we can see from this example, differences between the two approaches only arise in the year of net reversing timing differences.

Summary of the statement

Definitions

Key definitions are:

(a) *Deferred tax* is the tax attributable to timing differences.
(b) *Timing differences* are differences between profits or losses as computed for tax purposes and results as stated in financial statements, which arise from the inclusion of items of income and expenditure in tax computations in periods different from those in which they are included in financial statements. Timing differences originate in one period and are capable of reversal in one or more subsequent periods.
(c) The *liability method* is a method of computing deferred tax whereby it is calculated at the rate of tax that it is estimated will be applicable when the timing differences reverse. Under the liability method, deferred tax not provided is calculated at the expected long-term tax rate.

The definitions section of SSAP 15 considers three types of timing difference:

(a) Tax losses available for relief against future taxable profits are regarded as a timing difference.
(b) Revaluation surpluses on fixed assets are regarded as a timing difference, unless rollover relief is expected to defer tax indefinitely.
(c) Retention of overseas earnings leads to a timing difference only if there is an intention to remit them *and* remittance would result in a tax liability after taking into account double taxation relief.

Basis of provision

SSAP 15 takes a 'partial deferral' approach, requiring that deferred tax should be accounted for to 'the extent that it is probable' that a liability or asset will 'crystallise' and should not be accounted for to the extent that it 'is probable' that the item will 'not crystallise'.

In exercising judgement on the probability of crystallisation 'a prudent view should be taken'. Assumptions to be taken into account will include all information on events and management intentions up to the date the accounts are signed, including financial plans on projections.

The deferred tax provision should be computed by the liability method. Debit timing differences should be set off against credit timing differences, and ACT recoverable should be deducted from the deferred tax liability in so far as it can be offset against the liability.

Pension costs

In 1993 the ASB amended SSAP 15 to permit companies to use either the partial deferral or the full deferral approach for the deferred taxation effects of pension costs.

Debit balances

Net debit balances arising on deferred taxation should be written off unless they are expected to be recoverable without replacement by equivalent debit balances. ACT recoverable on proposed dividends should be carried forward to the extent that it is foreseen that it can be offset against tax on the profits of the next accounting period. ACT recoverable on earlier dividends should only be carried forward where recovery is 'assured beyond reasonable doubt', and SSAP 15 specifies that this will 'normally' only be the case where the offset is forecast on profits of the next accounting period.

Required disclosure

In the profit and loss account, deferred taxation should be shown separately as a part of the total tax charge for the year; there should also be an indication of the extent of any unprovided deferred tax for the year. Where there is a change in the rate of taxation, any resulting adjustment to the deferred taxation account should be disclosed separately as part of the total charge for the year.

The deferred tax balance and its major components should be disclosed in the accounts or the notes thereto, while transfers to or from deferred tax should be disclosed in a note.

Transfers to or from the deferred taxation account arising from reserve movements (e.g. fixed asset revaluations) should be shown as part of those movements. Where any note in or attached to the accounts shows that an asset has a value different from the related amount in the balance sheet then the note should also state the taxation effects of realising the asset at that value.

The total amount of any unprovided deferred tax should be shown in a note to the accounts, analysed into its component parts. If an asset revaluation has been regarded as not giving rise to a timing difference, the fact should be stated and the potential tax effect should be quantified.

Groups

In the case of a company in a group any assumptions made as to the impact of group relief in its effect on deferred tax should be stated, together with details of any payment due for group relief.

Making estimates

If a partial provision is to be made for deferred taxation then it is necessary to consider the circumstances in which each major category of timing difference is likely to crystallise.

(a) *Short-term timing differences* are those which arise from the use of the receipts and payments basis for tax purposes and the accruals basis in financial accounts. Some examples of short-term timing differences are:

(i) interest or royalties payable and receivable treated on a 'cash' basis for taxation purposes and on an 'accruals' basis in the financial accounts;

(ii) general provisions for bad debts in the financial accounts only allowed for taxation purposes where they become specific;

(iii) inter-company profits on stock deferred in the consolidated accounts until stock is sold to third parties but taxed when profit is taken in the accounts of the individual subsidiary.

By their nature such timing differences are likely to crystallise, although they may be offset by other timing differences.

(b) *Accelerated capital allowances timing differences* arise where capital allowances in the taxation computations exceed related depreciation charges in the financial accounts. Such timing differences were particularly significant from 1972 to 1984 when the first year allowance on plant and machinery was 100 per cent. This is a timing difference that can be of a recurring nature, in that the reversing difference may be offset or exceeded by new originating differences. Thus a company with a stable or growing investment in fixed assets may in each year enjoy capital allowances on purchases of fixed assets in that year in excess of the depreciation charge on fixed assets bought in previous years. The following example illustrates the nature of a recurring timing difference:

Example

Mercury Limited commenced business on 1 January 19X5 manufacturing gloves. The company used a standard type of glove-making machine that had a life of five years with no residual value at the end of that time. Over a period of five years the company steadily expanded its production capacity by acquiring a new machine each year and thereafter maintained that capacity level by replacing a machine each year.

Table 14.2 Mercury Limited

Year to	Machine purchased	Cost of machine	Capital allowances on machines					Depreciation on machine					Total allowance for year	Total depreciation for year
			A	B	C	D	E	A	B	C	D	E		
31.12.X5	A	100	100	—	—	—	—	20	—	—	—	—	100	20
31.12.X6	B	120	—	120	—	—	—	20	24	—	—	—	120	44
31.12.X7	C	150	—	—	150	—	—	20	24	30	—	—	150	74
31.12.X8	D	200	—	—	—	200	—	20	24	30	40	—	200	114
31.12.X9	E	250	—	—	—	—	250	20	24	30	40	50	250	164

Table 14.2 illustrates how accelerated capital allowances can lead to a recurring timing difference. If we look at each individual machine the originating timing difference in the year of purchase is reversed in the following years. However, in each year *total* capital allowances continue to exceed *total* depreciation, and as long as there is a stable and constant programme of fixed asset replacement, and fixed asset prices do not fall, the timing difference will continue to recur.

Assuming a steady increase in the price of glove-making machines and continuing first allowances of 100 per cent, total capital allowances and total depreciation in each of the first five years, might appear as shown in Table 14.2.

In this example an originating timing difference of £80 arises in respect of Machine A in 19X5. In 19X6 £20 of this difference reverses but a new originating timing difference of £96 arises in respect of Machine B. We can see that in each year the new originating timing difference exceeds the reversal of previous timing differences. Even if the cost of glove-making machines ceases to rise and stays steady at £250, depreciation provided in 19X4 at 20 per cent on five machines costing £250 each will be exactly equal to first year allowances of £250 on the machine purchased in that year. The timing difference will only cease to recur if the company ceases to replace its fixed assets or there is a reduction in the rate of first year allowance.

Under the current UK system of capital allowances this position is unlikely to occur, and the relatively small timing differences between capital allowances and depreciation will generally call for full provision. It is, nevertheless, important to appreciate the effect of high first-year allowances because:

(i)   these may still arise in the UK in the case of special regional incentives;
(ii) they may also arise in overseas subsidiaries;
(iii) in the history of the deferred tax debate it is important to be aware of the large timing differences attributable in the 1970s to accelerated capital allowances.

(c)   *A timing difference arises on the revaluation surpluses on fixed assets* in that a tax liability will arise at the time when the asset is disposed of at a price in excess of original cost (or tax written down in value) but this surplus, or part thereof, will already have been brought into the financial accounts at the time of revaluation. A taxation liability will only arise where a company disposes of the fixed asset and does not benefit from rollover relief. SSAP 15 therefore lays down that provision for deferred taxation on a revaluation surplus should be made as soon as a liability is foreseen, which would normally be the time when the company decides in principle to dispose of the fixed asset.

(d)   *A timing difference arising on rollover relief* in that tax on a capital gain arising on a disposal of a fixed asset may be deferred until the replacement asset is disposed of, although the capital gain will have been shown as a surplus in the financial accounts at the time of the original disposal. Deferred tax arising from rollover relief should be treated in the same way as on a revaluation surplus, provision being made as soon as it is foreseen that a liability will arise.

As we have seen, SSAP 15 specifies that in estimating whether a timing difference will crystallise 'reasonable assumptions' will involve use of financial plans or projections. An appendix suggests that a period of three to five years will often be adequate, but a longer period of forecasts may sometimes be needed.

Controversy over the statement

History of SSAP 15

The range of views relating to the subject of deferred taxation is reflected by the variations in official guidance published on the subject:

(a)   ICAEW recommends N19 (1958), and N27 (1968) advised that deferred taxation should be provided for by the liability method.
(b)   ED 11 issued in 1973 would have required provision in full for deferred taxation by the deferral method.

(c)   SSAP 11 issued in 1975 required provision in full for deferred taxation and allowed companies to use either the deferral method or the liability method.

(d)   ED 19 issued in 1977 laid down conditions for partial provision for deferred taxation similar to, though somewhat less precise than, those eventually adopted in SSAP 15, and prescribed the liability method.

(e)   SSAP 15 issued in 1978 required provision for deferred taxation on timing differences other than those that can be foreseen with reasonable probability. There was no guidance given in the statement on whether the liability or deferral methods should be used, but a technical release issued by the ASC advised that in most circumstances the liability method will be appropriate, but that companies may use the deferral method if they prefer.

(f)   ED 33 issued in 1983 proposed a change of emphasis in the criteria for partial deferral, based on the balance of probabilities, and argued the case for the liability method.

(g)   A revised SSAP 15, issued in 1985, followed ED 33 in prescribing partial deferral based on the balance of probabilities and prescribed the liability method.

Clearly there are two major areas of controversy over deferred taxation, the first relating to the appropriate method to be used in making a provision, and the second, which has overshadowed the first, being concerned with the more fundamental question of the extent to which it is appropriate to provide for deferred taxation at all.

Deferral versus liability method

The advantages of the deferral method may be summarised thus:

(a)   The deferral method is more in accordance with the 'accruals' concept, in that the actual benefit enjoyed from an originating timing difference is carried forward to the years of reversal.

(b)   Use of the deferral method avoids undue fluctuations in the deferred tax charge arising from changes in the tax rate.

(c)   The deferral method is required practice in the USA, so that for companies which are, or have, US subsidiaries this can be the more convenient method.

The advantages of the liability method are:

(a)   The figure for deferred taxation in the balance sheet represents the best current estimate of the future liability.

(b)   Since the liability method has been recommended practice in the UK for many years and has been adopted by most companies, its continuance will save companies from a change in accounting policy in this respect.

(c)   Calculations under the liability method are considerably more straightforward.

(d)   Under a system of partial deferral there are practical difficulties in making the specific identification of originating timing differences required for operating the deferral method.

(e)   Conceptually the liability method, representing an estimate of the liability which will actually arise, is more in line with the principles of partial deferral.

The debate over full deferral

As we have seen, the issue of SSAP 11, requiring a full deferral policy, caused considerable controversy leading to the eventual withdrawal of the statement. The arguments against a full deferral policy can be summarised as follows:

(a) Full deferral goes against the 'going concern' concept since in times of inflation increased costs of replacing stock and fixed assets will mean that deferred taxation will rarely in practice become payable unless the company goes into liquidation.

(b) If companies are required to provide for deferred tax in full then the benefits enjoyed by a company from good tax planning will not be reflected in the accounts.

(c) Similarly it can be argued that to require a full deferral policy is against the public interest, in that this frustrates the policy of the government in giving relief at an earlier date.

(d) The requirement to provide for deferred taxation in full had the effect of reducing the reserves of some companies to a point where their borrowing powers would be severely restricted. It is interesting to note that the CBI joined in the opposition to SSAP 11.

(e) Some commentators considered there to be a political danger in having companies show large balances of deferred taxation, since this might be seen as a form of government investment and as a result lead to some call for the government to exercise some form of voting right in proportion to the amount invested.

(f) Many companies were, in practice, likely to ignore SSAP 11 with a consequent danger to the authority of the ASC.

(g) The full deferral method ignores the advantages enjoyed by a company from postponing payment of tax for a considerable period; one suggestion made was that a prediction of the future cash flow relating to tax deferral be made and the tax liability discounted to present value.

Arguments for a full deferral policy included:

(a) That failure to provide for deferred taxation in full is against the 'prudence' concept, since there is always a risk that deferred taxation will become payable.

(b) Similarly, failure to provide deferred taxation goes against the 'accruals' concept, since it can be argued that a liability arises at the time of the originating timing difference.

(c) Any system of partial deferral involves an exercise of judgement which will result in the reported earnings of companies being heavily dependent on the attitude of the directors, with a resultant lack of comparability in earnings per share figures.

(d) Not to provide for deferred taxation results in a failure to account for a major source of company finance – postponement by the government of its demands for taxation. One suggestion made has been that deferred taxation should be described in the balance sheet as 'government funds invested by deferment of tax payments'.

(e) Since, in practice, the main reason why deferred taxation does not become payable is because of the effects of inflation, it can be argued that it is inconsistent to acknowledge this effect in historical cost accounts and that partial deferral should only be made in inflation adjusted accounts.

The ASC was eventually convinced of the merits of a partial deferral rather than a full deferral approach; the technical release accompanying SSAP 15 pointed out that there was a majority in favour of a partial deferral approach from those who commented on ED 19. It is, however, significant that the arguments against full deferral come mainly from those who present financial reports, and the arguments against come mainly from those who use published accounts. It can be argued that SSAP 15 is an example of the predominant influence of the former in setting accounting standards.

Audit problems

The auditor's responsibility under SSAP 15 can be considered in three parts:

(a) To check the accuracy of the calculation of the total liability for deferred taxation.

(b) To form an opinion as to whether the directors have based the actual provision made for deferred taxation on the requirements laid down in SSAP 15. Where the directors state that in their opinion the tax effects of originating timing differences cannot, in their opinion, be demonstrated with reasonable probability to continue in the future it is difficult to see how any auditor could in practice dispute this view and object to a full provision being made. Where the directors take the view that part of the potential deferred tax liability need not be provided, the auditors must examine the evidence advanced to justify this view, taking into account the success of forecasts made by the company in the past and secure written representations from the directors to support their action.

SSAP 15 does give opportunities to unscrupulous directors to manipulate the published results of a company; in particular a company might make a full provision for deferred taxation when the requirements of SSAP 15 are first complied with, and then increase the portion of the liability for which provision is not made over a period of time claiming that, with experience, increased confidence can be placed on forecasts. In such a case the auditor will have to form his or her own opinion on the motives and intentions of the directors in deciding whether SSAP 15 has been complied with in such a way as to give a true and fair view.

(c) To ensure that the accounts give full and clear disclosure as laid down in the accounting standard. Where a material part of the deferred tax charge arises from a change in forecasts made in previous years the auditor may wish to see the effects of such changes identified separately as an 'exceptional' item.

IAS 12: Accounting for Taxes on Income

Compliance with SSAP 15 ensures compliance with the above international standard.

EXAMINATION PRACTICE

14.1 The rules in SSAP 15

(a) Explain under what circumstances and to what extent SSAP 15 requires provision to be made for deferred taxation.

(b) Under what circumstances can a deferred tax charge be:
(i) shown as an extraordinary item;
(ii) shown as a prior year adjustment;
(iii) transferred direct to the reserves.

(c) Explain the difference between 'liability' and 'deferral' methods of computing deferred taxation.

14.2 Deferred taxation

In relation to Statement of Standard Accounting Practice No. 15 – Accounting for Deferred Taxation, you are required to:

(a) distinguish between:
(i) 'permanent differences', and
(ii) 'timing differences';

(b) outline five main categories under which timing differences may arise; and

(c) state the general criteria to be used in deciding whether a provision for deferred taxation is necessary. *(CIMA)*

15 | SSAP 16: Current Cost Accounting

Scope of chapter

SSAP 16 was withdrawn in 1986, the year in which the ASC issued a handbook entitled *Accounting for the Effects of Changing Prices*. There is no current UK accounting standard on the topic of *inflation accounting*. This chapter reviews the CCA system as put forward in SSAP 16 and in the ASC handbook. The topic continues to be a regular favourite with examiners, and there are good reasons why the UK accounting profession should have an interest in it:

(a)   Even at low levels of inflation, it has been shown that historical cost accounts include material distortions.

(b)   Internationally a number of countries, particularly in Latin America, continue to experience inflation rates at a level where unadjusted historical cost accounts are meaningless. Thus an understanding of approaches to inflation accounting is essential to the accountant working in an international environment.

(c)   Should inflation rates increase in the UK the accounting profession will be expected to respond with an appropriate system.

Background

UK inflation accounting proposals have included:

1973   ED 8 proposed a system of CPP accounting, whereby the effects of general price level movements on shareholders' funds would be shown in statements supplementary to the historical cost accounts.

1974   SSAP 7, issued as a provisional statement and therefore not binding on members of the professional accounting bodies as SSAPs usually are, followed ED 8.

1975   The 'Sandilands Report', being the report of a committee set up by the government to investigate the problem of accounting for inflation, rejected CPP as a solution on the grounds of being 'constrained by the deficiencies of the basic historic cost accounts' and recommended that 'accounts drawn up in accordance with the principles of current cost accounting should as soon as possible become the basic published accounts of companies'.

1976   The Inflation Accounting Steering Group presented ED 18, a proposal for a full system of CCA accounts to replace historical cost accounts.

1977 At a special meeting of the ICAEW members voted to reject ED 18.

1978 Following the vote against ED 18 the ASC published an interim report (The 'Hyde Guidelines') recommending that quoted companies should show a statement adjusting their historical cost profit to a current cost basis by means of three adjustments, these being one for depreciation, one for cost of sales and one for gearing.

1979 The ASC withdrew ED 18 and issued ED 24; ED 24 evolved from the Hyde guidelines, retaining the proposal for a separate statement giving current cost adjustments to the profit and loss account while separating from the gearing adjustment the working capital items into a separate monetary working capital adjustment, and in addition requiring presentation of a CCA balance sheet and disclosure by listed companies of CCA earnings per share.

1980 The accounting bodies agreed to the issue of SSAP 16, based on ED 24.

1984 ED 35 offered suggestions for amendments to SSAP 16.

1985 ED 35 withdrawn.
SSAP 16 ceases to be mandatory but is not officially withdrawn.

1986 ASC issued a handbook *Accounting for the Effects of Changing Prices* which considers a range of inflation accounting approaches.
ASC withdrew SSAP 16.

Forms of inflation accounting

An interesting analysis of forms of accounting considered in the UK is offered in the Accounting Standards Committee handbook on inflation accounting (ASC 1986). This argues that there are three elements to consider in distinguishing between approaches to inflation accounting:

(a) *The valuation base.* Two bases have been used in UK systems, historical cost and current cost (otherwise known as 'value to the business').

(b) *The capital maintenance concept.* All accounting systems arrive at profit after allowing for the maintenance of the opening capital of the business. This 'capital' to be maintained can be regarded in three ways:
  (i) as the physical operating capital of the company, referred to in SSAP 16 as 'operating capability';
  (ii) as the measure of opening capital in units of money (money capital);
  (iii) as the measure of opening capital measured in units of general purchasing power, often referred to as 'real capital'.

(c) *The unit of measurement.* The principal alternatives here are:
  (i) the monetary unit;
  (ii) a unit of constant purchasing power (CPP), usually defined as the purchasing power of the monetary unit at the closing balance sheet date.

Traditional historical cost accounting measures all items by reference to historical cost, uses money as a unit of measurement, and consistent with the unit of measurement uses a 'money capital' concept of capital maintenance.

The first response of the UK accounting profession to the problem of inflation was to put forward a CPP system in ED 8 (1973) and SSAP 7 (1974). This system also measures all items by reference to historical cost but uses a current purchasing power unit of measurement and, consistent with that unit, uses a 'real capital' concept of capital maintenance.

In 1975 the government appointed 'Sandilands Committee' argued against CPP and in favour of a CCA approach. After a number of proposals from the ASC an agreed CCA standard, SSAP 16, emerged in 1980. This used money as a unit of measurement, current cost as a valuation base, and consistent with the valuation base had an 'operating capability' capital maintenance concept. Compliance with SSAP 16 was made voluntary in 1985 but the standard was withdrawn in 1986.

In July 1984 the ASC published ED 35, offering some suggested amendments to SSAP 16, and in 1986 published a more wide ranging review of the inflation accounting issue. The 1986 review continued to support a CCA approach, but suggested that companies be permitted to choose either an 'operating capability' (as in SSAP 16) or a 'real capital' capital maintenance concept. It is interesting to note that the 'real capital' capital maintenance concept does not link to either the monetary unit of measurement or the current cost basis of measurement used in CCA.

Value to the business

The term *value to the business*, also known as *deprival value*, is of fundamental importance in current cost accounting, and is based on the concept of deprival value first expounded by Professor Bonbright in 1937. The deprival value approach is based on the assumption that the value to the business of an asset is measured in terms of the loss that the business would suffer if it was deprived of the asset. The value to the business of an asset can be related to money in three ways:

(a) current replacement cost;
(b) net realisable value;
(c) value receivable as a result of future use.

If the asset can be expected to produce, either by immediate sale or by future use, an amount in excess of the current replacement cost, then in the event of the destruction of the asset the business would be expected to buy a replacement, and the loss suffered would be this replacement cost. If this was not the case the asset would not be replaced and, assuming rational decision-making, the business would suffer a loss equal to what would have been earned by the more profitable option of selling the asset or continuing to use it.

In measuring the value receivable as a result of future use, it is usually argued that expected cash flows should be discounted to present values. However, the Guidance Notes to SSAP 16 argue in para. 29 against this approach 'as in HC accounts it is not usual to discount the future cash flows'.

In practice, in a going concern we would normally expect replacement cost to emerge as *value to the business*. This is because:

(a) we would expect a business to be able to sell stock at a price in excess of replacement cost;
(b) we would expect a fixed asset to be able to generate future earnings in excess of replacement cost.

The computational examples below will assume that replacement cost is value to the business. However, circumstances may arise where this is not the case.

Requirements of SSAP 16

SSAP 16 applied to all listed and some large companies, excluding certain value-based businesses. Various types of presentation were permitted, the most common being to include supplementary CCA statements with the main historical cost accounts.

SSAP 16 adjusts historical cost to current cost operating profit by making three adjustments:

(a)   A depreciation adjustment represents the difference between the current cost and historical cost of fixed assets consumed during the year.

(b)   A cost of sales adjustment represents the difference between the current cost and historical cost of stock consumed during the year.

(c)   A monetary working capital adjustment is made in respect of the net amount of monetary assets and liabilities that form part of the operating cycle of the business. These are basically trade debtors, trade creditors, and any cash or bank balances that fluctuate with the trading activities of the business.

If there is a net asset the adjustment represents the change in net finance needed to support the changing price level of the related stock. If there is a net liability then the adjustment represents an abatement of the cost of sales adjustment to the extent that changes in stock levels caused by price changes are financed by monetary working capital.

Once these three adjustments have been made a figure of current cost operating profit is arrived at. The next stage is to show the impact of borrowing on profit. This consists of the interest cost and the gearing adjustment. The gearing adjustment is an abatement of part of the CCA operating adjustments, in proportion to the part of total operating assets financed by net borrowing.

Having arrived at a figure of current cost profit before tax, deductions are then made for tax, dividends and other appropriations to arrive at retained current cost profit for the year.

In the current cost balance sheet tangible fixed assets and stock are shown at current cost. A current cost reserve shows revaluation surpluses which are of two kinds:

(a)   realised holding gains, being the various current cost adjustments transferred from profit and loss;

(b)   unrealised holding gains, being revaluation surpluses on fixed assets and stock shown in the balance sheet.

Computation in compliance with SSAP 16

The following example, Perla plc, is a fairly simple example of a CCA computation. It is assumed for the purposes of this example that for both fixed assets and stock their replacement cost represents *value to the business*, i.e. is lower than at least one of economic value or net realisable value. 19X9 is to be the first year of preparing CCA accounts.

Perla plc – Balance sheet as at 31 December 19X9

	19X9		19X8	
	£000	£000	£000	£000
Plant and machinery (Note 1)		1100		1000
Current assets:				
Stock	200		150	
Debtors	250		210	
Bank	20		30	
	470		390	
Current liabilities:				
Creditors	150		200	
Dividend	50		50	
Taxation	90		50	
Overdraft	70		180	
	360		480	
Net current assets/(liabilities)		110		(90)
		1210		910
Debentures		600		400
		610		510
Share capital		250		250
Retained profits		360		260
		710		510

Perla plc – Profit and loss account for the year ended 31 December 19X9

	19X9	
	£000	£000
Sales		2330
Cost of sales		1620
Gross profit		710
Administration	160	
Distribution	230	
		390
Operating profit		320
Interest		70
Profit before tax		250
Taxation		100
		150
Profit available to shareholders		
Proposed dividend		50
Retained profit		100

Note 1: Plant and machinery was acquired as follows:

	B/forward	Additions/ charge for year	Disposals	C/forward
Cost	£000	£000	£000	£000
19X8	1100	—	100	1000
19X9	—	330	—	330
	1100	330	100	1330
Depreciation				
19X8	100	100	10	190
19X9	—	40	—	40
	100	140	10	230
Net book value	1000			1100

Acquisitions and disposals should be assumed to take place at the mid point of the year.

Note 2: Relevant price indices moved as follows:

	Plant & machinery	Stock	General price level
Average 19X8	278	232	403
30.11.X8	312	256	420
31.12.X8	317	268	423
Average 19X9	347	288	506
30.11.X9	376	298	578
31.12.X9	380	310	592

Note 3: Monetary working capital consists of debtors less creditors. Both stock and monetary working capital are assumed to arise on average one month before the year end date.

Fixed assets

The first stage of the computation is to look at fixed assets. Here we need to compute:

(a)   The difference between historical cost depreciation and depreciation based on the *average* replacement cost of plant during the year. Average, rather than year end, cost is used because plant is assumed to be consumed evenly throughout the year. For this purpose historical cost depreciation for the year is analysed into the acquisition dates of related fixed assets. Each part of the historical cost depreciation is multiplied by the factor:

$$\frac{\text{Average index for year}}{\text{Index at acquisition date}}$$

in order to find the current cost depreciation for the year. Below is shown a simple form of working schedule that enables us to make these calculations. The difference between current cost and historical depreciation will be the *depreciation adjustment*.

Depreciation adjustment:
Year acquired

	HC	CCA factor	CCA
	£000		£000
19X8	100	347/278	125
19X9	40	1	40
	140		165
			140
Depreciation adjustment			25

(b) The difference between the depreciated historical cost and the depreciated replacement cost of plant sold in the year. Both cost and accumulated depreciation are uplifted by the factor:

$$\frac{\text{Index at disposal date}}{\text{Index at acquisition date}}$$

Plant disposal adjustment:

	HC	CCA factor	CCA
Cost	100	347/278	125
Depreciation	10	347/278	12
NBV	90		113
			90
Adjustment			23

(c) The balance sheet revaluation surplus on fixed assets both at the beginning and end of the year. This is required both for the balance sheet and for the computation of the gearing adjustment (discussed below).

The historical cost figures for cost and accumulated depreciation are adjusted to give the replacement cost by the factor:

$$\frac{\text{Balance sheet date index}}{\text{Acquisition date index}}$$

31.12.19X8 revaluation:

	HC			CCA	
	Cost £000	Depr. £000	CCA factor	Cost £000	Depr. £000
Acquisition date					
19X8	1100	100	317/278	1254	114
	100			114	
NBV	1000			1140	
				1000	
Revaluation surplus				140	

31.12.X9 adjustment

	HC			CCA	
	Cost £000	Depr. £000	CCA factor	Cost £000	Depr. £000
19X8	1000	190	380/278	1367	260
19X9	330	40	380/347	361	44
	1330	230		1728	304
	230			304	
	1100			1424	
				1100	
Revaluation surplus				324	

Stock

For stock two computations are required.

(a)   The opening and closing stock figures need to be adjusted from historical cost to replacement cost. This is necessary both to provide balance sheet figures and to provide details of the revaluation surplus to be taken into account when computing the gearing adjustment (see below). As shown below the adjustment involves applying to the historical cost figures the factor:

$$\frac{\text{Index at balance sheet date}}{\text{Index at acquisition date}}$$

Stock revaluation 31.12.X8:

	HC £000	CCA factor	CCA £000
Stock	150	268/256	157
			150
Revaluation surplus			7
31.12.X9:			
Stock	200	310/198	208
			200
			8

(b)   An estimate of the difference between the historical cost of stock consumed during the year, and its replacement cost at the time of sale, needs to be made. In practice it would not normally be practical to make such a calculation on an item by item basis. Accordingly an approximation is arrived at by using the 'averaging method'. This is computed by adjusting both opening and closing stocks from historical cost to the average price for the year, applying the factor:

$$\frac{\text{Average index for year}}{\text{Acquisition date index}}$$

Then the difference between opening and closing stock at average cost for the year represents the volume change, the difference between opening and closing historical cost represents total change, and the difference between the two is the cost of sales adjustment, being the change attributable to price level changes. The calculations are:

	HC £000	CCA factor £000	Average cost £000
Closing stock	200	288/298	193
Opening stock	150	288/256	169
Total change	50		24
Volume change	24		
Cost of sales adjustment	26		

Monetary working capital

The monetary working capital adjustment is generally computed by the same averaging method as the cost of sales adjustment. Since purchases and sales both relate to stock, an index relevant to stock is normally applied to opening and closing net monetary working capital. The calculation is:

Monetary working capital adjustment

	HC	CCA factor	Average cost
	£000	£000	£000
Closing net MWC (250 – 150)	100	288/298	97
Opening net MWC (210 – 200)	10	288/256	11
Total increase	90		
Volume increase	86		86
Monetary working capital adjustment	4		

Gearing

We have now computed all the SSAP 16 adjustments to operating profit. As we have seen, the gearing adjustment represents an abatement of the CCA operating adjustments to reflect the part of the total operating capacity of the business financed by borrowing. Thus it is necessary to compute both the net borrowing and the total equity of the business. Note that:

(a)   all items regarded as part of monetary working capital (in this case debtors and creditors) are excluded;

(b)   proposed dividends are taken as part of the equity;

(c)   revaluation surpluses on plant and stock are regarded as part of the CCA equity.

The gearing proportion:

	19X9		19X8	
	£000	£000	£000	£000
Bank		(20)		(30)
Taxation		90		50
Overdraft		70		180
Debentures		600		400
Net borrowing		740		600

	19X9		19X8	
	£000	£000	£000	£000
Share capital	250		250	
Retained profits	360		260	
Dividend	50		50	
Plant revaluation	324		140	
Stock revaluation	8		7	
Equity		992		707
		1732		1307

Average borrowing	$\dfrac{740+600}{2}$		=	670
Average net borrowing + equity	$\dfrac{1732+1307}{2}$		=	1519.5
Gearing proportion	$\dfrac{670}{1519.5}$		=	44%

Having computed the gearing proportion, we then compute the total CCA operating adjustments as:

	£000
Depreciation	25
Asset disposal	23
Cost of sales	26
Monetary working capital	4
	78
$44\% \times 78$ =	34

The profit and loss account

We can now prepare the CCA profit and loss account for our example. First, historical cost operating profit is adjusted by the CCA operating adjustments to give a figure of CCA operating profit. Then the impact of borrowing is shown with the gearing adjustment and the interest payable. Having found a figure of current cost profit before tax, appropriations are shown in the normal way.

Perla plc – CCA profit and loss account for the year ended 31 December 19X9

	£000	£000
Turnover		2330
Profit before interest and tax on historical cost basis		320
Less: current cost operating adjustments:		
Depreciation	25	
Asset disposal	23	
Cost of sales	26	
Monetary working capital	4	
		78
Current cost operating profit		242
Gearing adjustment	34	
Interest payable	(70)	
		36
Current cost profit before taxation		206
Taxation		100
Current cost profit attributable to shareholders		106
Proposed dividend		50
Retained current cost profit of the year		56

The balance sheet

In the balance sheet both plant and stock are shown at their revalued amount while all other assets and liabilities, being fixed in monetary terms, are shown at historical cost. The current cost reserve consists of:

	£000	£000
Unrealised surpluses:		
Fixed assets	324	
Stock	8	
		332
Realised surpluses:		
CCA operating adjustments	78	
Gearing adjustment	(34)	
		44
		376

Retained profits consist of historical cost retained profits up to the date when CCA accounts are first prepared, plus CCA retained profits thereafter. This may seem a strange mixture. However, a record of accumulated retained CCA profits over the life of the company could only be prepared by preparing CCA accounts in retrospect over each year of the company's life.

Thus the balance sheet will appear:

Perla plc – CCA balance sheet as at 31 December 19X9

	£000	£000
Plant and machinery		1424
Current assets:		
Stock	208	
Debtors	250	
Bank	20	
	478	
Current liabilities:		
Creditors	150	
Dividend	50	
Taxation	90	
Overdraft	70	
	360	
Net current assets		118
		1542
Debentures		600
		942
Share capital		250
Current cost reserve		376
Retained profits (260 + 56)		316
		942

The ASC handbook

The 1986 ASC handbook suggested a more flexible approach to CCA. Rather than presenting a full set of current cost accounts, the handbook suggests a minimum requirement of including in the notes to the accounts a supplementary statement of earnings on a CCA basis and a note of current costs of fixed assets, related depreciation and stocks. More complete CCA disclosure, such as a full set of CCA accounts or even use of CCA in the main accounts, would be permitted.

The handbook would allow companies to choose between an 'operating capability' and a 'real terms' capital maintenance concept. In either case the CCA profit and loss calculations would include both a depreciation adjustment and a cost of sales adjustment. However, the handbook suggests a wide range of options for the treatment of monetary items, depending on the capital maintenance concept chosen.

Under the 'operating capability' concept companies would be allowed to choose whether or not to apply the monetary working capital adjustment. Companies would also be allowed to choose whether or not to make a gearing adjustment. In calculating the gearing adjustment 'net borrowing' is computed as in SSAP 16, except that if no monetary working capital adjustment is computed then monetary working capital items will also form part of the net borrowing. The gearing proportion may then be applied to either:

(a) the CCA operating adjustments, as in SSAP 16, or
(b) the total of the CCA operating adjustments and the CCA unrealised revaluation surpluses arising during the year.

Under the 'real terms' capital maintenance concept an entirely different approach is taken to monetary items. No adjustment is made for monetary working capital or gearing. Instead both realised and unrealised holding gains are added on to profit, while an 'inflation adjustment to shareholders' funds' is deducted. This inflation adjustment is the uplift necessary to maintain opening CCA equity in 'real' terms, and is computed as:

$$\text{Opening CCA equity} \times \frac{\text{Closing RPI} - \text{Opening RPI}}{\text{Opening RPI}}$$

Computation of the ASC handbook's suggested system

Continuing our example Perla plc, the calculations for opening and closing CCA balance sheets, the depreciation adjustment and the cost of sales adjustment will continue as computed above whatever method is used.

If an 'operating capability' capital maintenance concept is used then four different approaches are possible:

(a) Inclusion of a monetary working capital adjustment, with a gearing adjustment applied to only *realised* holding gains. This is the SSAP 16 method already used above.
(b) No monetary working capital adjustment, with a gearing adjustment applied to only realised gains. Our computation must then be revised:
     (i) To include monetary working capital items in the net borrowing:

	19X9 £000	19X8 £000
Net borrowing as computed above	740	600
Add: Trade creditors	150	200
Less: Trade debtors	(250)	(210)
	640	590
CCA equity as computed above	992	707
	1632	1297

Average net borrowing	$\dfrac{640 + 590}{2}$	=	615
Average equity and net borrowing	$\dfrac{1632 + 1297}{2}$	=	1464.5
Gearing proportion	$\dfrac{615}{1464.5}$	=	42%

(ii) To exclude the monetary working capital adjustment, so that total CCA operating adjustments are:

	£000
Depreciation	25
Asset disposal	23
Cost of sales	26
	74

The gearing adjustment will be:

$$74 \times 42\% = 31$$

(c) Inclusion of a monetary working capital adjustment, with a gearing adjustment applied to all holding gains. In this case the CCA operating adjustments and the gearing proportion will continue to be computed as in SSAP 16. The only change will be to include the unrealised revaluation surpluses for 19X9 in the gearing adjustment:

	£000	£000
Plant – Closing revaluation surplus	324	
– Opening revaluation surplus	140	
		184
Stock – Closing revaluation surplus	8	
– Opening revaluation surplus	7	
		1
Total 19X9 unrealised gains		185
Realised gains as above		78
Total gains		263
Therefore:		
Gearing adjustment $263 \times 44\%$ =		116

(d) No monetary working capital adjustment, with a gearing adjustment applied to all holding gains. We have already seen the revised CCA realised gains and gearing proportion at (b) above. The gearing adjustment will therefore consist of:

	£000
19X9 unrealised gains as above	184
Realised gains	74
	258
× Gearing proportion	42%
	108

If a 'real terms' capital maintenance concept is used then the balance sheet figures and the profit and loss adjustments for fixed assets and stock are computed as in SSAP 16 above. The unrealised and realised revaluation surpluses are then added back to profit, and an 'inflation adjustment' is deducted, being:

$$\text{Opening CCA equity} \times \frac{\text{Closing RPI} - \text{Opening RPI}}{\text{Opening RPI}}$$

For our example Perla plc this is:

$$(707 - 50) \times \frac{592 - 423}{423} = 262$$

IAS 6: Accounting Responses to Changing Prices (issued June 1977) and IAS 15: Information Reflecting the Effects of Changing Prices (issued November 1981)

IAS 6 considered the topic of 'accounting responses to changing prices'. As we have already seen in considering SSAP 16, this is an issue that has caused considerable controversy in the UK. IAS 6 was therefore confined to a requirement that companies disclose, in their accounting policies noted, the procedures adopted to reflect the effects of general price changes, specific price changes, or both; where no procedures have been adopted the fact should be disclosed. A prediction was made in IAS 6 that a further IAS would be needed, and proposals for this are contained in IAS 15. The standard applies to 'large publicly traded enterprises and other entities that are economically significant'. These would be required, 'using a method that adjusts for the effects of changing prices', to disclose:

(a) the adjustment to or adjusted charge for depreciation;
(b) the adjustment to or adjusted charge for cost of sales;
(c) any financing adjustment arising from the method used;
(d) the results for the year recomputed to take into account all price level adjustments.

IAS 15 follows the approach of IAS 6 in requiring wider disclosure but not seeking to impose any specific approach.

Conclusion

The ASC has formulated both an accounting standard and a detailed discussion document on current cost accounting. Should a further attempt at producing such a system be undertaken in the UK issues to be resolved are likely to include:

(a) the choice of capital maintenance concept;
(b) the treatment of monetary items;
(c) the status of any CCA data to be included in the accounts;
(d) ways in which CCA might be simplified.

EXAMINATION PRACTICE

15.1 Preparing and presenting CCA

The historical cost accounts of Bun Ltd for the year 19X9 were as follows:

Profit and loss account	£000	£000
Turnover		137 000
Operating profit		9 670
Interest		2 320
Profit before taxation		7 350
Taxation		2 500
Profit after taxation		4 850
Dividends		
Ordinary – paid	520	
Ordinary – proposed	1 000	1 520
Retained profit for the year		3 330
Retained profit b/fwd		19 450
Retained profit c/fwd		22 780

Balance sheets

	19X9 £000	19X9 £000	19X8 £000	19X8 £000
Share capital				
£1 ordinary shares		10 000		10 000
Reserves		22 780		19 450
		32 780		29 450
10% debentures		15 500		11 000
		48 280		40 450
Represented by	£000	£000	£000	£000
Plant		23 740		19 550
Current assets:				
Stock	36 400		22 540	
Debtors	25 100		20 100	
	61 500		42 640	

Current liabilities:

Creditors	24 370		18 140	
Taxation	2 000		2 150	
Proposed dividends	1 000		950	
Bank overdraft	9 590		500	
	36 960		21 740	
Net current assets		24 540		20 900
		48 280		40 450

Notes

1. Plant cost:

	£000	£000	£000	£000
19X6	22 000	—	6 000	16 000
19X7	7 000	—	—	7 000
19X8	3 000	—	—	3 000
19X9	—	13 520	—	13 520
	32 000	13 520	6 000	39 520

Depreciation:

19X6	9 900	2 400	2 700	9 600
19X7	2 100	1 050	—	3 150
19X8	450	450	—	900
19X9	—	2 130	—	2 130
	12 450	6 030	2 700	15 780
NBV	19 550			23 740

2. Stock, debtors and creditors have all built up evenly over 2 months.

3. For the purpose of preparing CCA accounts the directors have selected two government indices, one appropriate to plant and the other to stock, debtors and creditors. Extracts from these indices show:

	Plant	Stock
Average 19X6	97	101
Average 19X7	109	132
Average 19X8	131	158
Average 19X9	162	185
October 19X8	142	168
November 19X8	144	170
December 19X8 (month end figures)	146	175
October 19X9	169	198
November 19X9	170	200
December 19X9	177	202

The company proposes to present, for the first time, supplementary CCA accounts for the year 19X9. You are required to prepare these in line with SSAP 16.

16 SSAP 17: Accounting for Post Balance Sheet Events

Background

In October 1978 the IASC issued IAS 10: Contingencies and Events Occurring after the Balance Sheet Date; in the UK the ASC responded by issuing SSAP 17 in rather more detail.

Summary of the statement

Definition of terms

The following definitions included in SSAP 17 are essential to an understanding of the statement.

Post balance sheet events are 'those events, both favourable and unfavourable, which occur between the balance sheet date and the date on which the financial statements are approved by the board of directors'. The statement draws a distinction between two types of post balance sheet event.

(a) *Adjusting events* are those which provide new or additional evidence of conditions existing at the balance sheet date, and therefore need to be reflected in the accounts. Specifically they include items decided on after the balance sheet date, such as the proposed dividend and reserve transfers for the period which, because of statutory requirements, are shown in the accounts.

(b) *Non-adjusting events* are those which concern conditions which did not exist at the balance sheet date, and have arisen since. Normally these events will not affect the accounts for the year but, nevertheless, it may be necessary to refer to them in the notes to the accounts.

It is clearly necessary in defining a 'post balance sheet event' to identify clearly the date when the accounts are approved by the directors. It is recognised in SSAP 17 that companies will have various procedures for approving the accounts, depending on the company's management structure. SSAP 17 defines the date of approval as the 'date of the board meeting at which the financial statements are formally approved', and requires disclosure of this date in the accounts.

Preparation of the accounts

SSAP 17 is based on the principle that the accounts must be prepared on the basis of conditions existing at the balance sheet date. Accordingly a post balance sheet event will only affect the amounts stated in the accounts in one of two circumstances:

(a) where it is an 'adjusting event', that is as we have seen above, where it provides or brings to light evidence of circumstances already existing at the balance sheet date;

(b) where the event indicates that it is not appropriate to apply the going concern concept to a material part of the company.

Disclosure of non-adjusting events

Although non-adjusting events should not be taken into account in computing the amounts in the accounts (unless and in so far as they provide evidence of the validity of applying the going concern concept) disclosure will be necessary in either of two cases:

(a) where the event is so material that non-disclosure would affect the ability of those using the accounts to have a proper understanding of the financial position of the company;

(b) where the nature of the post balance sheet event is to reverse or complete a transaction entered into before the year end, the substance of which was primarily to alter the appearance of the company's balance sheet, i.e. what is commonly known as 'window dressing'.

In such circumstances disclosure will consist of:

(a) the nature of the post balance sheet event;

(b) an estimate of the financial effect or a statement that it is not possible to quantify the effect. Such an estimate should be given before tax, the tax implications being explained where necessary for a proper understanding of the position.

Complying with the statement

'Window dressing'

The requirements of SSAP 17 relating to window dressing were not included in the original exposure draft on post balance sheet events, ED 22. SSAP 17 does not require that artificial transactions designed to alter the appearance of the company's balance sheet should be reversed in the accounts, instead requiring that the effect of such a transaction should be disclosed. It is interesting to reflect that a company can comply with SSAP 17 by presenting accounts showing amounts which are distorted in this way and, provided that the nature of the transaction is disclosed in the notes to the accounts, avoid any comment from the auditors on failure to comply with an SSAP. It is to be hoped that, in a material case of 'window dressing', the auditors would in any case draw the attention of shareholders to the consequent failure of the accounts to present a 'true and fair view'. Presumably the ASC has felt unable to lay down stricter rules on 'window dressing' because of the practical difficulties of defining and identifying such transactions.

Classification of post balance sheet events

An appendix to SSAP 17 gives some examples of 'adjusting' and 'non-adjusting' events. These examples can be summarised:

Adjusting events

(a) Where fixed assets purchased or sold *during* the year have a purchase or selling price determined *after* the year end date. SSAP 17 does not give any guidance on how to determine the date of sale. Purchases or sales after the year end date will be 'non-adjusting' events.

(b) A valuation of property which indicates a permanent diminution in value existing at the year end date; where it can be demonstrated that the decline in value took place after the year end date this will be a non-adjusting event.

(c) The receipt of the accounts of, or other information relating to, an unlisted company, providing evidence of a permanent loss of value of the investment; again, if it can be demonstrated that the loss in value took place after the year end date this will be a non-adjusting event.

(d) Evidence from transactions or events after the year end date as to the net realisable value attributable to stock and work in progress, or as to the accrued profit on a long-term contract.

(e) The insolvency of a debtor, or renegotiation of an amount owed by a debtor.

(f) The declaration of dividends by subsidiaries and associated companies relating to periods prior to the balance sheet date of the holding company. There is no specific guidance in SSAP 17 as to how a company should treat proposed dividends receivable from an investment other than in a subsidiary or associate.

(g) The announcement of the rates of taxation applicable to the accounting period.

(h) The receipt or agreement of amounts due in respect of insurance claims in the course of negotiation at the balance sheet date.

(i) The discovery of fraud or errors which had led to the accounts being incorrect.

Non-adjusting events

(a) Mergers and acquisitions.

(b) Proposals for any form of capital reconstruction scheme.

(c) Issues of shares and debentures. SSAP 3 only requires disclosure of a figure for diluted earnings per share where the company has already undertaken to issue the new shares at the balance sheet date. In order to comply with the requirement to disclose an estimate of the financial effect of a material post balance sheet event, it would seem reasonable to show the effect of a post balance sheet dilution on earnings per share.

(d) Losses of fixed assets or stocks arising from catastrophes such as fire or flood.

(e) Changes in trading activities.

(f) Fluctuations in exchange rates.

(g) Industrial disputes.

(h) Augmentation of pension benefits.

(i) Government action such as nationalisation.

EXAMINATION PRACTICE

16.1 SSAP 17 – Definitions

Define and give five examples of:

(a) an 'adjusting event';

(b) a 'non-adjusting event'.

16.2 SSAP 17 – Treatment

What is a post balance sheet event? Decribe the way in which such events should be treated in a set of accounts.

17 SSAP 18: Accounting for Contingencies

Background

As with SSAP 17, the issue of SSAP 18 became desirable following IAS 10. In the UK there is already a disclosure requirement laid down in the Companies Acts to disclose the nature and amount of any contingent liabilities. Thus SSAP 18 is unlikely to become a controversial statement.

Summary of the statement

Definitions

A 'contingency' is defined as a 'condition which exists at the balance sheet date, where the outcome will be confirmed only on the occurrence or non-occurrence of one or more uncertain future events'. A contingency can result in a 'contingent gain' or a 'contingent loss'.

Required practice and disclosure

SSAP 18 requires that a provision should be made for a material contingent loss where:

(a) it is *probable* that a future event will confirm the loss; and
(b) the loss can be estimated with reasonable accuracy at the date when the accounts are formally approved by the directors.

Provision should not be made in respect of any contingent gain.

Where no provision is made for a material contingent loss, full disclosure should be made unless the possibility of loss is remote. Disclosure should only be made in respect of a contingent gain where it is probable that the gain will be realised. The following information should be disclosed:

(a) the nature of the contingency;
(b) a summary of the elements of uncertainty which affect the anticipated outcome;
(c) an estimate, computed on a prudent basis, of the financial effects of contingency made at the date when the accounts are approved by the or a statement that such an estimate cannot be practically made.

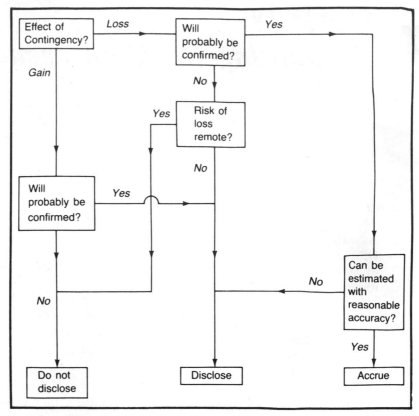

Fig. 17.1   Accounting for contingencies.

The estimate of the financial effect of the contingency should be given before taking into account any related taxation effects; where material the taxation implications should be shown separately. The potential financial effect of contingencies should be reduced for:

(a)   any amounts already accrued;
(b)   the extent to which any part of the contingent loss is considered remote.

Figure 17.1 illustrates the application of SSAP 18. Note how the prudence concept applies, in that contingent gains are never accrued for but probable contingent liabilities are provided for.

EXAMINATION PRACTICE

17.1   SSAP 18 – Requirements

(a)   Define the term 'contingency'.
(b)   Under what circumstances should provision be made in the accounts for a contingent gain or loss?
(c)   Where provision is not made for a contingent gain or loss what additional disclosure is necessary?

17.2   SSAP 18 – Example

The Denton Mousetrap Company Ltd has recently embarked on an export drive to the USA. Its sales campaign has been concentrated in the State of California where it has advertised its product as 'A girl's best friend'. Unhappily it has found itself, in that litigious nation, subject to the following lawsuits:

(a)   Mr G. Washington has lost his thumb as a result of handling a mouse trap with an excessively powerful spring, and is suing the company for £5000. The company's legal advisers are of the opinion that this claim is reasonable in amount and that no defence can be put forward.

(b)   The Californian Women's Liberation Group claims that the company's advertising is offensive to the dignity of women and are claiming £10 000 000 as damages. The company's legal advisers are of the opinion that the outcome of this action will depend upon which judge happens to hear the case, there being a 70 per cent chance that the company will be held free of blame and a 30 per cent chance that the company will be required to pay damages in full.

(c)   Mr A. Lincoln, a keen self-publicist, is suing the company for £1 000 000 000, on the grounds that he is widely known to have a great fear of mice, and the company's advertising has caused him to be accused of effeminacy in this respect. The company's legal advisers are of the opinion that the risk of any court upholding this claim is negligible.

What accounting treatment and disclosure is required in respect of each of these items in the accounts?

18 SSAP 19: Accounting for Investment Properties

Background

When ED 15, issued in January 1975, included a requirement to depreciate buildings, the proposal was highly controversial. As explained in Chapter 12, SSAP 12 excludes investment properties from this requirement. SSAP 19 offers a definition of investment property and defines the appropriate accounting treatment.

Summary of the statement

Definitions

SSAP 19 defines an 'investment property' as 'an interest in land and/or buildings':

(a) 'in respect of which construction work and development have been completed', and

(b) 'which is held for its investment potential, any rental income being negotiated at arm's length'.

The standard goes on to state that there are two exceptions:

(a) A property owned and occupied by a company for its own purposes is not an investment property.

(b) A property let to and occupied by another group company is not an investment property either in the company's own accounts or those of the group.

Required practice

SSAP 19 requires that depreciation on investment properties should not be provided as laid down in SSAP 12, except where a property is held on a lease, in which case, if the unexpired lease term is less than twenty years, depreciation must be provided.

Investment properties should be included in the balance sheet at their open market value. Changes in their value should be shown as a movement on an investment revaluation reserve, except where a revaluation deficit exceeds the balance on that reserve account; any excess deficit should be dealt with in the profit and loss account.

Special cases

SSAP 19 applies special rules to certain types of entity:

(a) Charities are excluded from the scope of SSAP 19.

(b) Investment trust companies and property unit trusts are permitted, in accordance with their articles of association, not to take revaluation deficits in excess of the investment revaluation reserve through the profit and loss account. Instead such deficits must be shown 'prominently' in the accounts.

(c) The rules on treatment of property revaluation surpluses and deficits do not apply to pension funds and the long-term business of insurance companies, where changes in value are dealt with in the relevant fund account.

Required disclosure

The accounts should disclose either the name or the qualifications of the valuer, together with the bases of valuation. Where the valuer is an employee or officer of the company or group this fact must be disclosed.

Background

As we have seen, the application of SSAP 19 is to all investment properties, not merely those held by property investment companies, but it was the special problems affecting those companies that caused the special treatment.

Certain special objections to the provision of depreciation have been put forward in relation to investment property, including:

(a) That where there is a clause in the lease requiring the tenant to keep the property in good repair then a depreciation provision becomes unnecessary. This objection fails to take into account the wearing out of the basic structure of the building and the obsolescence factor.

(b) That the total value of an investment property consists of the total of future rents to be received from it discounted to present value, and that a figure of cost less depreciation is meaningless. Now one measure of value of any asset is to take the total of the net future stream of income arising from it and discount this to present value; as each year passes, there is a reduction in the total expected income and a consequent reduction in value. Under our present accounting conventions we recognise that loss in value by making a depreciation charge.

(c) That the provision of depreciation on investment properties will reduce the distributable profits of property companies to such an extent as to reduce or eliminate their capacity to pay dividends. This, in practice, is the main reason for the opposition of the property companies to property depreciation, and it does seem unacceptable to say that companies should be exempted from following best accounting practice in order to show their results in a better light.

To understand the reasons why the ASC was willing to give special consideration to the problems of investment property it is necessary to consider the special circumstances of property companies. Traditionally such companies fall into two categories, property dealing and property investment. A property dealing company will acquire property with the intention of resale, treating both the rental received and the disposal proceeds as trading income, showing property held at the balance sheet date as a current asset akin to stock, and paying corporation tax in full on its profits; a property investment company will acquire property with the intention of continuing to hold it for the benefit of the rental received which will be shown as the only trading profit from the property, any surplus arising in the event of a disposal being taken direct to reserves and regarded as non-distributable, and corporation tax being payable at the full rate on trading income and at the capital gains tax rate on surpluses on property disposals.

In the early 1970s a rapid increase in property prices combined with a sharp rise in interest rates led to a situation where it was common for property companies to buy property at a price such that rental income was considerably less than the related interest charges, the commercial justification for such a transaction being the prospect of increased rental yields and property values in the future. This is known as deficit financing. Conventional measures of accounting income would result in the company showing substantial losses in the early years of such a venture, even though the transaction had been undertaken in the full knowledge of such losses with the expectation of their being exceeded by related income at a later date. To require the provision of depreciation in the early years of such a transaction would result in further distortion of the company's commercial intention, artificially increasing losses in the early years and increasing profit in later years.

Conclusion

SSAP 19 emerged as a response to vigorous lobbying from the property industry. It resulted in the presentation of useful information, but did so at the cost of a substantial departure from traditional accounting conventions.

EXAMINATION PRACTICE

18.1   Definition
You are required, in relation to Statement of Standard Accounting Practice No 19: Accounting for Investment Properties (SSAP 19), to define the term 'investment property'.

19 SSAP 20: Foreign Currency Translation

Background

When exchange rates are fixed and stable, perhaps with occasional orderly revaluations or devaluations of currency, the difficulties of accounting for exchange rate fluctuations are minimised. However, since the early 1970s most currency exchange rates have been 'floating', being allowed to fluctuate in line with market pressures on a day-to-day basis. In those countries, such as the UK, where companies tend to have substantial foreign trading links, foreign currency loans and foreign investments, the need to find an acceptable solution to the problem of accounting for foreign currency items is particularly important.

There are two main ways in which a company may engage in foreign currency operations:

(a) The company may enter directly into a foreign currency business transaction. It will be necessary to translate these transactions into the currency in which the company reports so that they can be included in the accounting records.

(b) Operations may be conducted through a foreign subsidiary company which maintains accounting records in terms of the local currency; in order to prepare consolidated accounts it will be necessary to translate the accounts of the foreign subsidiary into the currency in which the holding company presents its accounts.

When translating foreign currency items in the accounts the question arises as to what rate of exchange should be used. Generally there are two rates that might be considered:

(a) The 'historical rate', being the exchange rate applicable when the item first entered the accounts.

(b) The 'closing rate', being the exchange rate applicable at the balance sheet date.

SSAP 20 lays down circumstances in which each rate should be used.

The other main accounting problem in accounting for foreign currency translation is how to account for foreign exchange differences, which a company may be 'exposed' to in the two following ways.

Transaction exposure

Transaction exposure arises when there is a difference between the exchange rate at the time when a transaction is entered into and the time when it is completed. These realised gains or losses are quantified by the circumstances of the transaction, and there is general agreement that they should be taken through the profit and loss account.

Translation exposure

Translation exposure arises when there is a difference between the exchange rate at the time when an item is brought into the accounts and the exchange rate used to translate that item at the balance sheet date. Translation differences will only arise in relation to those items translated at the closing rate. There are a number of ways of treating translation differences in the accounts, and SSAP 20 tries to standardise practice in this area.

Summary of the statement

Definitions

SSAP 20 defines a number of terms including:

(a)   'A *foreign enterprise* is a subsidiary, associated company or branch whose operations are based in a country other than that of the investing company or whose assets and liabilities are denominated mainly in a foreign currency.'

(b)   'A company's *local currency* is the currency of the primary economic environment in which it operates and generates net cash flows.' Note that this definition, combined with the requirement that individual companies should translate their foreign currency balances into local currency, means that companies are required to report their accounts in the currency of the 'primary economic environment', even if this is different from the country of legal incorporation.

(c)   'The *closing rate* is the exchange rate for "spot" transactions ruling at the balance sheet date and is the mean of buying and selling rates at the close of business on the day for which the rate is to be ascertained.'

(d)   The *average rate* is not covered by the definitions section of SSAP 20. However, the introductory explanatory note to SSAP 20 does consider this issue, pointing out that where there are seasonal trade variations the use of a weighting procedure will be desirable.

(e)   '*Monetary items* are money held and amounts to be received or paid in money and, where a company is not an exempt company, should be categorised as either short-term or long-term. Short-term monetary items are those which fall due within one year of the balance sheet date.'

(f)   'The *net investment* which a company has in a foreign enterprise is its effective equity stake and comprises its proportion of such foreign enterprise's net assets; in appropriate circumstances, intra-group loans and other deferred balances may be regarded as part of the effective equity stake.'

(g)   The *temporal method* is not covered in the definitions section of SSAP 20; the explanatory note states that 'the mechanics of this method are identical with those used in preparing the accounts of an individual company.' SSAP 20 explains that this means translating monetary items at the closing rate and other items at the historical rate. Although SSAP 20 does not specifically mention revalued assets, it may be implied from the use of the term temporal method that revalued assets should be translated by reference to the exchange rate at the date of revaluation, not acquisition.

(h) The 'closing rate/net investment' method is again not covered in the definitions section of SSAP 20, but in the introduction to the standard is defined: 'Under this method the amounts in the balance sheet of a foreign enterprise should be translated into the reporting currency of the investing company using the rate of exchange ruling at the balance sheet date' (i.e. the closing rate).

Overview

SSAP 20 requires use of the temporal method in translating foreign currency balances in a company's own accounts. The closing rate method should be used when incorporating the accounts of foreign enterprises into the group accounts, except where the foreign enterprise is heavily dependent on the economic environment of the investing company's home currency when the temporal method should be used. Normally translation differences go through the profit and loss account where they arise from the temporal method and direct to reserves when they arise from the closing rate method, except where a foreign investment is financed by foreign borrowing where a 'cover' approach (see below) may be used.

Required practice – individual companies

In the accounts of individual companies all items should be translated at the exchange rate ruling when each transaction occurs (i.e. the historical rate). An average rate for each accounting period may be used as an approximation. At each balance sheet date all monetary items should be retranslated at the closing rate, while non-monetary items will not be altered except where a cover approach (see below) is adopted.

All translation differences will be reported as part of the results for the year arising from ordinary operations, except:

(a) differences arising on extraordinary items should be treated as part of the related extraordinary item;

(b) exchange gains on long-term monetary items normally go through the profit and loss account, but should be taken to reserves where there are doubts as to the convertibility of the currency in question;

(c) where a 'cover' approach is adopted.

The possibility of adopting a 'cover' approach arises when a company has used foreign currency borrowings to finance or provide a hedge against foreign equity investments. In such a case a company is permitted to adopt a policy of translating the foreign equity investment at the closing rate and taking differences on translation of the investment, net of translation differences on the related loan, direct to reserves. This approach is subject to the following conditions:

(a) In each accounting period translation differences on borrowings may only be offset to the extent of translation differences on the related investments.

(b) The foreign currency borrowings which are offset must not exceed the total cash expected to be generated from the investments.

(c) Where a company chooses to adopt a cover approach, the same accounting policy must be adopted in successive accounting periods.

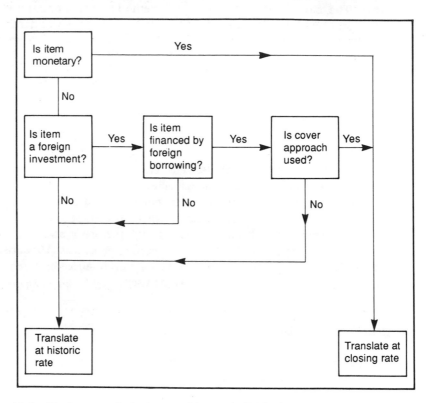

Fig. 19.1 Exchange rate to be used by an individual company.

Figure 19.1 shows the exchange rate to be used at the year end by an individual company.

Required practice – group accounts

When translating the accounts of foreign enterprises (as defined above), the closing rate method should normally be used. The one exception to this rule is that where the trade of the foreign enterprise is more dependent on the economic environment of the investing company's currency than that of its own reporting currency the temporal method should be used. The methods used should be applied consistently unless operational relationships with the investing company change.

When the closing rate method is used companies are allowed to translate the profit and loss account at either the average or the closing rate. Consequently translation differences can arise from two causes:

(a)   A difference will arise because of retranslation of the opening net investment from the opening to the closing rate.

(b)   Where the results for the year are translated at the average rate, a difference will arise when the results are retranslated at the closing rate for inclusion in the balance sheet.

Both types of difference should be recorded as reserve movements.

The conditions under which the 'cover' method can be adopted in the group accounts are rather different from those governing the individual company accounts. Where the investing company has adopted a cover approach, the same offset procedure can only be adopted in the consolidated accounts where the foreign equity investment is not a subsidiary or associated company; otherwise the accounting entries related to the cover approach in the individual company's accounts will be reversed on consolidation. SSAP 20 does permit a 'cover' approach to be adopted in the group accounts, whereby the exchange differences on foreign currency borrowings in a company's own accounts can be set off against exchange differences on the net equity investments in foreign enterprises, provided that:

(a)   The closing rate method is appropriate to translation of the accounts of the foreign enterprise.

(b)   The amount of exchange differences offset is limited to the extent of exchange differences on the net investment in the related foreign enterprises.

(c)   The foreign currency borrowings should not exceed the total amount of cash that the net investments are expected to generate.

(d)   The same accounting policy must be adopted in successive accounting periods.

We have seen that the SSAP 20 requires the accounts of foreign enterprises to be translated by the temporal method: 'in those circumstances where the trade of the foreign enterprise is more dependent on the economic environment of the investing company's currency than that of its own reporting currency'.

The explanatory note to SSAP 20 offers some detailed guidance on the factors to take into account in identifying this position:

(a)   The extent to which the cash flows of the foreign enterprise have a direct impact upon those of the investing company.

(b)   The extent to which the functioning of the foreign enterprise is directly dependent upon the investing company.

(c)   The currency in which most trading transactions are denominated.

(d)   The major currency to which the operation is exposed in its financing structure.

Examples of situations where the temporal method may be appropriate are where the foreign enterprise:

(a)   Acts as a selling agency of the investing company.

(b)   Produces raw materials or other products which are shipped to the investing company for inclusion in its own products.

(c)   Is located overseas to act as a vehicle for raising finance for other group companies.

SSAP 20 argues that where a foreign enterprise operates in an area of hyperinflation it is desirable that the local currency accounts be adjusted to reflect price level movements before translation takes place.

Required disclosure

SSAP 20 requires disclosure of the methods used in the translation of the accounts of foreign enterprises and the treatment accorded to foreign exchange differences. In practice, this information will normally be given in the accounting policies note.

All companies are required to disclose the net movement on reserves arising from exchange differences.

All companies other than exempt companies (as defined in CA 1985) are required to disclose the net gain or loss on foreign currency monetary items, identifying separately:

(a) amounts offset in reserves under the 'cover' method;
(b) the amount taken through the profit and loss account.

Computation in line with SSAP 20

The following example, Hathern Ltd, illustrates the main practical applications of SSAP 20.

Hathern Ltd, a UK company, set up a subsidiary, Hentzau Inc. in Ruritania on 1 January 19X1; the currency of Ruritania is the crown. At the end of the first year of trading Hentzau Inc. presented the following accounts:

Balance sheet as at 31 December 19X1

	Crowns
Share capital	750 000
Retained profit	50 000
	800 000
Plant (purchased 1.1.19X1)	
Cost	600 000
Depreciation	120 000
	480 000
Stock (purchased 30.11.19X1)	390 000
Net monetary current assets	80 000
	950 000
Long-term loan (raised 1.1.19X1)	150 000
	800 000

Profit and loss account year ended 31 December 19X1

	Crowns	Crowns
Sales		470 000
Depreciation	120 000	
Other expenses	280 000	
		400 000
		70 000
Taxation (payable 1.1.19X2)		20 000
		50 000

Exchange rates moved:	Crowns to the £1
1 January 19X1	3
Average for 19X1	2.8
30 November 19X1	2.6
31 December 19X1	2.5

In order to finance the investment in Hentzau Inc., Hathern Ltd had raised a long-term loan of 600 000 crowns in Ruritania on 1 January 19X1. The accounts of Hentzau Inc. will be converted to sterling as follows:

(a) By the temporal method:

Balance sheet	Crowns	Conversion factor	£
Share capital	750 000	1/3	250 000
Retained profit	50 000	*	32 000
	800 000		282 000
Plant: Cost	600 000	1/3	200 000
Depreciation	120 000	1/3	40 000
	480 000		160 000
Stock	390 000	1/2.6	150 000
Net monetary current assets	80 000	1/2.5	32 000
	950 000		342 000
Loan	150 000	1/2.5	60 000
	800 000		282 000

*Balancing figure

Profit and loss account	Crowns	Crowns	Conversion factor	£	£
Sales		470 000	1/2.8		167 857
Depreciation	120 000		1/3	40 000	
Other expenses	280 000		1/2.8	100 000	
		400 000			140 000
		70 000			27 857
Taxation		20 000	1/2.5		8 000
		50 000			19 857
Exchange difference					12 143
Profit					32 000

Note the principles of translation:
(i) All monetary items in the balance sheet translated at closing rate.
(ii) All non-monetary items in the balance sheet converted at historical rate.
(iii) All revenue and expenditure items are converted at historical rate or, where this is impractical, at average rate.
(iv) The exchange difference is taken through the profit and loss account.

(b) By the closing rate method:

Balance sheet	Crowns	Conversion factor	£
Share capital	750 000	1/3	250 000
Reserves	50 000	*	70 000
	800 000		320 000
Plant: Cost	600 000	1/2.5	240 000
Depreciation	120 000	1/2.5	48 000
	480 000		192 000
Stock	390 000	1/2.5	156 000
Net monetary current assets	80 000	1/2.5	32 000
	950 000		380 000
Loan	150 000	1/2.5	60 000
	800 000		320 000

*Balancing figure

Profit and loss account	Crowns	Crowns	Conversion factor	£	£
Sales		470 000	1/2.8		167 857
Depreciation	120 000		1/2.8	42 857	
Cost of sales	280 000		1/2.8	100 000	
	400 000				142 857
		70 000			25 000
Taxation		20 000	1/2.8		7 143
Retained profit		50 000			17 857

Note that it is necessary to translate share capital at the historical rate, and that any pre-acquisition reserves would also be translated at the exchange rate ruling at the date of acquisition. The exchange difference to be taken direct to reserves can be calculated:

	£	£
Opening net investment at closing rate:		
750 000 × 1/2.5	300 000	
at opening rate:		
750 000 × 1/3	250 000	
		50 000
Retained profit at closing rate:		
50 000 × 1/2.5	20 000	
at average rate:		
50 000 × 1/2.8	17 857	
		2 142
		52 143

So that the closing balance on the reserves is made up:

	£
Retained profit	17 857
Exchange difference	52 143
	70 000

Note that SSAP 20 would also have allowed the closing rate to be used in translation of the profit and loss account.

In the accounts of Hathern Ltd a loss on foreign currency transactions will arise made up as follows:

	£
Sterling proceeds of 600 000 crown loan @ 1/3	200 000
Year end liability 600 000 @ 1/2.5	240 000
Loss charged against operating profit	40 000

If the conditions for applying the 'cover' approach laid down in SSAP 20 apply, then Hathern Ltd would be allowed to choose an accounting policy for applying the cover approach as follows:

(a) In the company's own accounts the original investment of 750 000 crowns would be translated at the closing rate of 2.5 crowns instead of the historical rate of 3 crowns. A gain would arise of:

$$\left(750\ 000 \times \frac{1}{2.5}\right) - \left(750\ 000 \times \frac{1}{3}\right) = £50\ 000.$$

The loss on translating the loan (£40 000) would be offset against this gain, and the net gain (£10 000) is taken direct to reserves.

(b) On consolidation the loss on translating the loan would, if the closing rate method has been used, be offset directly against the translation gain of £52 143, the net gain or loss being taken directly to reserves. If the temporal method of translation has been used then, as we have already seen, use of the cover approach is not permitted.

Controversy over the statement

Economic relationships

Two economic principles are relevant to the controversy over foreign currency translation:

(a) The 'Fisher' effect, whereby it is argued that there is a link between interest rates and expectations as to future exchange rate movements, so that the weaker the currency the higher the interest rate. This relationship arises because lenders will expect to receive a high return in the form of interest to compensate for the loss which arises because when the foreign currency loan is repaid it will convert into fewer units of the home currency than when the loan was first made.

(b)   The purchasing power parity effect, whereby it is argued that there is a link between the rate of inflation and the strength of currency, so that the higher the rate of inflation the weaker the currency and vice versa.

It is not claimed that either of these relationships is cast iron, but research has shown that, over a number of years, both these effects tend to operate in practice.

Choice of translation method

The debate on foreign currency translation has tended to centre on the relative merits of the temporal and closing rate methods.

Benefits of the temporal method have been seen as:

(a)   The principles of historical cost accounting are maintained.

(b)   The activities of the foreign subsidiary are treated as an extension of those of the parent company, which is in line with the conceptual basis of consolidation.

(c)   The method recognises that the risk of translation differences being realised depends on the nature of the item being accounted for.

Benefits of the closing rate method have been seen as:

(a)   The accounting ratios in the accounts of the subsidiary are not distorted on consolidation.

(b)   The method is simple to operate and understand.

(c)   The most up-to-date information on exchange rates is used.

SSAP 20 attempts to justify the closing rate method for foreign subsidiaries with the argument that a company's investment in a quasi-independent foreign subsidiary 'is in the net worth of its foreign enterprise rather than a direct investment in the individual assets and liabilities'. This is why SSAP 20 focuses on the term 'net investment approach'. However, this is inconsistent conceptually with the consolidation of all the assets and liabilities of such a subsidiary into the group accounts on a line-by-line basis.

Translation exposure can be dramatically different for the two methods. For example, if a foreign subsidiary has substantial non-monetary assets but also has net monetary liabilities then under the closing rate method the net investment in the subsidiary, being a net asset, will be 'exposed', while if the temporal method is used then non-monetary assets will give rise to no translation gain or loss, being translated at the historical rate, and only the monetary items, being a net liability, will be exposed. To take a simple example: Nanpantan Ltd invested $100 000 on 1 January 19X6 in a wholly owned foreign subsidiary Bruges SA. Exchange rates moved from $5 to £1 on 1 January 19X6 to $4 to £1 on 31 January 19X6. During the year 19X6 no profit or loss arose, and at both the beginning and end of the year the balance sheet of Bruges SA showed:

	$
Freehold property	1 000 000
Loan	900 000
	100 000
Share capital	100 000

Translation of the balance sheet at 31 December 19X6 will show:

	$	Temporal Translation factor	£	Closing rate Translation factor	£
Freehold property	1 000 000	1/5	200 000	1/4	250 000
Loan	900 000	1/4	225 000	1/4	225 000
	100 000		(25 000)		25 000
Share capital	100 000	1/5	20 000		20 000
Gain/(loss) (on translation)	—	*	(45 000)	*	5 000
	100 000		(25 000)		25 000

*Balancing figure.

Translation differences

At different times various proposals on the treatment of translation differences have arisen. These include:

(a) taking translation differences into account when arriving at the figure for operating profit;

(b) showing translation differences on the face of the profit and loss account after the operating profit figure, possibly in conjunction with the extraordinary items;

(c) showing translation differences as a movement on the reserves.

As we have seen, SSAP 20 treats different types of translation difference in different ways. Arguments in favour of different views are taken into account in the SSAP 20 approach as follows:

(a) As we have seen, there is an economic relationship between interest rates and currency fluctuations. SSAP 20 recognises this in that translation differences in a company's own accounts, which relate to monetary items, are shown in the profit and loss account and are therefore matched with interest charges.

(b) Where an asset acquisition is financed by a loan it is desirable that translation differences on the two items be matched; SSAP 20 permits this to some extent via the cover method considered in detail above.

(c) Translation differences on investments abroad often reflect a form of revaluation adjustment; SSAP 20 normally takes such differences directly to reserve.

Areas of hyperinflation

Paragraph 26 of SSAP 20 argues that where a foreign enterprise operates in an area of hyperinflation it is desirable to adjust the accounts to reflect current price levels before translation of the foreign currency amounts.

We can illustrate the reason for this with a simple example. Supposing a UK company buys a company owning a piece of land in Ruritania for 100 000 crowns, and having no other assets or liabilities, at a time when the Ruritanian crown exchange rate is:

$2 \text{ Cr} = £1$

Let us suppose that in the following year rent from the land exactly covers expenses, while Ruritania has inflation of 100 per cent and, in line with the purchasing power parity effect, the exchange rate moves to:

$4 \text{ Cr} = £1$

Using the closing rate method of translation the investment in land would be translated for consolidation at:

Opening balance sheet:

	£
$\$100\ 000 \times \frac{1}{2} =$	50 000

Closing balance sheet:

	£
$\$100\ 000 \times \frac{1}{4} =$	25 000

Clearly it is not realistic to regard an unchanged piece of land as having halved in value over the year, since in practice one would expect such a non-monetary asset to maintain its value in real terms. The solution is to revalue the land in crowns before translation.

In the US, SFAS 52, the US accounting standard on currency translation, takes a different approach prescribing use of the temporal method for all companies operating in areas of hyperinflation.

IAS 21: Accounting for the Effects of Changes in Foreign Exchange Rates

Compliance with SSAP 20 will satisfy the requirements of IAS 21.

Conclusion

SSAP 20 tackles a highly complex area in which international harmonisation is particularly important. The provisions of SSAP 20 are very similar to those prescribed in the USA and Canada. Many of the difficult issues of principle involved in currency translation are attributable to differential inflation rates in different countries, and could be resolved more easily within the context of an inflation accounting system.

EXAMINATION PRACTICE

19.1 Foreign currency translation

(a) In terms of the definitions offered in SSAP 20 you are required to distinguish between
   (i)   the closing rate method
   (ii) the temporal method
   and to explain the circumstances under which each should be used.

(b) The following are the summary accounts of Overseas Ltd, in foreign currency (limas):

Balance sheet as at 31 December 19X9

	Limas
Ordinary share capital	630 000
Retained profits	80 000
	710 000
Plant and machinery, at cost	700 000
Less: Depreciation	70 000
	630 000
Stocks, at cost	210 000
Net monetary current assets	40 000
	880 000
Less: Long-term loan	170 000
	710 000

Profit and loss account, year to 31 December 19X9

		Limas
Sales		900 000
Less: Depreciation	70 000	
Other operating expenses	750 000	
		820 000
Net profit before taxation and appropriations		80 000

During the year, relevant exchange rates were:

	Limas to the £
1 January 19X9	14
Average for the year	12
Average at the acquisition of closing stock	11
31 December 19X9	10

Your UK company, Sterling Ltd, had acquired Overseas Ltd on 1 January 19X9 by subscribing £45 000 of share capital in cash when the exchange rate was 14 limas to the £. The long-term loan had been raised locally on the same date. On that date Overseas Ltd had purchased the plant and equipment for 700 000 limas. It is being depreciated by the straight line method over 10 years.

You are required to show the balance sheet, profit and loss account and reserve movement of Overseas Ltd in £s, using:

(i)   the closing rate method, and

(ii) the temporal method.

(*ACCA adapted*)

19.2   Translation

On 1 January 19X5 Chestnut Ltd, a UK company, acquired the entire share capital of Acorn SA, a company registered and trading in Ruritania, for a purchase consideration of 600 000 crowns. To help finance the purchase, a loan of 300 000 crowns was raised in Ruritania by Chestnut Ltd on 1 January 19X5. These were the only foreign currency items recorded in Chestnut's own accounts.

On 1 January 19X5 Acorn SA acquired all the plant currently shown in the balance sheet.

During the year to 31 December 19X5 exchange rates moved as follows:

1 January 19X5	20 crowns to £1
Average 19X5	18 crowns to £1
At date stock acquired	16 crowns to £1
31 December 19X5	15 crowns to £1

The accounts of Acorn for the year to 31 December 19X5 showed:

Acorn SA
Balance sheet as at 31 December 19X5

	Crowns	Crowns
Plant – Cost		604 800
– Depreciation		86 400
		518 400
Current assets		
Stock	129 600	
Cash	43 200	
		172 800
		691 200
Long-term loan		172 800
		518 400
Ordinary share capital		345 600
Retained profit – At 1 January 19X5	129 600	
– For year	43 200	
		172 800
		518 400

Profit and loss account for the year ended 31 December 19X5

	Crowns	Crowns
Sales		864 000
Cost of sales		561 600
Gross profit		302 400
Less:		
Depreciation	86 400	
Other expenses	172 800	
		259 200
Retained profit		43 200

Required

In compliance with SSAP 20:

(a) Translate the accounts of Acorn SA by the closing rate method. Apply the closing rate to profit and loss items.

(b) Translate the accounts of Acorn SA by the temporal method.

(c) Show the exchange differences taken in Chestnut Ltd's own accounts through the profit and loss account and direct to reserves respectively:

   (i)   taking a cover approach;
   (ii) not taking a cover approach.

20 SSAP 21: Accounting for Leases and Hire Purchase Agreements

Background

SSAP 21, issued in August 1984, has been one of the most difficult accounting standards on which to reach agreement. This is caused both by the technical complexity of the subject and by fierce controversy over the basic approach of the standard.

The growth of leasing

A lease is an agreement whereby a *lessor*, who owns an asset, conveys the right to use that asset to a *lessee* for an agreed period of time at an agreed rental. Most lessors in the UK are members of the Equipment Leasing Association, and Table 20.1 shows how the leasing industry had grown over a ten-year period.

Table 20.1 Assets acquired by members of the UK Equipment Leasing Association

	Assets* acquired	% increase in year
		£m
1975	340	6%
1976	421	24%
1977	675	60%
1978	1214	80%
1979	1802	48%
1980	2359	31%
1981	2674	13%
1982	2834	6%
1983	2894	2%
1984	4012	39%

*Source: *World Leasing Yearbook 1986*, Hawkins Publishers Ltd.

Leases can be divided into two broad categories:

(a) *Finance leases*, covering most of the life of the asset. Such a lease normally is designed as a mechanism whereby the lessor finances the acquisition of an asset which will in practice be used by the lessee.

(b) *Operating leases* where a lessor acquires an asset to be hired out for successive periods of time to successive users. Such a lease is normally entered into for operational reasons, in circumstances where the lessee does not require the asset for a sufficient length of time to warrant purchase.

The distinction between the two types of lease is obviously blurred, and we consider in detail below how SSAP 21 has tried to draw a distinction between the two.

A major reason for the growth of leasing in the UK has been the combination of the tax system and the economic climate. From 1972 to 1984 companies acquiring plant and machinery enjoyed 100 per cent first year allowances for tax purposes. Many manufacturing companies found that, with the high levels of inflation of the 1970s, their trading profits were insufficient to cover the full first year allowance; thus they were unable to enjoy the cash flow benefits on acquisition of new plant which the tax system was designed to give them. By contrast, in times of high inflation financial institutions tend to record high taxable profits. Thus where a financial institution financed asset acquisition for a client by means of a lease agreement rather than a simple loan then the lessor could enjoy a substantial cash flow benefit from accelerated capital allowances, and therefore would be willing to offer finance wtih lower finance charges than would apply to a simple loan.

The 1984 budget announced the phasing out of first year allowances and a phased reduction in the corporation tax rate from 50 per cent in 1984 to 35 per cent in 1987. The effect was to boost leasing business substantially in 1984, for two reasons:

(a)   Fixed assets were being leased early to enjoy the benefit of first year allowances before they were abolished.
(b)   During the transitional period first year allowances could be used to defer profit to later years with lower tax rates, giving a combination of cash flow benefits and a saving in actual tax paid.

The basic accounting problem

Accounting for leases presents a wide range of technical problems for both lessees and lessors. These are addressed in detail in SSAP 21, and are considered below. The major accounting problem that arises is that a finance lease is in legal form a rental agreement, while in commercial substance it is a device for borrowing the financial resources to obtain the use of a fixed asset. If we account for a finance lease in line with its legal form then in the accounts of a lessee we would expect the only accounting entry each year to be an item in the profit and loss account, writing off the rental charge. In the accounts of a lessor, following legal form, we would find the asset recorded initially at cost and depreciated systematically, with rental income credited to profit and loss. This approach was common practice in the UK up until the 1980s.

The traditional approach based on 'legal form' appears somewhat unsatisfactory if we consider the commercial substance of such a transaction. A lessee has effectively acquired the use of a fixed asset, and has incurred an obligation to pay a series of instalments, normally over a period of several years, to finance the acquisition. Accordingly, it is argued, the lease should be 'capitalised' by recording the asset as though it had been purchased, and the related obligation to pay future instalments as a liability. Similarly, lessors are regarded as owning a financial asset, the right to receive future payments under the lease agreement, rather than the fixed asset which is the subject of the lease. During the 1980s this 'capitalisation' approach has become more common, and it is the approach taken by SSAP 21.

Hire-purchase agreements

So far we have considered matters relating to lease agreements. A hire-purchase agreement is a special kind of rental contract under which the hirer has an option to purchase the asset at the end of the rental period.

SSAP 21 requires that hire-purchase agreements which are of a financing nature should be treated as finance leases, and other hire-purchase agreements should be treated as operating leases. Normally hire-purchase agreements involve transfer of the asset at the end of the agreement for a nominal sum, so that the hirer can be expected to exercise the option to purchase; such agreements are clearly similar in character to finance leases.

However, it sometimes happens that a hire-purchase agreement may set the option to purchase at a price so high as to raise doubts as to whether the option will be exercised; in such a case, the agreement will have the character of an operating lease.

It should be noted that a hire-purchase agreement is treated for tax purposes as the acquisition of an asset by the hirer, while under any form of lease agreement the tax system treats the lessor as acquiring the asset.

Definitions

A major problem in introducing a requirement to capitalise finance leases is that of drawing a distinction between a 'finance' lease and an 'operating' lease.

A *finance lease* is 'a lease that transfers substantially all the risks and rewards of ownership of an asset to the lessee'. Having defined a finance lease in principle SSAP 21 goes on to state that 'it should be presumed that such a transfer of risks and rewards occurs if at the *inception of a lease* the present value of the *minimum lease payments*, including any initial payment, amounts to substantially all (normally 90 per cent or more) of the *fair value* of the leased asset. The present value should be calculated by using the *interest rate implicit in the lease*. If the fair value of the asset is not determinable, an estimate thereof should be used'.

Four of the terms used above have been presented in italics, because SSAP 21 offers further definitions of these terms as follows:

(a)   The *inception of a lease* is 'the earlier of the time the asset is brought into use and the date from which rentals first accrue'.
(b)   The *minimum lease payments* are 'the minimum payments over the remaining part of the lease term (excluding charges for services and taxes to be paid by the lessor) and:
  (i)   in the case of the lessee, any residual amounts guaranteed by him or by a party related to him; or
  (ii)   in the case of the lessor, any residual amounts guaranteed by the lessee or by an independent third party'.

(c)   *Fair value* is 'the price at which an asset could be exchanged in an arm's length transaction less, where applicable, any grants receivable towards the purchase or use of the asset'.

(d)   The *interest rate implicit in the lease* is 'the discount rate that at the inception of a lease, when applied to the amounts which the lessor expects to receive and retain, produces an amount (the present value) equal to the fair value of the leased asset'. Where this interest rate is not determinable it should be estimated by reference to the rate which a lessee would be expected to pay on a similar lease.

Taking the above definitions together we can see that SSAP 21 both defines what in principle constitutes a finance lease and lays down detailed criteria for identifying such a lease. However, the standard makes it clear that it is the definition with reference to transfer of the 'risks and rewards of ownership' that is crucial, and provides that in exceptional circumstances a lease falling outside the detailed criteria may be shown to be a finance lease, and a lease falling inside the detailed criteria may be shown not to be a finance lease.

An *operating lease* is defined simply as 'a lease other than a finance lease'.

Other definitions in SSAP 21 include:

(a)   The *lease term* is 'the period for which the lessee has contracted to lease the asset and any further terms for which the lessee has the option to continue to lease the asset, with or without further payment, which option it is reasonably certain at the inception of the lease that the lessee will exercise'. Thus the definition of a 'lease term' involves not merely a reading of the minimum term provided in the lease, but also an assessment of how future rights to extend the lease are likely to be used.

(b)   The *net cash investment* in a lease 'is the amount of funds invested in a lease by a lessor, and comprises the cost of the asset plus or minus the following related payments or receipts:
    (i)   government or other grants receivable towards the purchase or use of the asset;
    (ii)   rentals received;
    (iii) taxation payments and receipts, including the effect of capital allowances;
    (iv)   residual values, if any, at the end of the lease term;
    (v)   interest payments (where applicable);
    (vi)   interest received on cash surplus;
    (vii) profit taken out of the lease'.
This definition is important in the allocation of finance charges by lessors, an issue that will be considered in detail below.

(c)   The *gross investment* in a lease is 'the total of the minimum lease payments and any unguaranteed residual value accruing to the lessor'.

(d)   The *net investment* in a lease is:
    (i)   'the gross investment in a lease . . . ; less
    (ii)   gross earnings allocated to future periods'.

Requirements for the lessee

A finance lease must be recorded by the lessee at the inception of the lease as an asset and as an obligation to pay future rentals. The asset and liability at the inception of the lease will both be of the same amount, and in principle the amount should be the present value of the minimum lease payments as discounted by the implicit interest rate. In practice, SSAP 21 points out that 'fair value' will normally closely approximate to 'present value' and so constitute an acceptable substitute.

The asset should be depreciated over the lesser of the useful life or the lease term; the logic of this is that the asset will only be of use to the lessee for the lesser of these two periods. There is an exception to this rule for hire-purchase agreements treated as finance leases, where the asset is simply depreciated over the useful life; the reason for this is that such an agreement carries an option to purchase, so that the asset will be available for use by the company indefinitely.

Rentals payable under the lease agreement should be split between the finance charge, shown as an expense in the profit and loss account, and the reduction of the outstanding lease obligation, being set off against the liability in the balance sheet. The total finance charge should be written off so as to produce a constant periodic rate of charge on the remaining balance of the lease obligation, or a 'reasonable approximation' thereto.

It may happen that a lessor offers lease terms whereby the minimum lease payments total less than the fair value of an asset, because of the benefits of government grants and capital allowances. In such a case the amount to be capitalised and depreciated will be restricted to the total of the minimum lease payments.

In the case of an operating lease the rental should be charged to profit and loss on a straight line basis over the lease term, even if the payments are not made on such a basis, unless another systematic and rational basis is more appropriate.

Disclosure by the lessee

For each major class of leased asset held under a finance lease there must be shown the gross amount and the accumulated depreciation. Alternatively, leased assets may be included in the totals disclosed relating to owned fixed assets; in this case the net amount relating to leased assets included in the fixed asset total must be disclosed. The amount of depreciation relating to assets held under finance leases must be disclosed.

The liabilities for finance lease obligations should be separately identified, either on the face of the balance sheet or in the notes to the accounts. These obligations should be analysed into three categories:

(a)   amounts due within one year.
(b)   amounts due in the second to fifth years.
(c)   amounts due after more than five years.

The analysis can be presented either as a separate analysis of finance lease obligations or, where such obligations are included with other items in the balance sheet, as an analysis of all those items. In the former case the lessee may, instead of showing net obligations, show gross lease payments due with future finance charges deducted from the total.

Total finance charges for the year relating to finance leases must be disclosed. Disclosure should be made of the amount of any commitment in respect of finance leases entered into at the balance sheet date where inception occurs after the year end.

In relation to operating leases the lessee must disclose total lease rentals for the year, split between hire of plant and machinery and other items. The lessee must also disclose total payments under operating leases committed for the coming year, analysed between:

(a)   agreements ending in the coming year;
(b)   agreements ending in years 2 to 5;
(c)   agreements lasting more than five years.

This analysis should further be split between commitments relating to land and buildings and other commitments.

Accounting policies relating both to finance leases and operating leases must be disclosed.

Requirements for the lessor

SSAP 21 requires that the amount due from a lessee under a finance lease should be shown as a debtor in the balance sheet, recorded at the net investment (see definitions above) in the lease, less any provision for bad or doubtful debts.

Total gross earnings under a finance lease should normally be allocated to accounting periods to give a constant periodic rate of return on the net cash investment in the lease; alternatively an allocation may be made out of gross earnings equal to the estimated cost of finance, with the balance recognised on a systematic basis. The practical problems of allocating the gross earnings on a finance lease are considered in detail below.

In the case of hire purchase agreements the same principles apply as in the case of a finance lease; in practice, because the lessor's cash flow position is not complicated by capital allowances or grants, SSAP 21 states that allocation of gross earnings to give a constant rate of return on the net investment in the lease will normally be acceptable.

Where a lessor receives tax-free grants against the purchase price of assets acquired for leasing these grants should be spread over the period of the lease, being dealt with by either:

(a)   treating the grant as non-taxable income, or
(b)   by grossing up the grant and including the grossed up amount in arriving at profit before tax. In this case the lessor should disclose the extent to which both pre-tax profit and the tax charge have been increased as a result of 'grossing up'.

In the case of an operating lease the asset should be recorded as a fixed asset and depreciated in the normal way. Rental income from an operating lease, excluding charges such as insurance and maintenance, should be recognised on a straight line basis over the period of the lease, even if payments are not made on such a basis, unless another more systematic and rational basis can be justified.

The initial direct costs of arranging any lease may be apportioned over the lease period on a 'systematic and rational' basis.

Disclosure by the lessor

At each balance sheet date there must be disclosed the net investment in finance leases and in hire-purchase contracts. The gross amounts of assets held for operating leases, and related accumulated depreciation, must be shown.

Disclosure must be made of the accounting policies on finance leases, operating leases and finance lease income.

Aggregate lease rentals receivable during the year must be disclosed both for finance and operating leases.

The cost of assets acquired for letting under finance leases during the year must be disclosed.

Special problems

So far we have addressed the basic rules laid down in SSAP 21 for the capitalisation of finance leases, and the techniques used to apply these rules. SSAP 21 also addresses a number of more detailed issues.

Manufacturer/dealer lessor

A manufacturer or dealer in goods may be the lessor of those goods. In such a case, a question may arise as to how the total profit on the transaction should be divided between a 'selling profit', to be taken as income on entering a firm agreement, and finance income, to be spread over the period of the lease. SSAP 21 lays down that a selling profit should be recognised under an operating lease. Under a finance lease a selling profit can be recognised, but is restricted to the excess of the 'fair value' of the asset over its cost, less any grants receivable relating to the asset.

Sale and leaseback transactions

Sometimes the owner of an asset will make an arrangement to sell the asset and lease it back from the purchaser. In such a transaction the sale cannot be regarded as being at an 'arm's length' price, so that it may be inappropriate to take account of any gain or loss in the sale in the normal way. Where the arrangement constitutes a finance lease SSAP 21 requires that the gain or loss be amortised over the shorter of the lease term and the useful life of the asset. In the case of an operating lease:

(a)   If the transaction is at fair value the gain or loss should be recorded immediately.

(b)   If the transaction is below fair value then again the gain or loss should be recorded immediately, unless the apparent loss is compensated by rentals below market price in which case the apparent loss should be deferred and amortised over the period at the low rentals.

(c)   If the sale price is above fair value the excess should be deferred and amortised over the shorter of the lease term and the period to the next rent review.

Application of SSAP 21 by the lessee

Example

Swithland Ltd is the lessee of an asset on a non-cancellable lease contract with a primary term of three years from 1 January 19X7. The rental is £5404 per quarter payable in advance. The lessee has the right after the end of the primary period to continue to lease the asset as long as the company wishes at a rent of £1 per year. The lessee bears all maintenance and insurance costs. The leased asset could have been bought for cash at the start of the lease for £55 404. The rate of interest implicit in the lease is 3 per cent per quarter. The company expects to continue to employ the asset for one year after the end of the primary term, and use the straight line method of depreciation.

This is a simple example of the terms of a lease agreement. It would clearly constitute a finance lease, since the company will be able to retain the asset indefinitely after the end of the primary period. The cash price of the asset will be taken as fair value, being £55 404, so that total finance charges to be allocated will be:

	£
Total instalments: 12 × £5404	64 848
Less fair value	55 404
Total finance charge	9 444

Table 20.2

Quarter	(a) Initial capital sum before instalment £	(b) Instalment £	(c) Capital sum after instalment £	(d) Finance charge @ 3% £	(e) Capital sum at end of period £
1/X7	55 404	5 404	50 000	1 500	51 500
2/X7	51 500	5 404	46 096	1 383	47 479
3/X7	47 479	5 404	42 075	1 262	43 337
4/X7	43 333	5 404	37 933	1 138	39 071
				5 283	
1/X8	39 071	5 404	33 667	1 010	34 677
2/X8	34 677	5 404	29 273	878	30 151
3/X8	30 151	5 404	24 747	742	25 489
4/X8	25 489	5 404	20 085	603	20 688
				3 233	
1/X9	20 688	5 404	15 284	459	15 743
2/X9	15 743	5 404	10 339	310	10 649
3/X9	10 649	5 404	5 245	157	5 402
4/X9	5 402	5 404	(2)*	2*	—
				928	

* Should be zero — attributable to rounding.

SSAP 21 requires that this charge be allocated in a way that gives a constant periodic rate of finance charge on the outstanding lease obligation. Table 20.2 shows how the finance charge would be apportioned by the *actuarial* method. Column (a) commences on the first line with the opening value of the asset. Column (b) shows on line 1 the first instalment, paid at the beginning of the first quarter. Column (c) shows in line 1 the amount outstanding at the beginning of the first quarter, being the amount in column (a) less the amount in column (b). Column (d) shows the finance charge, computed as the quarterly interest rate applied to the outstanding capital sum as shown in column (c). This finance charge is added to the lease obligation shown in column (c) to give the total capital sum outstanding at the end of the period shown in column (e). This then becomes the opening amount of the following quarter, shown in column (a). If the correct interest rate is used then in the final quarter the instalment should exactly clear the final balance. In practice, because of rounding, a small balance will often be outstanding after the final instalment and should be added to or deducted from the finance charge for that year.

The actuarial method is long-winded and complex to apply, particularly if the implicit interest rate in the finance charge is not given and has to be computed. A simpler method of approximating a fair allocation of finance charges is to use a 'sum of the digits' method as illustrated in Table 20.3. For each quarter we state the number of rental payments outstanding at the end of the quarter, as shown in column (a). For each year the finance charge is then computed as:

$$\frac{\text{Sum of digits for year}}{\text{Total sum of digits}} \times \text{Total finance charge}$$

Table 20.3 Swithland Ltd – allocation of finance charged by the 'sum of the digits'

	(a) Rentals not yet due	(b) Sum of digits for year	(c) Total sum of digits	(d) Total finance charge	(e) Finance charge for year
1/87	11				
2/87	10	(38	÷ 66)	× 9444	= 5437
3/87	9				
4/87	8				
1/88	7				
2/88	6	(22	÷ 66)	× 9444	= 3148
3/88	5				
4/88	4				
1/89	3				
2/89	2	(6	÷ 66)	× 9444	= 859
3/89	1				
4/89	0				9444
	66				

Finally, the guidance notes to SSAP 21 envisage the possibility of finance charges being apportioned on a simple straight line basis, in circumstances where total finance charges are not a material item in the accounts.

Table 20.4 shows a comparison of finance charges under each method for our example. We can see how the actuarial and sum of digit methods give similar figures, while the straight line method gives a very different picture.

Depreciation on a leased asset is governed by the same principles applied to other fixed assets in SSAP 12. The period over which the asset is depreciated is the lower of:

(a) the lease term, being the primary period of the lease plus any secondary periods which may reasonably be expected to be used by the lessee;
(b) the expected useful life of the asset.

Table 20.4 Swithland Ltd – annual finance charges by each method

	Actuarial	*Sum of digits*	*Straight line*
1987	5283	5437	3148
1988	3233	3148	3148
1989	928	659	3148

In our example, Swithland Ltd, we are told that the asset is to be leased for a primary period of three years, and that the company expects to lease and use the asset, at a nominal rent, for one further year. Thus the period over which the asset should be depreciated is four years, and using the straight line method annual depreciation will be:

$$\frac{£55\ 404}{4} = £13\ 851$$

Table 20.5 shows balance sheet extracts for our example Swithland Ltd, assuming that the actuarial method has been used to apportion finance charges (see Table 20.2). Note that to comply with the Companies Act 1985 we must split obligations within one year and over one year.

Table 20.5 Swithland Ltd – Balance sheet extracts

Asset held under finance lease

	19X7 £	*19X8* £	*19X9* £	*19X0* £
Cost	55 404	55 404	55 404	55 404
Less: Depreciation	13 851	27 702	41 553	55 404
Net book value	41 553	27 702	13 851	—

Finance lease obligations:

	19X7 £	*19X8* £	*19X9* £
Payable within one year	18 383	20 688	—
Payable in more than one year	20 688	—	—

Application of SSAP 21 by the lessor

As we have seen, SSAP 21 requires the lessor to allocate total gross earnings to accounting periods so as to give a constant periodic rate of return on the lessor's net cash investment in the lease. Alternatively an allocation out of gross earnings equal to the lessor's cost of finance may be made, with the balance allocated as above. An example in the guidance notes accompanying SSAP 21 helps both to explain this requirement and to show how figures are computed. The example is summarised below.

Example

A company leases an asset on a non-cancellable lease contract from 1 January 19X7. The rental is £650 per quarter payable in advance. The primary term of the lease is five years, at the end of which it is expected that the asset will be sold for £2373 and the proceeds will be passed to the lessee as a rebate of rental. The leased asset could have been purchased for cash at the start of the lease for £10 000.

Profit should be taken out of the lease at the following quarterly rate:

Assuming no interest	*Assuming quarterly interest @ 2.5%*
2.06%	0.36%

Tax at the rate of 35 per cent is payable at the beginning of the fourth quarter, 9 months after the balance sheet date. A writing down allowance of 25 per cent applies to plant.

In order to compute the net cash investment in the lease we have to identify the cash flows, which will consist of:

(a)   the initial outflow of £10 000 to purchase the asset;
(b)   the inflow from rentals of £650 at the beginning of each quarter for five years;
(c)   corporation tax, based on rental received less capital allowances.

Note that the sale of the asset at the end of the agreement has no cash flow effect, since cash is passed on to the lessee.

Capital allowances are summarised in Table 20.6, as are the annual tax charges payable in the following year. The ASC introduced a rather artificial assumption about the expected sale of the asset at tax written down value into this example to get round

Table 20.6 Capital allowances

19X7	Cost	10 000
	Less: WDA	2 500
19X8	WDV b/fwd	7 500
	Less: WDA	1 875
19X9	WDV c/fwd	5 625
	Less: WDA	1 406
19Y0	WDV b/fwd	4 219
	Less: WDA	1 055
19Y1	WDV b/fwd	3 164
	Less: WDA	791
		2 373
	Less: Balancing allowance	2 373
		0

Tax computation:

	19X7	*19X8*	*19X9*	*19Y0*	*19Y1*
Rentals	2600	2600	2600	2600	2600
Capital allowance	2500	1875	1406	1055	3164
Taxable profit @ 35%	100	725	1194	1545	(564)
Tax payable	35	254	418	541	(197)

the problem that, unless there is such a sale of the asset, writing down allowances on a reducing balance basis would continue indefinitely.

Having computed these cash flows we can now consider one method of allocating finance charges, the 'actuarial method after tax', ignoring interest payments. Table 20.7 shows how this would be computed. Column (a) shows the opening net cash investment. Column (b) shows the net cash flow at the beginning of the quarter. Column (c) shows the opening net investment adjusted for this cash flow. Column (d) shows the quarterly profit of 2.06 per cent applied to the figure in column (c); this is then added on to the outstanding net cash investment to give the closing net cash investment in column (e).

Table 20.7 Actuarial method after tax – no interest payments

Period	Opening net cash investment (a) £	Cash flow in period (b) £	Net cash investment after cash flows (c) £	Profit @ 2.06% (d) £	Closing net cash investment (e) £
1/X7	10 000	650	9 350	193	9 543
2/X7	9 543	650	8 893	183	9 076
3/X7	9 076	650	8 426	174	8 600
4/X7	8 600	650	7 950	164	8 114
				714	
1/X8	8 114	650	7 464	154	7 618
2/X8	7 618	650	6 968	144	7 112
3/X8	7 112	650	6 462	133	6 595
4/X8	6 595	615 (650–35)	5 980	123	6 103
				554	
1/X9	6 103	650	5 453	112	5 565
2/X9	5 565	650	4 915	101	5 016
3/X9	5 016	650	4 366	90	4 456
4/X9	4 456	396 (650–253)	4 060	84	4 144
				387	
1/X0	4 144	650	3 494	72	3 566
2/X0	3 566	650	2 916	60	2 976
3/X0	2 976	650	2 326	48	2 374
4/X0	2 374	232 (650–418)	2 142	44	2 186
				224	
1/X1	2 186	650	1 536	32	1 568
2/X1	1 568	650	918	19	937
3/X1	937	650	287	6	293
4/X1	293	109 (650–541)	184	4	188
				61	
1/X2	188	—	188	4	192
2/X2	192	—	192	4	196
3/X2	196	—	196	4	200
4/X2	200	197	(3)	(3)	—
				9	96 618

The percentage profit to be taken out in each quarter will be the amount to be applied to come to a final nil balance of net cash investment when all cash flows are completed. There is no formula to compute this percentage, and a 'trial and error' process, or some form of iteration, must be used. In practice, computer programs would be used to find this percentage. Note that in our example, as a result of 'rounding', a balance of £3 is left at the end of the agreement; this is not material, and would simply be adjusted against profit allocated to the final year. The total of the closing net investment figures is not needed to apply this method but is shown in the figure because it is relevant to the investment period method considered below.

As we have seen above, SSAP 21 allows finance charges to be allocated either by applying a constant periodic rate of return on the net cash investment to allocate gross earnings, or alternatively by deeming interest to be paid to support the borrowings financing the net cash investment and apportioning the finance charge. Table 20.8 shows how profit to be taken out of the lease would be computed on the basis of the ASC's example for 19X7.

Table 20.8 Actuarial method after tax — including interest

Period	Opening net cash investment £	Cash flow in period £	Net cash investment after cash flows £	Interest @ 2.5% £	Profit @ 0.36% £	Closing net cash investment £
1/X7	10 000	650	9 350	234	34	9 618
2/X7	9 618	650	8 968	224	32	9 224
3/X7	9 224	650	8 574	214	31	8 819
4/X7	8 819	650	8 169	204	29	8 402
				876	126	

The interest for 19X7 would be regarded as an expense reducing the company's tax charge for that year. Thus in the fourth quarter of 19X8 this would be treated as leading to an additional cash inflow of:

$$£876 \times 35\% = £307$$

The effect of taking interest charges into account is to run down the net cash investment regarded as tied up in the lease more quickly, because of tax relief on the interest; consequently finance income will be credited to profit and loss more rapidly by this method.

In our example, Table 20.7 shows how, ignoring interest, the income credited for 19X7 would be £714. By contrast, Table 20.8 shows how, taking interest into account, income taken to profit and loss would be:

	£
Interest	876
Profit	126
	1002

An alternative to the 'actuarial method after tax' is the 'investment period method'. This method is based on the figures calculated for the actuarial method after tax, either with or without interest taken into account. The profit taken on the lease for each period is computed as:

$$\frac{\text{Closing net investment at end of period}}{\text{Total of closing net investment at end of all periods}} \times \text{Total profit to be taken}$$

Total profit to be taken on our example is

$$(\pounds 650 \times 12) = \pounds 10\ 000$$
$$= \pounds 3000$$

Based on our figures for the actuarial method before tax and ignoring interest, as shown in Table 20.7 above, the profit taken in the first quarter of 19X7 would be:

$$\frac{9\ 543}{96\ 618} \times 3\ 000 = \pounds 296$$

Background

From the mid 1970s onwards, the ASC was acutely aware of the need for an accounting standard on leasing, yet SSAP 21 only emerged in August 1984. The main reason for this delay was a protracted debate over the principle of capitalising finance leases, a principle opposed vigorously by the major lessors.

The major conceptual issue has been an argument about the 'substance over form' concept on which capitalisation is based. This concept, that transactions should be accounted for in accordance with their commercial substance rather than their legal form, is discussed in IAS 1. Opponents of capitalisation questioned the validity of this concept, and also questioned whether a lease could in substance possess the characteristics of a secured loan.

ED 29 on leasing was the first UK exposure draft to refer explicitly to the potential economic consequences of a proposed accounting standard. Three potential consequences were identified:

(a) The ASC referred to the possibility that the capitalisation of finance leases might have an adverse effect on company borrowing powers, because the obligations under finance leases will be regarded as a form of borrowing.

In ED 29 the ASC stated: 'The lawyers we have consulted have advised generally that it is not capitalisation as such which would affect borrowing powers, but the entering into a lease agreement in the first place – if the item is relevant at all. However, borrowing power clauses may vary from document to document and the general advice may not be applicable in every case. Accordingly ASC particularly request submissions from any persons or companies who believe that their position might be affected in their own specific circumstances.' In fact no special problem emerged from this enquiry.

(b) The ASC referred to the argument that a requirement to capitalise finance leases might inhibit companies from entering such agreements, because of the loss of the attractions of 'off balance sheet' finance. In the absence of research on the effect of SSAP 21 in the UK, it is not possible to reach a conclusion on the significance of this issue. In the US a study found a significant number of companies claimed in reply to a questionnaire to have decided to buy assets instead of leasing because of the lease capitalisation requirements of a similar US standard.

(c) In ED 29 the ASC considered the possibility that in response to any requirement to capitalise finance leases the UK tax authorities might change the tax rules to give capital allowances on leased assets to the lessee instead of the lessor.

The ASC corresponded on this question with the Inland Revenue, and were informed that the publication of an accounting standard on leasing would not in itself lead to any change in the tax treatment of leased assets. However, in ED 29 the ASC recognised that an accounting standard might have an influence on government thinking on any review of tax law on leasing. The ASC made the point that: 'It is fair to assume that the UK Treasury and government would take into account the possible economic consequences of any change in rules before deciding upon such a change.'

In fact prior to the issue of SSAP 21 the UK tax system was changed so that the tax benefits of leasing were substantially removed. This change in tax policy had no apparent connection with the accounting debate over leasing.

In the Republic of Ireland, a special set of conditions applied at the time of ED 29 which included a paragraph: 'By reason of the law at present obtaining in the Republic of Ireland, this exposure draft is not intended to apply to financial statements prepared or audited in the Republic of Ireland.' This exclusion was inserted because tax law in the Republic of Ireland gave capital allowances on leased assets to the party recording depreciation in the accounts. In the Irish Budget in 1984 the tax benefits of leasing were effectively removed, so that accounting practice on leasing would no longer have any effect on the tax position. As a result SSAP 21 now applies in the Irish Republic.

Conclusion

The emergence of an accounting standard on leasing has been marked both by the economic issues raised and some knotty technical problems.

EXAMINATION PRACTICE

20.1 SSAP 21 rules

In relation to SSAP 21: Accounting for Leases and Hire Purchase Payments:

(a) What is the difference between a finance lease and an operating lease?

(b) In preparing both the balance sheet and the profit and loss account of a finance company (the lessor) how should you treat:

    (i) an asset subject to a financial lease?

    (ii) an asset subject to an operating lease?

20.2   Lease calculations

K C Ltd leases a computer from T F Ltd. The terms of the lease are that K C Ltd pays four annual rental payments of £10 000 each, the first payment to be made on 1 January 19X7. Thereafter the computer can be rented indefinitely for a nominal sum of £1 per year. The cost of the computer new would be £34 868, and the finance cost implicit in the lease is 10% per year.

Compute the amount of the lease obligation to be shown at the end of each year in the balance sheet.

21 SSAP 22: Accounting for Goodwill

Background

The value of a business at any point in time is likely to be different from the total value of the identifiable assets, both tangible and intangible, owned by the business. This is because the value of the business as a whole will be estimated by reference to the expected future flows of income from the business. This difference is generally referred to as 'goodwill'. In practice we would expect a successful business to build up substantial 'goodwill' as a result of such factors as a trained skilled workforce and trading connections with customers and suppliers.

Goodwill is normally only identified and quantified when a business is sold as a whole. This can be reflected either in the acquirer's own accounts when an unincorporated business is acquired or in the group accounts when another company is acquired. SSAP 22 deals with the question of how goodwill should be accounted for.

Summary of the statement

Definitions

Goodwill is the difference between the value of a business as a whole and the aggregate of the fair values of its separable net assets.

Separable net assets are those assets (and liabilities) which can be identified and sold (or discharged) separately without necessarily disposing of the business as a whole. They include identifiable intangibles.

Purchased goodwill is goodwill which is established as a result of the purchase of a business accounted for as an acquisition. Goodwill arising on consolidation is one form of purchased goodwill.

Non-purchased goodwill is any goodwill other than purchased goodwill.

Fair value is the amount for which an asset (or liability) could be exchanged in an arm's length transaction.

Useful economic life of purchased goodwill is the best estimate of the life of such goodwill at the date of purchase.

Computation of goodwill

SSAP 22 requires that in computing purchased goodwill the 'fair value' of the assets acquired should be used, including identifiable intangibles. This is similar to the requirement in relation to consolidation goodwill. When computing fair values at the date of acquisition, SSAP 22 points out the need to estimate any anticipated future losses taken into account in arriving at the purchase price of the business, and record these as a provision in the accounts; previously such amounts have often been regarded as part of negative goodwill.

Where negative goodwill arises the explanatory note to SSAP 22 recommends that the 'fair values' attributed to assets acquired should be reviewed to see if they are overstated.

Non-purchased goodwill

SSAP 22 states that non-purchased goodwill should not be included in the accounts.

Positive goodwill

Where the goodwill figure is positive SSAP 22 requires that one of two policies should be applied:

(a) An 'immediate write-off policy' of writing off goodwill immediately on acquisition directly against reserves.
(b) An 'amortisation policy' of charging amortisation through the profit and loss account as an expense in arriving at the result of ordinary activities, over its useful estimated economic life.

SSAP 22 states that the write-off policy should 'normally' be followed, but permits the amortisation policy. It is unusual for the ASC to express a positive preference for one approach while continuing to permit an alternative. Companies are allowed to choose different accounting policies for different acquisitions.

SSAP 22 requires that where an amortisation policy is chosen the following rules should apply:

(a) Purchased goodwill should not be revalued.
(b) If there is a permanent diminution in the value of goodwill, it should be written down immediately through the profit and loss account to the estimated recoverable amount.
(c) Purchased goodwill should be classified as a separate item under intangible fixed assets in the balance sheet.
(d) When estimating the useful economic life at the time of acquisition, no account should be taken of the effects of future expenditure or circumstances leading to the creation of non-purchased goodwill.
(e) The estimated useful economic life of goodwill may be shortened but may not be increased.

It is necessary to estimate the useful economic life of goodwill relating to each acquisition separately.

Negative goodwill

Where the goodwill figure is negative, SSAP 22 requires that it should be taken direct to reserves.

Disclosure

The notes to the accounts should include an explanation of the accounting policy followed in relation to goodwill. Goodwill recognised as a result of acquisitions during the year should, where material, be shown separately for each acquisition, whatever the accounting policy applied.

Where the amortisation treatment is chosen purchased goodwill will be shown separately as an intangible fixed asset.

The notes to the accounts should show:

(a)   the movements on goodwill during the year with a breakdown of cost, accumulated amortisation and net book value at the beginning and end of the year;

(b)   the amount of goodwill amortised through the profit and loss account for the year;

(c)   the amortisation period for goodwill on each major acquisition.

The following disclosures should be made separately for each 'material' acquisition during the year, and in total for others which are not material individually:

(a)   The fair value of the consideration and the amount of purchased goodwill. The method of dealing with goodwill should be identified, stating whether it has been carried forward as an asset or written off against reserves (specifying if merger reserve has been used).

(b)   A table should show the pre-acquisition book values and the deemed fair values of major categories of asset and liability, analysed between:
   (i)   revaluations;
   (ii)   provisions for future trading losses;
   (iii)   other provisions;
   (iv)   adjustments to accounting policies;
   (v)   other major items.

(c)   Movements on provisions relating to acquisitions should be disclosed and analysed.

(d)   Where fair values can only be determined on a provisional basis this should be stated and explained. Subsequent material adjustments should be disclosed and explained.

For each material disposal of a previously acquired business or business segment there should be disclosed:

(a)   the profit or loss on disposal;

(b)   related purchased goodwill, and how this has been treated in computing profit or loss;

(c)   accounting treatment and amount of disposal proceeds when no profit or loss is recorded and the proceeds have been accounted for as a reduction in cost of the acquisition.

Where the relevant information is unobtainable this should be stated and explained.

ED 47: Accounting for Goodwill

The first edition of SSAP 22 came out in December 1984. A revised edition, on which this chapter is based, came out in July 1989. The main difference between the two is a substantial expansion of disclosure requirements.

ED 47, issued in February 1990, proposes a radical change in ruling out the immediate write-off policy favoured by SSAP 22 and prescribing an amortisation policy with a normal maximum of 20 years, and up to 40 years allowed in special circumstances.

Background

Nature of goodwill

There are two broad views as to the nature of goodwill. One view regards goodwill as an asset that has been purchased, being the right to receive future profits in excess of what might reasonably be expected from the assets employed. Logically this view leads to an amortisation approach. The alternative view regards goodwill as an accounting anomaly. This leads to an approach that involves treating goodwill in a way that has the minimum impact on the accounts. Thus the two alternative methods permitted by SSAP 22 are based on contrasting views as to the basic nature of goodwill. Critics of the standard make two points on this:

(a)   How can a standard that permits two such different approaches be regarded as narrowing areas of accounting practice?
(b)   Why should companies be allowed to adopt inconsistent policies, treating goodwill on different acquisitions in different ways?

Reserves for write-off

Where goodwill is subject to an immediate write-off, companies must choose which reserve should be chosen.

Some companies have written off goodwill against a revaluation reserve. However, there does not seem to be any authority to justify this approach in the Companies Act, and the Department of Trade has indicated that it does not regard this practice as legal.

Similarly, use of the share premium account would appear to be illegal. An exception arises in the case of shares issued in an acquisition which meets the requirements of company law for merger relief (see p. 203) and the company has not chosen to use merger accounting.

A further approach has been to 'invent' a reserve against which to set off goodwill, so as to carry forward a permanent debit balance on that reserve. This is similar to what used to be called the 'dangling debit' approach whereby goodwill was shown as a simple deduction from reserves.

The simplest approach, of course, is to write off goodwill against retained profits. This is common practice, but can be inconvenient for some companies!

IAS 22: Accounting for Business Combinations

SSAP 22 is closely in line with the above international standard.

Conclusion

SSAP 22 tackles a long-standing area of difficulty. It is by no means without critics, and may well be subject to review in order to achieve a more consistent approach.

EXAMINATION PRACTICE

21.1   Goodwill calculations

(a)   On 1 April 19X0 Cab Ltd acquired the entire share capital of Horse Ltd. The summarised balance sheets of the two companies immediately after the transaction were:

	Cab Ltd	Horse Ltd
	£000	£000
Share capital	1500	500
Retained profits	500	200
	2000	700
Tangible assets	800	700
Investment in Horse Ltd	1200	
	2000	700

The fair value of the tangible assets of Horse Ltd was one million pounds.

You are required to prepare a consolidated balance sheet for the Cab group as at 1 April 19X0, prior to any goodwill write off.

(b)   The consolidated profit and loss account for the Cab group, before taking goodwill into account, for the two years to 31 March 19X1 and 31 March 19X2 showed:

	19X1	19X2
	£000	£000
Profit before taxation	320	350
Taxation	160	175
Profit after taxation	160	175
Dividend	130	140
Retained profit	30	35

You are required to prepare predicted balance sheets and profit and loss accounts for the two years to 31 March 19X1 and 31 March 19X2 under each of the methods of treating goodwill permitted in SSAP 22, assuming a ten-year life for goodwill.

22 | SSAP 23: Accounting for Acquisitions and Mergers

Introduction

Normal practice in the preparation of consolidated accounts reflects the legal form of the amalgamation of businesses, in that the investment in a subsidiary is recorded at cost in the books of the holding company while in the group accounts only profits earned by the subsidiary after the acquisition date are treated as distributable. This treatment is acceptable when the substance of the transaction is the acquisition of one business by another, but may be regarded as less acceptable when the substance of the transaction is a merger of businesses. The problems can be illustrated by the merger of two companies, Top Ltd and Hat Ltd:

	Top Ltd £000	Hat Ltd £000
Ordinary share capital	20	30
Retained profits	30	20
	50	50
Net assets	50	50
	50	50

Three methods of merging the two businesses are proposed:

(a) A new company, Tophat Ltd, is to be formed with an issued share capital of £100 000, half of which will be issued to the shareholders of each company.

(b) Top Ltd will issue £20 000 of ordinary shares, at a premium of £30 000, to the shareholders of Hat Ltd in exchange for their shareholding.

(c) Hat Ltd will issue £30 000 of ordinary shares at a premium of £20 000 to the shareholders of Top Ltd in exchange for their shareholding.

Each of these methods has the same commercial effect, that of merging two similarly sized businesses and sharing the expanded business equally between the former proprietors. Consolidated accounts under each scheme will appear as follows:

	(a) Tophat Ltd £000	(b) Top Ltd £000	(c) Hat Ltd £000
Share capital	100	40	60
Share premium	–	30	20
Retained profits	–	30	20
	100	100	100
Net assets	100	100	100
	100	100	100

Thus we can observe that, although the commercial substance of each scheme is the same, the normal method of accounting for acquisitions produces three very different amounts of distributable reserves; further, none of the figures we have produced is equal to the combined distributable reserves of the businesses that have been merged.

'Merger accounting' offers an alternative mechanism for consolidation that 'pools' the distributable reserves of the merged companies. SSAP 23 offers guidance on the situations where this practice is acceptable and the ways in which it should be applied.

Definitions

A *business combination* arises when one or more companies become subsidiaries of another company. A *merger* is a business combination which meets the following conditions:

(a) The business combination must result from an offer to the holders of all equity and all voting shares not already held by the offeror.

(b) The offer must be accepted by the holders of 90 per cent of the equity and 90 per cent of the voting shares of the offeree company. For this purpose convertible stock is not regarded as equity except in so far as it is converted into equity as a result of the business combination.

(c) Immediately prior to the offer the offeror must not hold more than 20 per cent of the equity or voting shares of the offeree.

(d) Not less than 90 per cent of the fair value of the total consideration given for the equity share capital (including shares already held) must be in the form of equity capital; not less than 90 per cent of the fair value of the consideration given for voting non-equity share capital (including shares already held) must be in the form of equity and/or non-voting equity share capital.

Any business combination not meeting these conditions will be an *acquisition*.

Other relevant definitions within SSAP 23 are:

(a) An *offer* is any offer made by or on behalf of a company ('the offeror') for shares in another company ('the offeree'). A number of separate offers constituting in substance a composite transaction is considered to be a single offer.

The provisions of this standard which are set out in relation to 'an offer' and the results thereof apply also to any scheme or arrangement having similar effect.

(b) The *effective date of acquisition or merger* is the earlier of:
  (i)   the date on which the consideration passes; or
  (ii) the date on which an offer becomes or is declared unconditional.
  This applies even if the acquiring company has the right under the agreement to share in the profits of the acquired business from an earlier date.

(c) *Equity share capital* is as defined in s. 744, Companies Act 1985, namely, 'in relation to a company, its issued share capital excluding any part of that capital which, neither as respects dividends nor as respects capital, carries any right to participate beyond a specified amount in a distribution'.

Merger accounting

When a business combination meets the conditions that define it as a merger, then companies are allowed to use merger accounting. The acquiring company will record the cost of the new investment in its books as the nominal value of the shares issued plus the fair value of any additional consideration. On consolidation, the book value of assets, liabilities and reserves will be added together and the only difference arising will be any difference between the amount of the investment recorded in the books of the holding company and the nominal value of the acquired shares. If the surplus is a credit balance this will be treated as an unrealised reserve, while a debit balance will be deducted from consolidation reserves. The consolidated profit and loss account for the year of the merger will include the profits of all the merged companies for the whole year and the corresponding amounts will be computed on the same basis.

Adjustments to the accounts must also be made if necessary to reflect common accounting policies.

Acquisition accounting

All acquisitions must, and mergers may, be accounted for by conventional acquisition accounting, in line with FRS 2 and SSAP 22.

Disclosure

For all business combinations, however they are accounted for, there must be shown:

(a) the names of the combining companies;
(b) the number and class of securities issued in respect of the combination and details of any other consideration.

Background

Evolution

Merger accounting was an issue on the ASC's agenda as early as 1971, with the issue of ED 3 on the subject. However, doubts about the legality of merger accounting, confirmed by the case of *Shearer* v. *Bercain* (1980), delayed any development until a change in company law. The Companies Act 1985, s. 131, gives relief from the normal requirement for a share premium account to reflect the full value of the consideration for which shares are issued when at least 90 per cent of the shares in the investee are acquired.

The basic principle of SSAP 23 is that a merger is regarded as occurring where 'only limited resources leave the group'. This contrasts with ED 3 which laid down more stringent conditions, including a requirement that in the amalgamated undertaking shareholders in no one of the constituent companies should have more than three times the equity in the new undertaking than shareholders from any other constituent company.

Avoiding the restrictions

Commentators on SSAP 23 have pointed out that there are techniques whereby the criteria for merger accounting can be met, although in practice the shareholders in the acquired company do not continue to hold shares in the merged undertaking. These arrangements involve acquisition by the issue of shares in the acquiring company with a related agreement for their immediate sale, either to an arranged third party in the case of a 'vendor placing', or to the existing shareholders of the acquiring company in the case of 'vendor rights'. The net effect of either arrangement is that a company has been acquired for cash raised by a share issue.

The requirement that immediately prior to the acquisition the acquirer must not hold more than 20 per cent of the acquiree can be avoided by disposal of part of an existing shareholding to a financial adviser with an agreement for repurchase.

Both these measures have been used in practice since the introduction of SSAP 23.

Choice of policy

Critics of SSAP 23 question the choice of policy allowed for companies meeting the merger criteria. They point to the US rules which define mergers more strictly but then prescribe merger accounting.

ED 48: Accounting for Acquisitions and Mergers

In February 1990 the ASC issued ED 48. This proposes:

(a) a very much more restrictive definition of a merger;
(b) a requirement that where the definition of a merger is met then the use of merger accounting should be compulsory.

A merger is defined as:

The coming together of two or more enterprises for the mutual sharing of the risks and rewards, of the combined enterprise, where no party to the combination can be identified as acquiror or acquiree. There must be a substantially equal partnership, with the pre-combination enterprises sharing influence in the new economic unit. If a dominant partner (i.e. an acquiror) or a subordinate partner (i.e. an acquiree) can be identified, then the combination will be an acquisition regardless of the form by which the combination was transacted.

Six conditions are then considered to test whether a merger exists. Each of these conditions must be met to justify merger treatment:

(a) None of the parties must see itself as acquiror or acquiree.

(b) No party must dominate the management of the combined entity.

(c) None of the equity shareholders of any of the combined parties can have disposed of any material part of their shareholding for shares with significantly reduced rights or any other non equity consideration, or be able to do so. This includes arrangements where any arrangements have been made for the disposal of shares for cash.

(d) No minority interest in excess of 10 per cent in any of the combining parties must remain.

(e) None of the parties must be more than 50 per cent larger than any other party in the combination.

(f) The share of the equity in the combination allocated to any party must not be dependent on subsequent business performance.

While it is as yet unclear whether the new ASB will develop ED 48 into a standard, the exposure draft does offer an interesting example of how a more rigorous definition of a merger can be developed.

IAS 22: Accounting for Business Combinations

SSAP 23 is in line with the provisions of IAS 22 on merger accounting.

Conclusion

SSAP 23 is a controversial standard. Both the definition of a merger and the permitted choice of accounting policy are likely to come under continued scrutiny.

EXAMINATION PRACTICE

22.1 Definitions
Describe what is meant by the following terms:

(i)   equity method of accounting;
(ii) acquisition accounting techniques;
(iii) pooling of interests method of accounting.

(Society of Company and Commercial Accountants)

22.2 Merger accounting
The summarised balance sheet of Sid Limited at 31 December 19X0 was as follows:

	£		£
Share capital issued and fully paid			
980 000 shares of £0.25 each	245 000	Fixed assets	180 000
Reserves	300 000	Current assets	565 000
Current liabilities	200 000		
	£745 000		£745 000

At that date the company acquired the whole issued share capital of Toad Limited by the issue of 300 000 new ordinary shares, at the day's market price of £0.80.

The balance sheet of Toad Limited immediately prior to acquisition was:

	£		£
Share capital, 70 000 shares of			
£1 each	70 000	Fixed assets	90 000
Reserves	50 000	Current assets	55 000
Current liabilities	25 000		
	£145 000		£145 000

You are required to prepare the consolidated balance sheet of Sid Ltd:

(a) by the acquisition method;
(b) by the merger method.

(ICMA adapted)

23 | SSAP 24: Accounting for Pension Costs

The basic problem

The provision of a pension is part of the benefits provided to many employees. Two types of scheme arise:

(a) A defined contribution scheme involves an employer in making agreed contributions to a pension scheme. The benefits paid to the employee will then depend on these contributions and related investment earnings. This type of scheme is common in smaller businesses. The cost to the employer is easy to identify.

(b) In a defined benefit scheme the benefits to be paid are defined, often in terms of the employee's final pay. Such schemes are common in larger enterprises. The level of contributions needed to meet benefit requirements is necessarily a matter for estimate. In this case, because of the uncertainty as to the final cost, a number of accounting problems arise.

Actuarial issues

In a defined benefit scheme the choices of assumptions and valuation method made by an actuary can have a major impact on the estimated necessary level of contributions. Major matters to estimate include:

(a) future rates of inflation and pay increases;
(b) increases to pensions in payment;
(c) number of employees joining and leaving the scheme;
(d) deaths of employees before retirement age;
(e) the age profile of employees;
(f) earnings on investments.

Some of these estimates may be related and offsetting. One example is that income from investment yields and costs of pension increases may both be related to inflation.

Funding

Pension schemes are often financed from a special fund managed by independent trustees. Payments into the fund are likely to be linked to actuarial estimates of the required level of funding. From time to time a revised estimate may lead to:

(a) changes in the levels of contribution made into the fund;

(b) lump sum payments by the enterprise to the fund or vice versa reflecting changed requirements.

Key definitions

Definitions in SSAP 24 include:

(a) An *ex gratia pension* or *a discretionary or ex gratia increase in a pension* is one which the employer has no legal, contractual or implied commitment to provide.

(b) A *defined benefit scheme* is a pension scheme in which the rules specify the benefits to be paid and the scheme is financed accordingly.

(c) A *defined contribution scheme* is a pension scheme in which the benefits are directly determined by the value of contributions paid in respect of each member. Normally the rate of contribution is specified in the rules of the scheme.

(d) An *experience surplus or deficiency* is that part of the excess or deficiency of the actuarial value of assets over the actuarial value of liabilities, on the basis of the valuation method used, which arises because events have not coincided with the actuarial assumptions made for the last valuation.

(e) A *funding plan* is the timing of payments in an orderly fashion to meet the future cost of a given set of benefits.

(f) A *funded scheme* is a pension scheme where the future liabilities for benefits are provided for by the accumulation of assets held externally to the employing company's business.

(g) The *level of funding* is the proportion at a given date of the actuarial value of liabilities for pensioners' and deferred pensioners' benefits and for members' accrued benefits that is covered by the actuarial value of assets. For this purpose the actuarial value of future contributions is excluded from the value of assets.

(h) An *ongoing actuarial valuation* is a valuation in which it is assumed that the pension scheme will continue in existence and (where appropriate) that new members will be admitted. The liabilities allow for expected increases in earnings.

(i) *Past service* is used in the statement to denote service before a given date. It is often used, however, to denote service before entry into the pension scheme.

(j) *Pensionable payroll/earnings* are the earnings on which benefits and/or contributions are calculated. One or more elements of earnings (e.g. overtime) may be excluded, and/or there may be a reduction to take account of all or part of the state scheme benefits which the member is deemed to receive.

(k) A *pension scheme* is an arrangement (other than accident insurance) to provide pension and/or other benefits for members on leaving service or retiring and, after a member's death, for his/her dependents.

Required practice

The principles

SSAP 24 applies to any situation where an employer is committed to a pension scheme. Commitment may arise from legal requirements or contract, it may be implicit in the employer's actions and may arise from discretionary or *ex gratia* payments. The accounting objective is to ensure that the accounts recognise the expected cost of providing pensions on a systematic and rational basis over the period of the employees' services.

Defined contribution schemes

In this case the charge against profits should be the amount of contributions payable to the pension scheme for the accounting period.

Defined benefit schemes

In this case actuarial valuation methods should be used. The actuarial assumptions must be compatible 'taken as a whole', giving the actuary's 'best estimate'.

On the basis of these actuarial assumptions pension costs should be allocated over employees' service lives by a 'substantially level percentage' of the pensionable payroll.

Where variations from the regular cost arise these should normally be allocated over the expected remaining service lives of current employees in the scheme. Exceptions to this rule are:

(a) Charges arise because of a significant reduction in the number of employees in the scheme. Reductions in these circumstances should be recognised as they occur.

(b) Prudence may dictate that a material deficit be recognised over a shorter period than the expected remaining service lives of employees in the scheme.

(c) Where a refund to the employer is subject to deduction of tax then the surplus or deficiency may be accounted for in the period in which the refund occurs.

Ex gratia *arrangements*

The capital costs of granting *ex gratia* pensions or increases, to the extent that these are not covered by a surplus, should be recognised in the period when they are granted.

Balance sheet

The balance sheet should show a 'net pension provision' or prepayment for the difference between the cumulative pension cost recognised in the profit and loss account and total of contributions made into the pension fund and pensions paid directly.

Required disclosure

The accounts should state whether the pension scheme is on a 'defined benefit' or 'defined contribution' basis.

For a defined contribution scheme there should be disclosed:

(a)   the accounting policy;
(b)   the pension cost charge for the period;
(c)   any outstanding or prepaid contributions at the balance sheet date.

For a defined benefit scheme there should be stated:

(a)   whether it is funded or unfunded;
(b)   the accounting policy and, if different, the funding policy;
(c)   whether pension arrangements are assessed on the advice of a professionally qualified actuary, together with the date of the most recent formal actuarial valuation. Where the actuary is an employee of the company or of a group of which the company is part, this fact should be disclosed;
(d)   the pension cost charge for the period, with an expansion of significant variations in comparing with the previous accounting period;
(e)   any provisions or prepayments in the balance sheet arising from differences between the costs shown in the accounts and payments to the fund;
(f)   any commitment to make additional payments over a limited number of years;
(g)   the accounting treatment adopted for a refund made subject to deduction of tax.

The following disclosures must also be made, except in the case of a subsidiary company which is a member of a group scheme and has a UK or Irish holding company:

(a)   the amount of any deficiency on a current funding level basis, indicating any action being taken on the matter;
(b)   an outline of the results of the most recent actuarial valuation or formal review including:
   (i)   the actuarial method and main assumptions,
   (ii)   the market value of scheme assets,
   (iii) the level of funding expressed in percentage terms,
   (iv)   comments on any material actuarial surplus or deficiency.

A subsidiary company which is a member of a group scheme should state this fact and report if contributions are based on the group scheme as a whole. The accounts should state the name of the holding company in whose accounts details of the scheme will be found.

International standards

SSAP 24 is in line with IAS 19: Accounting for Retirement Benefits in the Financial Statements of Employers.

Conclusion

Pension costs are a difficult topic for the accountant because they constitute a major expense subject to fluctuation in the light of events in the long-term future. While the job of making estimates and computing their effects is the responsibility of the actuary, the accountant's role is to report the impact of changes in actuarial valuation in a consistent way.

EXAMINATION PRACTICE

23.1   **Pension costs**

In conjunction with SSAP 24: Accounting for Pension Costs:

(a)   Explain the objective in accounting for pension costs.

(b)   How are the following items defined:

    (i)   a defined contribution scheme?

    (ii)   a defined benefit scheme?

    (iii)   an experience deficiency?

(c)   What information should be disclosed concerning a formal actuarial valuation of a defined benefit scheme?

24 SSAP 25: Segmental Reporting

The need for a standard

(The Companies Act 1985 requires disclosure of certain segmented information where a company carries on two or more classes of business that differ substantially from each other, or supplies geographical markets that differ substantially from each other.) The International Stock Exchange also requires certain segmental information. SSAP 25 provides detailed guidance on the provision of such information, together with some additional requirements.

Definition of terms

SSAP 25 offers the following definitions:

(a) A *class of business* is a distinguishable component of an entity that provides a separate product or service or a separate group of related products or services.
(b) A *geographical segment* is a geographical area comprising an individual country or group of countries in which an entity operates, or to which it supplies products or services.
(c) *Origin* of turnover is the geographical segment from which products or services are supplied to a third party or to another segment.
(d) *Destination* of turnover is the geographical segment to which products or services are supplied.

Basic requirements

If an entity has two or more classes of business, or operates in two or more geographical segments which differ substantially from each other, then it should define these classes in the accounts and report with respect to each class the following:

(a) turnover, distinguishing between turnover from external customers and turnover from other segments of the entity;
(b) profit or loss before tax, minority interests and extraordinary items;
(c) net assets.

The disclosure of geographical segmentation of turnover should be based on origin. Where materially different turnover to third parties by destination should also be disclosed; if this is excluded on grounds of not being materially different that fact should be stated.

The segment profit or loss before tax should normally be before interest earned or incurred; similarly net assets will normally be non-interest bearing operating assets less non-interest bearing operating liabilities.

However, where any part of the entity's business is to earn or incur interest, or interest income/expense is central to the business, then interest should be taken into account in arriving at the reported segmental profit/loss and related assets/liabilities will form part of reported net assets.

If the total of segmented amounts does not equal the related total in the accounts then a reconciliation between the two shall be provided.

Comparative figures for the previous year should be provided. The directors should redefine segments when appropriate, and the nature and effects of any change should be reported with an appropriate restatement of the previous year's figures.

Associated companies

If associated companies account for at least 20 per cent of either total profit/loss or total net assets then the segmental report should include details of:

(a)   the group's share of profit/loss on the same basis as above.
(b)   the group's share of net assets, including unamortised goodwill, where possible attributing 'fair value' to assets at the acquisition date.

Such information need not be published if it is unobtainable or prejudicial to the associate. In such a case the reason for non-disclosure should be given in a note, with a brief description of the omitted business.

Exemptions

All companies are required to comply with SSAP 25 to the extent that the requirements coincide with company law. The additional requirements only apply where:

(a)   the entity is a plc or has a plc subsidiary, or
(b)   is a banking or insurance company or group, or
(c)   exceeds the criteria, multiplied by ten, for defining a medium size company under company law.

Practical problems of compliance

SSAP 25 contains some useful guidance on practical problems of compliance.

In deciding whether a separate class of business is a distinguishable segment factors to consider include:

(a)   the nature of the products;
(b)   the nature of the production process;
(c)   the markets in which output is sold;
(d)   the distribution channels for products;

(e)   the manner in which the entity's activities are organised;

(f)   any separate legislative framework relating to part of the business.

A geographical segment is an individual country or group of countries where the entity either operates or supplies goods and services. The geographical analysis should enable the user of the accounts to assess the impact of:

(a)   expansionist or restrictive economic climates;

(b)   stable or unstable political regimes;

(c)   exchange control regulations;

(d)   exchange rate fluctuations.

Overall, in the case of both business and geographical segments, the user needs to distinguish between areas that:

(a)   earn a rate of return out of line with the entity as a whole;

(b)   are subject to different degrees of risk;

(c)   have experienced different rates of growth;

(d)   have different potential for future development.

It is suggested that a segment should be reported on separately if:

(a)   third-party turnover is 10 per cent or more of total turnover,

(b)   profit or loss is 10 per cent or more of total profits or total losses, whichever is greater, or

(c)   net assets are 10 per cent or more of total net assets.

SSAP 25 also considers the situation where common costs or common net assets cannot be apportioned to segments on a basis that is other than misleading, and argues that these should be identified separately.

The example below shows how business segment information might be disclosed:

Fulke plc – Segmental report

	Hotels 19X9 £000	Hotels 19X8 £000	Brewing 19X9 £000	Brewing 19X8 £000	Group 19X9 £000	Group 19X8 £000
Turnover						
Total sales	33 000	20 000	38 000	36 000	71 000	56 000
Inter-segment sales	—	—	1 000	1 000	1 000	1 000
Sales to third parties	33 000	20 000	37 000	35 000	70 000	55 000
Profit before tax						
Segment profit	5 400	4 000	3 600	3 500	9 400	7 500
Common costs					100	100
Operating profit					9 500	7 600
Net interest					(500)	(500)
					10 000	8 100
Group share of associated company profits			1 000	900	1 000	900
Group profit before tax					11 000	9 000

Net assets

Segment net assets	58 000	41 000	37 000	36 000	95 000	77 000
Unallocated net assets					3 000	3 000
					98 000	80 000
Group share of associates' net assets			10 000	9 000	10 000	9 000
Total net assets					108 000	89 000

Geographical segments would be analysed on a similar basis.

IAS 14: Reporting Financial Information by Segment

IAS 14 includes an additional requirement to disclose the basis of inter-segment pricing, and does not allow the same range of exemptions as SSAP 25. IAS 14 also refers to 'assets employed' rather than 'net assets'. In other respects IAS 14 is similar to SSAP 25.

EXAMINATION PRACTICE

24.1   **In relation to SSAP 25 'Segmental Reporting':**
(a)   Explain the basis on which disclosure of geographical segmentation of turnover should be made.
(b)   Outline the issues to be considered in deciding whether a separate class of business is a distinguished segment.

25 Exposure Drafts and Financial Reporting Exposure Drafts

Introduction

A number of exposure drafts, both from the ASC and the ASB, are outstanding at the end of 1992. It is important to note that the Financial Reporting Review Panel have made it clear that they do not regard it as acceptable for a company to depart from an existing accounting standard on the grounds of a proposed amendment in an exposure draft. Below is a brief summary of outstanding EDs and FREDs.

ED 46: Related Party Transactions

The idea that a business entity is separate and distinct both from the owners and from other enterprises means that transactions reported in the acounts can normally be assumed to arise on an 'arm's length' basis between independent parties. The reasoning behind the proposals in ED 46 is that when this is not the case then the users of accounts need information on the situation. Accordingly ED 46 requires disclosure of details of any *abnormal* transaction with a *related* party.

Two or more parties are considered to be 'related' when:

(a) one party is able to exercise either direct or indirect control or significant influence, over the other party or over the assets or resources of the other party; or

(b) such parties are subject to common control or significant influence from the same source.

In deciding whether parties are related, it is necessary to consider the substance of the relationship. This is determined by identifying all its aspects and implications and by giving greater weight to those likely to have commercial effect in practice.

An 'abnormal transaction' is one which is not 'normal', while a 'normal transaction' is defined as 'one which is undertaken by the reporting enterprise in the ordinary course of business on normal commercial terms except where it is so material that it has a significant impact on the financial statements. Transactions entered into the ordinary course of business are those which are usually, frequently or regularly undertaken by the enterprise.'

Details of transactions to be disclosed include:

(a) the name of the related party;

(b) the relationship between the parties;

(c) the extent of any ownership interest (in percentage terms) in the related party or by it in the reporting enterprise;

(d)   the nature of the transaction;

(e)   the amounts involved, either in percentage or in monetary terms;

(f)   the amount due to or from the related party at the balance sheet date;

(g)   the basis on which the transaction price has been determined; and

(h)   any other information necessary for an understanding of the commercial substance of the transaction and of its effects on the financial statements.

The proposals in ED 46 are similar to IAS 24: Related Party Transactions, except that IAS 24 requires disclosure of normal as well as abnormal transactions.

ED 51: Accounting for Fixed Assets and Revaluations

This very full and detailed exposure draft, issued in May 1990, considers a number of issues on fixed asset accounting. The aim is to cover all categories of fixed asset other than investments, development expenditure and goodwill. Issues covered include the following.

Recognition

A fixed asset should be shown in the balance sheet if, and only if:

(a)   it is probable that future economic benefits associated with the asset will flow to the enterprise;

(b)   the asset has a cost and, if valued, a value that can be measured with reliability.

Cost

Detailed guidance on determining purchase price or production cost is provided.

Capitalisation of borrowing costs

When a substantial period of time is involved in bringing a fixed asset into use ED 51 proposes to permit a choice of accounting policy on whether or not to capitalise borrowing costs. Detailed guidance on how to identify such costs is given.

Enhancement costs

Guidance on the extent to which improvement costs should be capitalised is given.

Exchange of fair assets

The amounts at which cost and selling price of the assets involved in an exchange or part exchange deal are stated in a contract are not necessarily at 'market value', since the stated amounts may both be artificially enhanced or depressed by agreement.

ED 51 spells out a requirement that the cost of the fixed asset acquired must be stated at 'fair value'.

Permanent diminution

A permanent diminution in the value of a fixed asset below the carrying amount in the accounts must be accounted for as soon as it is observed, being deemed to occur before any revaluation in the same accounting period.

Valuations and revaluation reserve

Detailed guidance on accounting for valuations is provided.

ED 52: Accounting for Intangible Fixed Assets

The subject matter of ED 52 is defined as follows: 'An intangible fixed asset is a fixed asset that is non-monetary in nature and without physical substance.' The exposure draft excludes from its coverage development expenditure, leases of tangible assets, goodwill and investments.

ED 52 proposes that an intangible fixed asset should only be recognised in the balance sheet if:

(a)   historical costs incurred in its creation are known or readily ascertained;
(b)   its characteristics can clearly be distinguished from other assets, particularly goodwill;
(c)   cost can be measured independently of goodwill, other assets, and the earnings of the relevant business or segment.

Where an intangible fixed asset is recognised in the balance sheet it should be amortised over its useful economic life, normally up to a maximum of 20 years. In exceptional circumstances, a longer life up to 40 years may be used, but reasons to justify this must be disclosed.

Revaluation of intangibles is only permitted if:

(a)   it is based on depreciated replacement cost and this can be measured with 'reasonable certainty';
(b)   depreciated replacement cost equals current cost.

The explanatory note to ED 52 spells out the view that brands cannot be separately identified as an intangible fixed asset on the basis of the definition above and accordingly should be accounted for as part of goodwill.

ED 53: Fair Value in the Context of Acquisition Accounting

This exposure draft, issued in July 1990, addresses the question of how 'fair value' should be computed. This is necessary when looking both at the purchase consideration and the assets acquired, in the context of SSAP 1, FRS 2 and SSAP 22.

Fair value is defined as 'the amount for which an asset or liability could be exchanged in an arm's length transaction as at the date relevant for the evaluation.

Practical guidance relating to the fair value of the purchase consideration includes the following:

(a)   Fair value of securities issued should be based on market values over a time period – 10 days is suggested – so as to avoid distortion from short-term market fluctuations.

(b)   Where market price is unavailable or regarded as an unfair measure, fair value should be estimated by comparison with the market price of shares in other similar businesses.

(c)   Monetary items in the consideration should be at their cash amount, subject to discounting where appropriate.

(d)   Non-monetary assets should be valued at net realisable value unless they are to be replaced by the donor, in which case valuation will be at replacement cost.

(e)   The value of conversion rights depends on their likelihood of conversion. The higher that likelihood, the closer fair value will be to the security into which conversion is expected.

(f)   Deferred cash consideration should be discounted to present value.

(g)   Deferred consideration in the form of shares should be taken into account in computing earnings per share under SSAP 3.

(h)   The best estimate should be made of contingent consideration, adjusting this and the related goodwill figure in the light of experience.

(i)   Acquisition costs should be included in the cost of the investment unless they have been set off against share premium.

Practical guidance relating to the fair value of assets and liabilities acquired is based on the principle that it should equal the amount it would have cost the company directly to acquire those items individually in their current location and condition.

ED 55: Account for Investments

The exposure draft considers the accounting treatment of investments other than investment properties (already covered by SSAP 19). The three main issues addressed are:

(a)   whether investments should be classified as fixed assets or current assets;
(b)   whether investments should be shown at cost or at market value;
(c)   whether revaluation gains and losses should be taken to profit and loss or to revaluation reserve.

ED 55 offers this definition of a fixed asset investment: 'an investment that is intended to be held for use on a continuing basis in the activities of the enterprise. An investment should be classified as a fixed asset only where an intention to hold the investment for the long term can be demonstrated or where there are restrictions as to the investor's ability to dispose of the investment.' Any other investment should be classified as a current asset.

Current asset investments that are 'readily marketable' should be shown at their current market value. Gains or losses on revaluation should be taken to profit and loss.

Other current asset investments should be shown at current cost or at the lower of cost and net realisable value. Revaluation gains should be credited to revaluation reserve while losses should be:

(a) written off against previous related revaluation surpluses;
(b) any excess loss should be written off in the profit and loss account.

Fixed asset investments should be carried at cost less provision for any permanent diminution in value. Alternatively they may be carried at a valuation, reviewed annually. In that case revaluation surpluses and deficits should be treated in line with ED 51.

FRED 3: Accounting for Capital Instruments

This exposure draft covers problems in accounting for 'capital instruments', being:

> All instruments issued by reporting entities which are a means of raising finance, including shares, debentures, loans and debt instruments, options and warrants which give the holder the right to subscribe for or obtain capital instruments. In the case of consolidated financial statements, the term includes capital instruments issued by subsidiaries, except those which are held by another member of the group that is included in the consolidation.

Problems that arise in accounting for such instruments are:

(a) The distinction between 'equity' and 'borrowing' is not always clear. On the one hand, some types of share might carry a right to a fixed level of dividend, be restricted to recovery of the original sum invested on liquidation, and be redeemable on a future date. On the other hand, convertible loan stocks might be issues on terms where conversion is so attractive as to be likely to occur.
(b) Various types of cost arise in relation to different kinds of capital instrument. Allocation of these between the accounting periods in which the finance is available to the business is necessary.

FRED 3 identifies three types of item to be analysed:

Type of item:	*Analysed between:*	
Shareholders' funds	Equity	Non-equity
Minority interest in subsidiaries	Equity	Non-equity
Liabilities	Convertible	Non-convertible

'Non-equity' shares are those where any of the following conditions apply:

(a) The right to dividends or payments on redemption is limited other than by reference to profits or assets.
(b) Rights on winding up of the company are limited.
(c) The shares are redeemable.

The broad principle of FRED 3 is that capital instruments are liabilities if they give rise to an obligation to transfer economic benefits and otherwise are part of the shareholders' funds. Finance costs on debt should be allocated over the term of the debt to give a constant rate on the carrying amount. FRED 3 gives detailed guidance on how to achieve these objectives.

UITF pronouncements

These tend to be brief statements on technical issues, which may well be superseded by future FRSs embracing the relevant topic:

UITF abstract 1: Convertible Bonds – Supplementary Interest/Premium

This addresses the situation where some companies have only charged the coupon rate of interest on convertible bonds to profit and loss rather than the higher market rate which may be payable on redemption. The abstract requires that the full finance cost be charged annually.

UITF abstract 2: Restructuring Costs

This is now superseded by FRS 3, covered in Chapter 4.

UITF abstract 3: Treatment of Goodwill on Disposal of a Business

Where goodwill on acquisition of a business is written off directly to reserves then a subsequent sale of that business may show a misleadingly low cost figure for the disposal. This abstract requires that attributable goodwill should be taken into account in computing the gain or loss on disposal.

UITF abstract 4: Presentation of Long-term Debtors in Current Assets

Under the Companies Act, the current assets figure may include debtors payable after more than one year, with separate disclosure of these in the notes. The abstract requires disclosure of such debtors on the face of the balance sheet where the amount is so material that otherwise 'readers may misinterpret the accounts'.

UITF abstract 5: Transfers from Current Assets to Fixed Assets

This abstract deals with the situation where a decision is taken to use a current asset on a continuing basis in the company's activities. At this stage the fixed asset should be recorded at the lower of cost and net realisable value.

UITF abstract 6: Accounting for Post-retirement Benefits other than Pensions

This abstract explicitly responds to a new standard in the USA, FAS 106, that requires companies to account for all post-retirement benefits on an accruals basis, in the same way as pensions are treated under SSAP 24. The abstract requires similar treatment in the UK for accounts ending on or after 23 December 1994, while encouraging earlier compliance.

UITF abstract 7: True and Fair View Override Disclosures

The abstract addresses in detail what disclosure companies should make when invoking the 'true and fair view override' provisions of the Companies Act 1985. This comprises:

(a)   A statement of the treatment normally required and that actually adopted.

(b)   A statement as to why the treatment normally required fails to give a true and fair view.

(c)   A description of the effect of departing from the normal rules, with a quantification of the effect if this is not shown in the accounts and is practicable.

Answers

Answers for the examination practice questions have been carefully written to provide the student with clear answer guides and key facts that would be needed to pass professional accountancy examinations. Additional detail for a fully comprehensive answer is given in the relevant chapter.

1.1 Compliance with accounting standards

The CCAB bodies require their members to observe accounting standards. Members having a responsibility as directors or officers of a company for the publication of accounts have a duty to ensure that the board are fully aware of the existence and purpose of accounting standards, and should use their best endeavours to ensure that the accounts comply with accounting standards. Members acting as auditors or as reporting accountants are required to ensure that any significant departures from accounting standards are disclosed, and must justify any departures in which they concur. The tradition in the UK that a 'clean' audit report is a brief document has made this a powerful factor in persuading companies to comply with accounting standards.

The Stock Exchange expects listed companies to comply with accounting standards.

The Companies Act 1989 has introduced a new provision for large companies, which are now required to state in their accounts whether these have been prepared in accordance with applicable accounting standards. Any material departure from SSAPs must be disclosed and justified.

In the case of a material departure from a SSAP either the Secretary for Trade or the Review Panel may refer this to the court. If the court takes the view that non-compliance results in a failure to give a true and fair view then it may order the company to circulate appropriately revised accounts.

Company directors may be personally concerned at the risk that any costs falling on the company as a result of such an order may be regarded as arising from their failure to perform a legal duty, and so fall on them personally.

2.1 **Forecast cash flow statement**

Chiron Ltd — cash flow statement for the year ended 31 March 19X7

	£000	£000
Net cash inflow from operating activities		89
Returns on investments and servicing of finance:		
Bank interest paid	(2)	
Dividends paid	(16)	
Net cash outflow from returns on investments and servicing of finance		(18)
Taxation (16 + 26 − 26)		(16)
Investing activities:		
Premises	(30)	
Plant purchased	(105)	
Net cash outflow from investing activities		(135)
Net cash outflow before financing		(80)
Financing:		
Issue of ordinary shares	75	
Net cash inflow from financing		75
Decrease in cash and cash equivalents		5

Notes to the cash flow statement:

1. Reconciliation of operating profit to net cash inflow from operating activities:

	£000
Operating profit	86
Depreciation	28
Stock increase	(30)
Debtor increase	(20)
Creditor increase	24
Accrual increase	1
	89

2. Analysis of changes in cash and cash equivalents during the year:

	£000
Balance at 1 April 19X6	(5)
Net cash flow	(5)
Balance at 31 March 19X7	(10)

3. Analysis of the balances of cash and cash equivalents as shown in the balance sheet:

	19X7 *£000*	*19X6* *£000*	*Change in Year* *£000*
Cash in hand	2	1	1
Bank overdraft	(12)	(6)	(6)
	(10)	(5)	(5)

4. Analysis of changes in financing during the year:

	Share capital *including premium* *£000*
Balance at 1 April 19X6	200
Cash inflow from financing	75
Balance at 31 March 19X7	275

2.2 Preparation of cash flow statement

Beatem Ltd – cash flow statement for the year ended 31 March 19X8

	£000	£000
Net cash inflow from operating activities		1295
Returns on investments and servicing of finance:		
Dividend	(180)	
Debenture interest	(80)	
Overdraft interest	(140)	
Net cash outflow from returns on investments and servicing of finance		(400)
Taxation		(1000)
Investing activities:		
Plant disposal	565	
Plant acquired	(1500)	
Land and buildings acquired	(1700)	
Net cash outflow from investing activities		(2635)
Net cash outflow before financing		(2740)
Financing:		
Share issue	150	
Debenture issue	2000	
Net cash inflow from financing		2150
Decrease in cash and cash equivalents		(590)

Notes to the cash flow statement:

1. Reconciliation of operating profit to net cash flow from operating activities:

	£000
Operating profit	1375
Depreciation	640
Creditors (100 + 80)	(180)
Stock	(285)
Debtors	(300)
Loss on plant disposal	45
Net cash inflow from operating activities	1295

2. Analysis of changes in cash and cash equivalents during the year:

	£000
Balance at 1 April 19X7	(1000)
Net cash outflow	(590)
Balance at 31 March 19X8	(1590)

3. Analysis of the balances in cash and cash equivalents as shown in the balance sheet:

	19X8	19X7	Change in Year
	£000	£000	£000
Bank overdraft	(1750)	(1500)	(250)
Cash and bank	160	500	(340)
	(1590)	(1000)	(590)

4. Analysis of changes in financing during the year:

	Share capital and premium	Debentures
	£000	£000
Balance at 1 April 19X7	1600	—
Cash inflow and financing	150	2000
Balance at 31 March 19X8	1750	2000

Workings:

Retained profit movement:

	£000
Profit per question	2015
Depreciation*	640
Operating profit	1375

* Balancing figure

Interest	300
Taxation	670
Dividends	180
Retained profit	225

Tax paid:

	£000
B/f	1150
+ Change for year	670
− Loss paid in year	(1000)
C/f	820

2.3   Treatment of items in the cash flow statement

1.	DO	6.	I
2.	N	7.	N
3.	R	8.	F
4.	I	9.	AO
5.	N	10.	N

3.1   Exclusion from consolidation

A subsidiary may only be excluded from the consolidated accounts in the following circumstances:

(a)   Company law permits, and FRS 2 requires, that a subsidiary be excluded from consolidation where severe long-term restrictions substantially hinder the exercise of the rights of the parent undertaking over the assets or management of the subsidiary. If the restrictions were in force at the acquisition date then the subsidiary is carried in the accounts initially at cost; if the restrictions come into force after the accounting date then the investment in the subsidiary at that point in time is shown as though the equity method applied. No further accruals for profit or loss of the subsidiary should then be made unless the restrictions allow 'significant influence', in which case the subsidiary should be treated as an associate.

(b)   Company law permits, and FRS 2 requires, exclusion from consolidation for a subsidiary held exclusively with a view to resale. Such an investment should be shown at the lower of cost and net realisable value.

(c)   Company law permits exclusion from consolidation on the grounds that the subsidiary's activities are so different from those of other group undertakings as to make inclusion incompatible with the obligation to give a true and fair view. FRS 2 argues that such cases are 'exceptional' since a true and fair view of different activities can be given by segmental reporting. Where this situation does arise then equity accounting should be used.

(d)   Company law allows exclusion of subsidiaries where 'disproportionate expense or undue delay' would arise from their inclusion. FRS 2 restricts this exemption to situations where the subsidiary is not material to the consolidated accounts.

4.1   FRS 3 − allocation of items

(a)   This is part of the gain or loss on termination of an operation, shown on the face of the profit and loss account after operating profit and loss interest as an exceptional item.

(b) This is an exceptional item. To give a true and fair view it should be shown on the face of the profit and loss account under the appropriate format heading.

(c) This is shown as a gain relating to discontinued operations, as an exceptional item shown on the face of the profit and loss account after operating profit and before interest.

4.2 FRS 3 – presentation

(a) The £320 000 is shown as an exceptional item after operating profit and before interest. The related taxation is shown as part of the tax charge.

(b) This is a 'fundamental error' giving rise to a prior period adjustment. The comparative figures for the previous period should be adjusted accordingly. The effect of the adjustment will also be shown at the foot of the statement of total recognised gains and losses.

(c) The whole £980 000 is an exceptional item to be included under the appropriate format headings within operating profit.

(d) This is a gain on a fixed asset disposal, and accordingly appears as an exceptional item between the operating profit and the interest charge.

4.3 FRS 3 – conceptual basis

The 'all-inclusive' income approach shows on the face of the profit and loss account all extraordinary items and all prior period adjustments, as well as ordinary trading profit. The advantages of this approach are:

(a) analysts can select for themselves the aspect of performance they wish to focus on;

(b) since all income and expenditure is revealed, management does not have the opportunity to manipulate the disclosure in the profit and loss account;

(c) the risk of analysts failing to observe significant non-trading items is reduced.

The 'current operating income' approach shows only items relating to the normal recurring activities of the company on the face of the profit and loss account. This has the following advantages:

(a) the profit figure provides a more meaningful guide to future profits, since non-recurring items are excluded;

(b) the profit figure gives a useful indication of management's achievement in running the business.

5.1 Definition of associated company

SSAP 1 defines an 'associated company' as one which is not a subsidiary and where either:

(a) the interest is effectively that of a partner in a joint venture or a consortium, and the investing group exercises a significant influence over the associate; or

(b) the interest is long term, substantial, and having regard to the disposition of other shareholdings, the investing group exercises significant influence over the investee.

'Significant influence' is defined as participation in the policy discussions of the company. There is an assumption, which applies unless the contrary can be clearly demonstrated, that where the equity holding is 20 per cent or greater the investing company can exercise significant influence. Where the equity holding is less than 20 per cent there is an assumption that the investing company cannot exercise significant influence unless:

(a) the investing company can demonstrate otherwise, and
(b) the investee company concurs.

5.2 Consolidating an associate's results

Crust Ltd – Consolidated profit and loss account for the year to 31 December 1980

	£	£
Turnover		6 800 000
Profit for the year		702 000
Share of profit of associate		168 000
		870 000
Taxation:		
Crust Ltd and subsidiaries	282 000	
Associated company	68 000	350 000
		520 000
Profit attributable to the members of Crust Ltd of which £x is dealt with in the books of the holding company		
Proposed dividend		264 000
Retained profit		256 000
By the holding company	123 600	
By subsidiaries	70 000	
In the associate	62 400	
	256 000	

6.1 Defining the terms

(a) Fundamental accounting concepts are the broad basic assumptions which underlie the periodic financial accounts of business enterprises.

(b) Accounting bases are the methods developed for applying fundamental accounting concepts to financial transactions and items, for the purpose of financial accounts, and in particular (i) for determining the accounting periods in which revenue and costs should be recognised in the profit and loss accounts and (ii) for determining the amounts at which material items should be stated in the balance sheet.

(c) Accounting policies are the specific accounting bases selected and consistently followed by a business enterprise as being, in the opinion of the management, appropriate to its circumstances and best suited to present fairly its results and financial position.

6.2 **Understanding the concepts**

   (a) The 'going concern' concept that the enterprise will continue in operational existence for the foreseeable future. This means in particular that the profit and loss account and balance sheet assume no intention or necessity to liquidate or curtail significantly the scale of operation.

   (b) The 'accruals' concept that revenue and costs are accrued (that is, recognised as they are earned or incurred, not as money is received or paid), matched with one another so far as their relationship can be established or justifiably assumed, and dealt with in the profit and loss account of the period to which they relate.

   (c) The 'consistency' concept that there is consistency of accounting treatment of like items within each accounting period and from one period to the next.

   (d) The 'prudence' concept that revenue and profits are not anticipated, but are recognised by inclusion in the profit and loss account only when realised in the form either of cash or of other assets the ultimate cash realisation of which can be assessed with reasonable certainty; provision is made for all known liabilities (expenses and losses) whether the amount of these is known with certainty or is a best estimate in the light of the information available.

   The relative importance of these concepts will vary according to the circumstances of the particular case. The only provision for putting the four fundamental accounting concepts in any order of priority in SSAP 2 is a requirement that where the accruals concept is inconsistent with the prudence concept the latter should prevail.

6.3 **Accounting bases**

   Examples might include:

Subject-matter	*Different bases*
Depreciation	(a) Write off over estimated useful life by the straight line method.
	(b) Write off over estimated useful life by the reducing balance method.
Development expenditure	(a) Write off in the year incurred.
	(b) Write off over the period of commercial exploitation of the related project.
Stock	(a) Value at the lower of cost and net realisable value on a FIFO basis.
	(b) Value at the lower of cost and net realisable value on an average cost basis.
Government grants	(a) Reduce the cost of acquisition of fixed assets by the amount of any related government grant.
	(b) Show government grants relating to fixed assets as a deferred credit, to be transferred to the profit and loss account over the life of the asset.

6.4 **Accounting policies**

   (a) *Turnover.* Turnover represents amounts received and receivable for goods and services supplied exclusive of inter-group sales and VAT.

(b) *Depreciation*. Depreciation is calculated to write off buildings, plant and machinery during their expected normal lives by equal annual instalments. The rates used by the group are:

Buildings	2%
Plant	15%
Motor vehicles	25%

(c) *Stocks*. Stocks are stated at the lower of cost including factory overheads and net realisable value.

(d) *Research and development*. Costs are written off to revenue in the year during which they are incurred.

(e) *Government grants*. Grants relating to fixed assets are treated as deferred credits and are transferred to revenue in equal amounts over the expected life of the asset.

7.1 Net and nil EPS

In computing a figure for earnings per share the amount 'earnings' is defined as the consolidated profit of the period after *taxation*, after deducting minority interests and preference dividends, and after taking into account extraordinary items. The amount for 'taxation' included in this definition may, under the imputation system, include an amount of irrecoverable ACT. Since irrecoverable ACT arises from the payment of dividends (see Chapter 10 on SSAP 8) it follows that the company's dividend policy may affect the earnings per share ratio. The 'net' basis includes irrecoverable ACT in the taxation charge, while the 'nil' basis excludes irrecoverable ACT from the taxation charge for the purposes of computing earnings per share.

7.2 Dilution of EPS

The possibility of 'dilution' of earnings per share arises when at the year end the company has entered into a commitment which may result in an increase in the number of shares over which earnings will be spread. Three specific circumstances are considered in SSAP 3:

(a) where the company has issued a separate class of equity shares which do not rank for dividend in the period under review but will do so in the future;

(b) where the company has issued loans or preference shares convertible into equity of the company;

(c) where options to subscribe for equity shares have been granted.

7.3 Computation of EPS

Camborne Ltd

(a) Basic net EPS:

$$\frac{5\ 206\ 000\ \text{(w(i))}}{27\ 898\ 265\ \text{(w(ii))}} = 18.7\text{p}$$

Basic nil EPS:

$$\frac{5\ 318\ 000\ \text{(w(i))}}{27\ 898\ 265\ \text{(w(ii))}} = 19.1\text{p}$$

Diluted net EPS:

$$\frac{5\ 260\ 750\ \ (w(iii))}{28\ 628\ 265\ \ (w(iii))} = 18.4p$$

Diluted nil EPS:

$$\frac{5\ 372\ 750\ \ (w(iii))}{28\ 628\ 265\ \ (w(iii))} = 18.8p$$

(b) The earnings per share of previous years will have to be adjusted to allow for the bonus element in the rights issue. This will be done by applying to the previously reported EPS figure the factor 86/90.

Workings

(i) *Calculation of earnings:*

	£000
Profit after tax and minority interest	5 290
Less: Preference dividends	84
Earnings on the 'net' basis	5 206
Irrecoverable ACT	112
Earnings on the 'nil' basis	5 318

(ii) *Calculation of number of shares:*
Theoretical ex rights price:

	Number of shares		£
Market value prior to share issue	24 316 000	× 90p	21 884 400
Cash raised by issue	6 079 000	× 70p	4 255 300
	30 395 000		26 139 700

$$\frac{26\ 139\ 700}{30\ 395\ 000} = 86p$$

Portion of year	Fraction of year	Shares in issue	Rights factor	Number of shares
1.1.X1 to 5.5.X1	$\frac{125}{365}$ ×	23 500 000 ×	$\frac{90}{86}$ =	8 422 268
6.5.X1 to 14.6.X1	$\frac{40}{365}$ ×	24 316 000 ×	$\frac{90}{86}$ =	2 788 710
15.6.X1 to 11.11.X1	$\frac{150}{365}$ ×	30 395 000	=	12 491 095
12.11.X1 to 31.12.X1	$\frac{50}{365}$ ×	30 632 200	=	4 196 192
				27 898 265

(iii)   *Effects of dilution:*
Cash to be raised — 730 000 × £1.20 = £876 000
Earnings:

$$\frac{876\ 000}{20} \times £2.50 = 109\ 500$$

Tax @ 50%   =   54 750

Increase in earnings   54 750

	Net	Nil
Basic earnings	5 206 000	5 318 000
Increase on dilution	54 750	54 750
	5 260 750	5 372 750
Shares in issue		
Basis calculation	27 898 265	
Prospective dilution	730 000	
	28 628 265	

7.4   Computation of two years' EPS
Gnome Ltd
(a)   In the accounts to 31.12.X6
      Basic earnings per share   7.9p
      Diluted earnings per share   6.6p
(b)   In the accounts to 31.12.X7

Earnings per share:	*19X7*	*19X6*
Basic	5.9p	7.4p
Diluted	5.1p	6.2p

Workings

(a) *19X6*	£
Basic earnings	220 000
Number of shares in issue:	
280 000 × 10	2 800 000

Basic EPS $\dfrac{220\ 000}{2\ 800\ 000} = 7.9\text{p}$

Earnings from dilution:

	£
$\frac{100}{25} \times 2.5 \times £60\ 000 = $	6 000
Less: Tax @ 50%	3 000
	3 000

Diluted EPS $\dfrac{220\ 000 + 3\ 000}{2\ 800\ 000 + 600\ 000} = 6.6\text{p}$

(b) *19X7*

Theoretical ex rights price:

	Number of shares	£
Market capitalisation before issue	2 800 000 × 60p	1 680 000
Cash raised	700 000 × 40p	280 000
	3 500 000	1 960 000

$$\frac{1\ 960\ 000}{3\ 500\ 000} = 56p$$

Number of shares:

Portion of year	Fraction of year		Shares in issue		Rights factor		Number of shares
1.1.X6 to 31.3.X7	$\frac{3}{12}$	×	2 800 000	×	$\frac{60}{56}$	=	750 000
1.4.X7 to 31.12.X7	$\frac{9}{12}$	×	3 500 000			=	2 625 000
							£3 375 000

Basic EPS $\dfrac{200\ 000}{3\ 375\ 000} = 5.9p$

Earnings from dilution:

$$\frac{100}{20} \times 2.5 \times £60\ 000 = \quad 7\ 500$$

Less: Tax @ 50%	3 750
	3 750

Diluted EPS $= \dfrac{200\ 000 + 3\ 750}{3\ 375\ 000 + 600\ 000} = 5.1p$

Comparative figures altered:

Basic EPS $\quad 7.9p \times \dfrac{56}{60} = 7.4p$

Diluted EPS $\quad 6.6p \times \dfrac{56}{60} = 6.2p$

7.5 EPS

(a) The earnings per share figure relates the profit figure to the individual shareholder, and is widely reported as a component of the 'price/earnings ratio'. SSAP 3 defines earnings as profit after tax, extraordinary items, minority interest and preference dividends.

(b) The nil distribution basis excludes irrecoverable ACT and unrelieved overseas tax from the tax figure used in computation of the earnings figure, where these are attributable to payment of the ordinary dividend. The advantage of this is that company earnings are comparable irrespective of the dividend level. The net basis includes the full tax charge in computing the earnings. The advantage of this approach is that the impact of dividend policy on the earnings position is fully recognised.

(c) (i) The basic EPS figure will be computed on the basis of the number of shares in issue and ranking for dividend. In addition a diluted EPS figure, including the impact of the new share issue, will be disclosed if materially different (i.e. more than 5 per cent).

(ii) A bonus issue of shares will be treated as though the shares had been in issue throughout the year. In addition, the comparative EPS figure will be adjusted on to the same basis.

(iii) The number of shares will be computed on a weighted average basis, bringing the new shares into account from the date when profits of the subsidiary are brought into account.

(d) Compute theoretical ex rights price:

$$\begin{array}{ll} 2 \times 2 & = 4.00 \\ 1 \times 1.5 & = 1.50 \\ \hline 3 & 5.50 \end{array}$$

$$= \frac{5.50}{3} = £1.833$$

Number of shares:

$$\begin{array}{ll} 6/12 \times 3\,000\,000 \times 2.0/1.833 & = 1\,636\,393 \\ 6/12 \times 4\,500\,000 & = 2\,250\,000 \\ \hline & 3\,886\,393 \end{array}$$

$$\text{EPS} = \frac{750\,000}{3\,886\,393} = 19.3\text{p}$$

8.1 Accounting for grants

Investment Grant Deferred Credit

		Approach (a) £000	Approach (b) £000			Approach (a) £000	Approach (b) £000
31.12.X4	Profit and loss	—	4	31.1.X4	Cash	—	20
31.12.X4	C/f	—	16				
			20				20

Plant Account

		Approach (a) £000	Approach (b) £000			Approach (a) £000	Approach (b) £000
1.1.X4	Bank	100	100	31.1.X4	Bank	20	—
				31.12.X4	Depreciation	16	20
31.12.X4	C/f depreciation	16	20	31.12.X4	C/f cost	80	100
		116	120			116	120

Balance sheet extracts:

	Approach (a) £000	Approach (b) £000
Fixed assets:		
Plant: Cost	80	100
Depreciation	16	20
	64	80
Deferred liabilities		
Investment grant	—	16

Notes:
Approach (a): Reduce the cost of the acquisition of the fixed asset by the amount of the grant.
Approach (b): Treat the amount of the grant as a deferred credit, a portion of which is transferred to revenue annually.
For solution see discussion in text.

9.1 VAT and turnover
The turnover figure in a set of published accounts must be shown net of VAT. If a company wishes to show the gross turnover it must also show the related VAT as a deduction to arrive at a net turnover figure.

9.2 VAT and fixed assets
VAT will only be added to the cost of fixed assets where the VAT is irrecoverable, that is where the company is not registered for VAT or is partially exempt.

10.1 Tax in published accounts
Chatham Ltd

Profit and loss account
Taxation

	£	£
UK corporation tax (£17 000 – 248)	16 752	
Transfer to deferred tax	50 600	
		67 352
Dividends		
Interim paid	9 600	
Final proposed	14 400	24 000
Balance sheet		
Current liabilities	£	
Corporation tax	31 752	
Dividends	14 400	
ACT	7 418	
Deferred liabilities		
Tax payable 1 Jan X2	5 873	
Deferred tax	102 084	
Deferred tax – note		
Tax deferred by virtue of accelerated capital allowances	109 502	
ACT recoverable	(7 418)	
	102 084	

Workings

Corporation Tax

	£		£
B/f	4 945	B/f	32 000
Profit and loss	248	Profit and loss	17 000
Deferred tax – ACT	6 182	Deferred tax – ACT	7 418
C/f ACT 7 418			
19X9 tax 31 752			
19X0 5 873			
	45 043		
	56 418		56 418

Deferred Tax

	£		£
B/f	6 182	B/f	58 902
Corporation tax – ACT	7 418	Profit and loss	50 600
		Corporation tax – ACT	6 182
C/f	109 502	C/f	7 418
	123 102		123 102

10.2   Tax in the ledger
Pitt Ltd

(a)

Corporation Tax

	£		£
Jan 19X7 Cash	16 300	1 Jan X7 B/f 1975 16 300	
		1976 5 000	
			21 300
Oct 19X7 – ACT paid	6 800	Dec 19X7 Profit and loss	36 000
Dec 19X7 Profit and loss	1 200	Dec 19X7 Deferred tax – ACT	17 000
Dec 19X7 c/f			
19X6 3 800			
19X7 29 200			
ACT 17 000			
	50 000		
	74 300		74 300

Deferred Taxation

	£		£
Dec 19X7 ACT	17 000	1 Jan X7 B/f	29 400
		Dec 19X7 Profit and loss	7 000
Dec 19X7 C/f	36 400	Dec 19X7 C/f	17 000
	53 400		53 400

Profit and loss account for year ended 31 December 19X7

	£	£
Profit before tax		88 800
Taxation:		
UK tax at %	34 800	
UK deferred tax	7 000	41 800
Profit after tax		47 000
Ordinary dividends		
Interim paid	13 200	
Final proposed	33 000	46 200
		800
Balance at 1.1.X7		43 000
Retained profits 31.12.X7		43 800

Balance sheet extracts

	£
Current liabilities	
Proposed dividends	33 000
Corporation tax	3 800
ACT	17 000
Deferred liabilities	
Deferred taxation	19 400*
Corporation tax	
(payable Jan X9)	29 200

* If information were available we would show a split of this item into its component parts.

(b)   The shareholder will have received an interim dividend of £66 carrying a related tax credit of £34 and will receive a final dividend of £165 carrying a related tax credit of £85. Thus his income will be:

	Cash received	*Tax credit*	*Total*
Interim	66	34	100
Final	165	85	250
	£231	£119	£350

For tax purposes the shareholder will be deemed to have an income of £350, and an amount of £119 of his tax liability will be deemed to have been paid. Thus if the shareholder pays tax at 34 per cent, then he will have discharged his liability on this income; if he pays tax at a higher rate he will have a further tax liability; while if he is not liable to tax in full at 34 per cent on this income, then he will receive a refund.

10.3   Definitions

(i)   Franked investment income should be shown in the profit and loss account grossed up to include the related tax credit, which should be shown as part of the tax charge.

(ii) Proposed dividends should be shown in the profit and loss account as part of the appropriations for the year, and as a liability in the 'creditors: amounts falling due within one year' section of the balance sheet. Related ACT should also be shown as a creditor due within one year.

(iii) Recoverable ACT should be set off against deferred taxation, or to the extent this cannot be done should be shown as a deferred item in the current asset part of the balance sheet.

(iv) Irrecoverable ACT should be included in the tax charge for the year and disclosed if material.

(v) Turnover should be shown excluding VAT, while the output tax should be credited to the VAT account in the ledger.

(vi) Irrecoverable input tax on a fixed asset should be included in the cost of that asset as recorded in the accounts.

(vii) Receipt or payment of VAT should be recorded in the VAT account, the balance of which will be a debtor or creditor in the balance sheet.

11.1   SSAP 9

(a) A long-term contract is defined in SSAP 9 as a contract entered into for the design, manufacture or construction of a single substantial asset or the provision of a service (or of a combination of assets or services which together constitute a single project) where the time taken to complete the contract is such that the contract actively falls into different accounting periods. A contract that is required to be accounted for as long term will usually extend for a period exceeding one year, but this duration is not an essential feature. Some contracts with a shorter duration should be accounted for as long term if they are so material that exclusion of their turnover and results would result in the accounts failing to give a true and fair view; such a policy must be applied consistently.

(b) The profit and loss account will include:

	£
Sales	1770
Cost of sales (1680 + 70)	1750
	20

The balance sheet will include:

	£
Debtors (classified as amounts recoverable on contracts)	240
Stock (classified as long-term contract balances)	150
Provision for liabilities and charges (classified as long-term contract foreseeable losses)	60

A note to the balance sheet will analyse the stock item:

	£
Net cost less foreseeable losses	190
Applicable payment on account	40
	150

	1	2	3	4	B/S	P&L
Value of work done	500	350	700	220		1770 (Sales)
Payments on account	525	200	610	235		
			150	90	240 (Debtors)	
Excess payments on account	25			15		
Offset	(25)			(15)		
	—			—		
Total costs incurred	600	400	720	280		
Transfer to cost of sales	450	400	600	230		1680 (Cost of sales)
Provision for foreseeable loss			(60)	(10)		70 (Cost of sales)
Classify as provision			(60)		(60)	
Offset	(25)			(15)		
Classify in stock	125			25	150	

11.2 SSAP 9 terminology

(a) Net realisable value is the estimated selling price less all costs to completion and all cost relating to the sale of the product.

(b) Replacement cost is not in itself an acceptable basis of valuation, in that to value stock at replacement cost when net realisable value is greater will result in increasing the loss in the current period in order to create a future artificial profit; however, SSAP 9 acknowledges that there are occasions when replacement cost will form the best guide to net realisable value.

(c) 'Cost' as defined in SSAP 9 consists of both the 'cost of purchase' and the 'cost of conversion'. Cost of conversion consists of all the expenses, both direct and indirect, attributable to bringing the product to its present location and condition. Thus production overheads will be included in cost, absorption being based on normal production levels and excluding abnormal costs. Normally other overheads will not be included, with certain exceptions including:

   (i) costs of service departments, e.g. the accounting department, will be apportioned between the main functions of the business, so that a portion of these costs will be included in production overheads and consequently in stock;

   (ii) interest charges on borrowings specifically relating to long-term contracts may be included in the cost of related work in progress;

   (iii) expenses of obtaining firm sales contracts, including marketing and design costs, may be included in the cost of related work in progress.

(d) (i) Adjusted selling price, a technique used mainly by retail stores, is calculated by deducting from stock valued at selling price the estimated gross profit percentage. This method is acceptable under SSAP 9 only where no other method is practical and where it can be demonstrated that the result gives a reasonable approximation of the actual cost.

(ii)   First in, first out is a method whereby the cost of stock and work in progress is calculated on the basis that the quantities in hand represent the latest purchases or production.

(iii)   Last in, first out is a method whereby the cost of stock and work in progress is calculated on the basis that the quantities in hand represent the earliest purchases or production.

(iv)   Base stock is a method whereby the cost of stock and work in progress is calculated on the basis that a fixed unit value is ascribed to a predetermined number of units of stock, any excess over this number being valued on the basis of some other method. If the number of units in stock is less than the predetermined minimum, the fixed unit value is applied to the number in stock.

12.1 Depreciation policies

(a)   The accounting policies of the two companies are deficient in the following respects:

(i)   SSAP 12 requires that the method of depreciation and the useful life should be disclosed in respect of each major class of asset. Policy 1 has failed to relate depreciation rates to the specific related fixed assets, while Policy 2 has failed to provide details either of depreciation methods used or of lives of major classes of asset.

(ii)   SSAP 4 requires that capital-based grants should be credited to the profit and loss account over the lives of the related assets; this should be achieved by showing the investment grant as a deferred liability which will be credited to the profit and loss account over the life of the asset. Company 1 is in breach of SSAP 4 both in writing back investment grants over a period of 12 years rather than by reference to the lives of the specific related assets and in showing grants not yet written back as part of shareholders' funds rather than as a deferred liability.

(iii)   SSAP 12 specifically requires that depreciation should be provided on freehold and long lease properties, these being assets having a finite useful life. Therefore Company 2 is in breach of SSAP 12 in this respect, unless the properties held are investment properties.

(iv)   Company 2's policy of amortising short leases over the unexpired term may appear reasonable on the grounds that leases have a predetermined maximum life. However, it may on occasion happen that the useful life of a lease may expire before the end of its term, and a sound accounting policy would allow for amortisation over the shorter period in that case.

(b)   The purpose of the depreciation charge in the profit and loss account is to provide a measure of the wearing out, consumption or other loss of value of fixed assets whether arising from use, effluxion of time or obsolescence through technology and market changes.

(c)   An accounting standard on depreciation was required:

(i)   because depreciation is one of the two major areas (the other being the valuation of stock and work in progress) which have produced the widest differences in practice in the preparation of financial accounts; an accounting standard was required to narrow these areas of difference;

(ii)   because prior to the issue of SSAP 12 disclosure of accounting policies on depreciation was often vague to the point of being meaningless;

(iii) a number of specific problems, including change of depreciation method, asset life and revaluation, required specific guidance.

12.2 Depreciaton adjustments

(a) A revision of the useful life of a depreciable asset will normally be accounted for by writing off the net book amount over the remaining useful economic life. If this is likely to result in material distortion of future results then an immediate adjustment to accumulated depreciation should be made; this adjustment will be an exceptional, not an extraordinary, item, unless the circumstances leading to the revision are themselves extraordinary.

(b) A change in the basis of computing depreciation should be accounted for by writing off the net book value of the asset by the new method over the estimated life.

(c) Where a depreciable asset is disposed of the gain or loss on disposal can be computed in two ways:
   (i)   as the difference between net book value and sale proceeds;
   (ii) as the difference between net book value and sale proceeds, adjusted for any revaluation surplus or deficit on the asset.

(d) When a depreciable asset is revalued no adjustment should be made in the profit and loss account in respect of accumulated depreciation. Depreciation should be provided on the revalued amount over any revised estimated life and be charged through the profit and loss account.

13.1 Allocation of R&D items

Simple Ltd

SSAP 13 divides research and development expenditure into the following categories:

(a) pure research, being original investigation undertaken to gain new scientific or technical knowledge, not aimed at a specific objective;

(b) applied research, being original investigation undertaken to gain new scientific or technical knowledge directed at a specific objective;

(c) development, being the use of scientific or technical knowledge in order to produce new or substantially improved materials, devices, products, processes, systems or services prior to the commencement of commercial production.

The statement requires that pure and applied research expenditure be written off in the year that it is incurred. Development expenditure must also be written off in the year that it is incurred unless the following conditions are met:

(a) There must be a clearly defined project.

(b) Expenditure relating to the project must be separately identified.

(c) There must be a 'reasonable certainty' as to the technical feasibility and commercial viability of the project.

(d) There must be a reasonable expectation that the total of further development costs and related production, selling and administration costs will be covered by revenues arising from the project.

(e) Adequate resources must be available to cover completion of the project, including working capital requirements.

If these conditions are met then the company is allowed to defer development expenditure to the extent that its recovery can 'reasonably be regarded as assured', being amortised over the period of commercial production. Even where the conditions are met in full, the company may choose to write off development expenditure. The policy chosen must be applied consistently.

In choosing between a write-off and a deferral policy for development expenditure meeting these conditions, a company will consider:

(a) whether its planning and forecasting systems are adequate to comply with the conditions for deferral;

(b) the policy followed by other companies in the same industry, since it is desirable that accounts be comparable;

(c) since deferment of development expenditure involves disclosure of movements in the balance on the deferred asset account, companies anxious to preserve commercial secrecy may prefer a write-off policy;

(d) where development expenditure fluctuates substantially from year to year, it may be particularly desirable to follow a deferral policy;

(e) a deferral policy is only worth pursuing where the amounts involved are material.

Considering the problem posed by the Research and Development suspense account of Simple Ltd:

1. The term 'applied research' has been used in the question to describe expenditure of £500 000 relating to a specific project. If the description used is correct, then this expenditure must be written off as it is incurred. Even if the description 'development expenditure' would be more accurate, 'cautious' optimism does not sound a strong enough expression of expectation to justify deferral.

2. Expenditure of £50 000 in pure research must clearly be written off when it is incurred.

3. Project Y clearly falls within the definition of 'development expenditure' given in SSAP 13. If the project meets the conditions laid down in SSAP 13, therefore, the expenditure may be deferred.

4. Similarly expenditure in Project Z may, if it meets the conditions laid down in SSAP 13, be deferred. The company must be consistent in its choice of policy. In amortising the expenditure it should be borne in mind that patents have a maximum life of 16 years.

5. Purchased 'know-how' is similar in character to development expenditure, although not, strictly speaking, falling within the scope of SSAP 13. It would, therefore, be reasonable to defer this expenditure upon the same conditions as development expenditure.

13.2 Treatment of R&D
Venture Ltd

(a) *Definitions:*

(i) Pure research expenditure is on original investigation undertaken in order to gain new scientific or technical knowledge or understanding, not directed towards any specific practical objective.

(ii) Applied research expenditure is on original investigation undertaken in order to gain new scientific or technical knowledge directed towards a specific practical objective.

(iii) Development expenditure relates to the use of scientific or technical knowledge in order to produce new or substantially improved materials, devices, products, processes, systems or services prior to the commencement of commercial use or production.

(b) *Deferral.* Expenditure on fixed assets for the purpose of research and development should be capitalised and depreciated over their estimated useful life. Expenditure fully recoverable under a firm contract from a customer should, in so far as it has not been reimbursed at the balance sheet date, be carried forward as work in progress.

All other expenditure on pure and applied research must be written off in the year it is incurred. Development expenditure should normally be written off in the year it is incurred but *may* be written off under the following conditions:

(i) There must be a clearly defined project, expenditure on which should be separately identifiable.

(ii) The project must be technically feasible and commercially viable, bearing in mind market conditions and legal requirements.

(iii) Total revenues from the project must be reasonably expected to cover total costs.

(iv) There must be good reason to believe that adequate resources exist, or will become available, to carry through the project.

The policy chosen in respect of development expenditure must be applied consistently.

(c) *Treatment.* Projects 3 and 4 both fall within the scope of development expenditure, while Project 5 will be included in work in progress. Treatment of Projects 3 and 4 will depend on:

(i) whether the projects meet the criteria for deferral laid down by SSAP 13;

(ii) whether the company has chosen to adopt a deferral or a write-off policy in respect of such expenditure.

Expenditure on Projects 3, 4 and 5 will therefore be reflected in the accounts as follows:

(i) The balance sheet will include £35 000 additions to plant.

(ii) The balance sheet will, if the deferral method is used, include a note as follows:

	£	£
Deferred development expenditure at the beginning of the year		x
Development expenditure incurred (including £36 000 relating to Projects 3 and 4)	x	
Development expenditure amortised	<u>x</u>	<u>x</u>
Deferred development expenditure at the end of the year		x

(iii) The amount for work in progress in the balance sheet will include £44 500 in respect of Project 5, less any payments on account received.

(iv) The figure for depreciation shown in the published profit and loss account will include £3500 relating to fixed assets used on Projects 3, 4 and 5.

(v) The notes on the company's accounting policies will include a note on the policy adopted in respect of research and development expenditure and on stock and work in progress.

Workings

1. Projects 3 and 4 – Deferred expenditure

	3	*4*	*Total*
Salaries	5 000	10 000	15 000
Overheads	6 000	12 000	18 000
Depreciation	1 000	2 000	3 000
	12 000	24 000	36 000

2. Project 5 – Work in progress

Salaries	20 000
Overheads	24 000
Depreciation	500
	44 500

14.1 The rules in SSAP 15

(a) SSAP 15 requires that deferred tax should be provided if it is 'probable' that a liability or asset will crystallise.

(b) (i) Deferred taxation will only be shown as an extraordinary item where it arises from an extraordinary item.

  (ii) Deferred taxation will be shown as a prior year item only when it arises from a change in accounting policy or correction of a fundamental error.

  (iii) Deferred taxation arising from a reserve movement, e.g. a fixed asset revaluation, will be taken direct to reserves.

(c) Under the liability method the taxation effects of timing differences are regarded as liabilities for taxes payable in the future; thus the deferred tax balance each year will be calculated on the basis of the most recent rate of tax. Under the deferral method the taxation effects of timing differences are regarded as deferrals of taxation payable or recoverable to be allocated to future periods when the differences reverse; thus the deferred tax balance will not change in line with changes in the rate of taxation.

14.2 Deferred taxation

(a) (i) 'Permanent' differences arise because certain types of income or expenditure shown in the accounts are tax free or disallowable, while there may also be certain types of tax charge or allowance which are not reflected in the accounts.

  (ii) 'Timing differences' arise because there are items which are included in the financial statements of a period different from that in which they are dealt with for tax purposes.

(b) (i) Short-term timing differences arise from the use of the receipts and payments basis for tax purposes and the accruals basis in the accounts. Examples include interest receivable, interest or royalties payable, and bad debt provisions.

(ii) Accelerated capital allowances arise when capital allowances in the tax computation differ from the related depreciation charges in the accounts.

(iii) Revaluation of fixed assets leads to a timing difference in that the realisation of the asset might lead to a tax liability on the surplus.

(iv) Rollover relief leads to a timing difference in that the relief is subject to potential clawback in the event of a replacement asset being disposed of without further replacement.

(v) Losses lead to a timing difference in that tax relief may only be obtained by offset against profits of a future accounting period.

(c) Deferred tax should be provided for to the extent that it is probable that a liability or asset will crystallise, and should not be provided for to the extent that it is probable that crystallisation will not occur. A prudent view should be taken in the assessment of the probability of crystallisation.

15.1 Preparing and presenting CCA

Bun Ltd – profit and loss account for the year ended
31 December 19X9

	£000	£000
Turnover		137 000
Historic cost operating profit		9 670
Less: Depreciation adjustment	2 225	
Asset disposal adjustment	2 212	
Cost of sales adjustment	4 575	
Money working capital adjustment	215	
		9 227
Current cost operating profit		443
Interest payable	(2 320)	
Gearing adjustment	2 934	
		614
Current profit before tax		1 057
Tax		2 500
		(1 443)
Dividend		1 520
		(2 963)
Retained profit b/fwd		19 450
Retained profit c/fwd		16 487

Bun Ltd – balance sheet for the year ended
31 December 19X9

	£000	£000
Plant		33 212
Current assets:		
Stock	36 764	
Debtors	25 100	
	61 864	

	£000	£000
Current liabilities:		
Creditors	24 370	
Tax	2 000	
Dividend	1 000	
Overdraft	9 590	
	36 960	
Net current assets		24 904
		58 116
Debentures		15 500
		42 616
Ordinary shares		10 000
Current cost reserve (9472 + 364 + 9227 − 2934)		16 129
Retained profit		16 487
		42 616

Workings
(a) *Fixed assets:*

Plant	Year acquired	Cost £000	HC Depreciation £000	CCA factor	CCA Cost £000	CCA Depreciation £000
31.12.X8						
	19X6	22 000	9 900	$\frac{146}{97}$	33 113	14 901
	19X7	7 000	2 100	$\frac{146}{109}$	9 376	2 813
	19X8	3 000	450	$\frac{146}{131}$	3 344	502
		32 000	12 450		45 833	18 216
		12 450			18 216	
Written down value		19 550			27 617	
Revaluation surplus					8 067	
31.12.X9						
	19X6	16 000	9 600	$\frac{177}{97}$	29 196	15 518
	19X7	7 000	3 150	$\frac{177}{109}$	11 367	5 115
	19X8	3 000	900	$\frac{}{131}$	4 053	1 216

Plant	Year acquired	Cost	HC Depreciation	CCA factor	Cost	CCA Depreciation
		£000	£000		£000	£000
	19X9	13 520	2 130	$\dfrac{177}{162}$	14 772	2 327
		39 520	15 780		59 388	26 176
		15 780			26 176	
Written down value		23 740			33 212	
					23 740	
Revaluation surplus					9 472	

Depreciation charge:

Year acquired	HC charge	CCA factor	CCA charge
	£000		£000
19X6	2 400	$\dfrac{162}{97}$	4 008
19X7	1 050	$\dfrac{162}{109}$	1 561
19X8	450	$\dfrac{162}{131}$	556
19X9	2 130	$\dfrac{162}{162}$	2 130
	6 030		8 255
			6 030
Depreciation adjustment			2 225

Plant disposal:

	HC £000	CCA factor	CCA £000
Cost of plant sold	6 000	$\dfrac{162}{97}$	10 021
Less: Accumulated depreciation	2 700	$\dfrac{162}{97}$	4 509
	3 300		5 512
			3 300
Asset disposal adjustment			2 212

(b) *Stock:*
Average index − last 2 months 19X8:

$$\frac{168 + 170 + 175}{3} = 171$$

Average index − last 2 months 19X9:

$$\frac{198 + 200 + 202}{3} = 200$$

	HC £000	CCA factor	CCA £000
Stock 31.12.X8	22 540	$\frac{175}{171}$	23 067
			22 540
Revaluation surplus			527
Stock 12.12.X9	36 400	$\frac{202}{200}$	36 764
			36 400
Revaluation surplus			364

COSA

	HC £000	Averaging factor	CCA £000
Opening stock	22 540	$\frac{185}{171}$	24 385
Closing stock	36 400	$\frac{185}{200}$	33 670
	(13 860)		(9 285)
			(13 860)
Cost of sales adjustment			4 575

(c) *Monetary working capital:*

	HC £000	Averaging factor	CCA £000
Opening MWC (20 100 – 18 140)	1 960	$\frac{185}{171}$	2 120
Closing MWC (25 100 – 24 370)	730	$\frac{185}{200}$	675
	(1 230)		(1 445)
			(1 230)
MWCA			215

(d) *Gearing adjustment:*

	19X9 £000	19X9 £000	19X8 £000	19X8 £000
Debentures		15 500		11 000
Taxation		2 000		2 150
Overdraft		9 590		500
		27 090		13 650
Share capital	12 400		12 400	
Reserves	22 780		19 450	
Dividends	1 000		950	

	19X9			*19X8*	
	£000	£000		£000	£000
Revaluation surplus:					
Plant	9 472			8 067	
Stock	364	46 016		527	41 394
		73 106			55 044

$$\text{Gearing proportion} = \frac{27\ 090 + 13\ 650}{73\ 106 + 55\ 044} = 31.8\%$$

	£000
Depreciation adjustment	2 225
Fixed asset disposal	2 212
COSA	4 575
MWCA	215
Total CCA adjustments	9 227

Gearing adjustment: $9\ 227 \times 31.8\% = \quad$ 2 934

16.1 SSAP 17 – definitions

(a) An 'adjusting event' may be defined as a post balance sheet event which provides new or additional evidence of conditions existing at the balance sheet date. Examples include:

(i) A valuation of property showing a permanent diminution in value.

(ii) The receipt of information regarding rates of taxation.

(iii) The discovery of errors or frauds which show that the accounts were incorrect.

(iv) The receipt of the accounts from a company in which an investment is held giving evidence of a permanent diminution in the value of the investment.

(v) The receipt of evidence after the year end showing the net realisable value of stock held at the year end.

(b) A 'non-adjusting event' may be defined as a post balance sheet event concerning conditions which did not exist at the balance sheet date. Examples include:

(i) Issues of shares or debentures.

(ii) A decline in the value of property which occurs after the year end.

(iii) Strikes or other labour disputes.

(iv) Losses of assets as a result of some type of catastrophe.

(v) Nationalisation.

Note: Chapter 16 lists further example of 'adjusting' and 'non-adjusting' events.

16.2 SSAP 17 – treatment

Post balance sheet events may be defined as 'those events, both favourable and unfavourable, which occur between the balance sheet date and the date on which the financial statements are approved by the board of directors'. Such events fall into two categories:

(a) 'Adjusting events' are those which provide new or additional evidence of conditions existing at the balance sheet date. Where the effect is material the amounts stated in the accounts should be adjusted for these items.

(b) 'Non-adjusting events' are those which concern conditions which did not exist at the balance sheet date. Disclosure of these items should be made in the accounts in either of two cases:

(i) where the event is so material that non-disclosure would affect the ability of those using the accounts to have a proper understanding of the financial position of the company;

(ii) where the nature of the event is to reverse or complete a transaction entered into before the year end, the substance of which was primarily to alter the appearance of the company's balance sheet.

In these cases disclosure will consist of:

(i) a description of the nature of the estimate;

(ii) an estimate of the financial effect before tax and of the taxation implications.

17.1   SSAP 18 – requirements

(a) A contingency may be defined as 'a condition which exists at the balance sheet date, where the outcome will be confirmed only on the occurrence or non-occurrence of one or more uncertain future events'.

(b) No provision should be made for a contingent gain. Provision should be made for a contingent loss where it is probable that a future event will confirm the loss, and the loss can be estimated with reasonable accuracy at the date when the accounts are approved by the directors.

(c) Where provision is not made for the effects of a contingency, further disclosure should be made in respect of a contingent gain which is likely to be realised and any contingent loss unless the possibility of loss is remote. Further disclosure will consist of:

(i) a description of the nature of the contingency;

(ii) detail of the uncertainties which are expected to affect the final outcome;

(iii) a prudent estimate of the financial effect of the contingency, or a statement that such an estimate is impracticable.

17.2   SSAP 18 – example

Item (a), being a loss which will probably occur, should be provided for in full.

Item (b) is an item where the possibility of loss cannot be regarded as remote. Accordingly the accounts should give details of the nature of the legal action, an explanation that the outcome depends on the attitude taken by the courts of the State of California, and a statement that the financial effect of the contingency is estimated to be £10 000 000.

In the case of item (c) the possibility of loss is so remote that no disclosure is required.

18.1   Definition

An 'investment property' is defined in SSAP 19 as 'an interest in land and/or buildings:

(a) 'in respect of which construction work and development have been completed', and

(b) 'which is held for its investment potential, any rental income being negotiated at arm's length'.

This definition excludes any property occupied by a company for its own purposes or rented out to any other member of the same group of companies.

19.1 Foreign currency translation

(a) (i) The 'closing rate' method is a method whereby assets and liabilities denominated in foreign currencies are translated using the closing rate. Revenue items are translated using an average rate of exchange for the period.

(ii) The 'temporal' method is a method whereby 'assets, liabilities, revenues and expenses are translated at the rate of exchange ruling at the date on which the amount recorded in the financial statements was established at the balance sheet date. Any assets or liabilities which are carried at current values are retranslated at the closing rate'. The 'temporal' method must be used where the trade of a foreign subsidiary is a direct extension of the trade of the holding company; in all other circumstances the 'closing rate' method must be used.

(b) (i) *Closing rate method:*

Balance sheet 31 December 19X9

	Limas	Conversion factor	£
Ordinary share capital	630 000	$\frac{1}{14}$	45 000
Retained profits	80 000	*	26 000
	710 000		71 000
Plant and machinery:			
Cost	700 000	$\frac{1}{10}$	70 000
Depreciation	70 000	$\frac{1}{10}$	7 000
	630 000		63 000
Stock	210 000	$\frac{1}{10}$	21 000
Net monetary current assets	40 000	$\frac{1}{10}$	4 000
	880 000		88 000
Less: Long-term loan	170 000	$\frac{1}{10}$	17 000
	710 000		71 000

* Balancing figure

Profit and loss account for the year ended 31 December 19X9

	Limas	Limas	Conversion factor	£	£
Sales		900 000	$\frac{1}{12}$		75 000
Depreciation	70 000		$\frac{1}{12}$	5 833	
Other operating expenses	750 000			62 500	
		820 000			68 333
		80 000			6 667

Retained profit movements	£
B/fwd	0
Exchange differences*	19 333
Profit for the year	6 667
C/fwd	26 000

* Balancing figure

	£	£
Opening share capital and reserves at closing rate:	63 000	
$630\ 000 \times \frac{1}{10}$		
Less: Opening share capital and reserves at opening rate:		
$630\ 000 \times \frac{1}{14}$	45 000	
		18 000
Profit for year at closing rate:	8 000	
$80\ 000 \times \frac{1}{10}$		
Profit for year at average rate		1 333
$80\ 000 \times \frac{1}{12}$	6 667	19 333

(ii) *Temporal method:*

Balance sheet 31 December 19X9

	Limas	Conversion factor	£
Ordinary share capital	630 000	$\frac{1}{14}$	45 000
Retained profits	80 000	*	6 091
	710 000		51 091
Plant and machinery:			
Cost	700 000	$\frac{1}{14}$	50 000
Depreciation	70 000	$\frac{1}{14}$	5 000
	630 000		45 000
Stock	210 000	$\frac{1}{11}$	19 091
Net monetary current assets	40 000	$\frac{1}{10}$	4 000
	880 000		68 091
Less: Long-term loan	170 000	$\frac{1}{10}$	17 000
	710 000		51 091

* Balancing figure

Profit and loss account for the year ended 31 December 19X9

	Limas	Limas	Conversion factor	£	£
Sales		900 000	$\frac{1}{12}$		75 000
Depreciation	70 000		$\frac{1}{14}$	5 000	
Other operating expenses	750 000	820 000	$\frac{1}{12}$	62 500	67 500
					7 500
Exchange differences					1 419
					6 091

19.2 Translation

(a) *and* (b) *Translation of the accounts of Acorn*

Balance sheet:

	Crowns	Crowns	Conversion factor	Closing rate £	£	Conversion factor	Temporal £	£
Plant – Cost		604 800	$\frac{1}{15}$		40 320	$\frac{1}{20}$		30 240
– Depreciation		86 400	$\frac{1}{15}$		5 760	$\frac{1}{20}$		4 320
		518 400			34 560			25 920
Current assets								
Stock	129 600		$\frac{1}{15}$	8 640		$\frac{1}{16}$	8 100	
Cash	43 200		$\frac{1}{15}$	2 880		$\frac{1}{15}$	2 880	
		172 800			11 520			19 980
		691 200			46 080			36 900
Loan		(172 800)	$\frac{1}{15}$		(11 520)	$\frac{1}{15}$		(11 520)
		518 400			34 560			25 380
Ordinary share capital		345 600	$\frac{1}{20}$		17 280	$\frac{1}{20}$		17 280
Retained profit – 1.1.X5	129 600		$\frac{1}{20}$	6 480		$\frac{1}{20}$	6 480	
– For year	43 200		*	10 800		*	1 620	
		172 800			17 280			8 100
		518 400			34 560			25 380

* Balancing figure

Profit and loss:

	Crowns	Crowns	Conversion factor	Closing rate £	£	Conversion factor	Temporal £	£
Sales		864 000	$\frac{1}{15}$		57 600	$\frac{1}{18}$		48 000
Cost of sales		561 600	$\frac{1}{15}$		37 440	$\frac{1}{18}$		31 200
		302 400			20 160			16 800
Less:								
Depreciation	86 400		$\frac{1}{15}$	5 760		$\frac{1}{20}$	4 320	
Expenses	172 800		$\frac{1}{15}$	11 520		$\frac{1}{18}$	9 600	
		259 200			17 280			13 920
Net profit		43 200			2 880			2 880
Exchange gain/(loss)		—	*		7 920	*		(1 260)
		43 200			10 800			1 620

* Balancing figure to balance sheet retained profit

(c) (i) *Taking a cover approach:*

	Crowns	£	£
Investment:			
As originally translated	$600\ 000 \times \frac{1}{20} = 30\ 000$		
As retranslated	$600\ 000 \times \frac{1}{15} = 40\ 000$		
Gain			10 000
Loan:			
Originally	$300\ 000 \times \frac{1}{20} = 15\ 000$		
At 31.12.X5	$300\ 000 \times \frac{1}{15} = 20\ 000$		
Loss			(5 000)
Net gain taken direct to translation reserve			5 000

      (ii)   *Not taking a cover approach:*
Investment not retranslated − loss of £5000 taken through profit and loss account.

20.1 SSAP 21 rules

(a)   A finance lease is defined in SSAP 21 as a lease that transfers substantially all the risks and rewards of ownership of an asset to the lessee.

    Such a transfer is normally assumed to have taken place when at the inception of the lease the present value of the minimum lease payments amounts to substantially all (90 per cent or more) of the fair value of the leased asset. Present value is computed using the interest rate implicit in the lease. This assumption may be refuted by other evidence.

    An operating lease is any lease other than a finance lease, i.e. one that fails to meet the above conditions.

(b)   (i)   An asset subject to a finance lease will be regarded as a debtor, recorded in the balance sheet at the net investment in the lease. Total gross earnings under the lease should be allocated to accounting periods to give a constant periodic rate of return on the net cash investment.

      (ii)   An asset subject to an operating lease should be recorded as a fixed asset, with depreciation provided over the estimated useful life. Rental income from the asset should be recognised on a straight line basis over the period of the lease, even if payments are not made on such a basis, unless another more systematic and rational basis can be justified.

20.2 Lease calculations

Balance sheet extracts:

Lease obligations

	£
Opening obligation	34 868
Less: First payment	10 000
	24 868
Interest at 10%	2 487
Outstanding loan − end year 1	27 355
Second payment	10 000
	17 355
Interest at 10%	1 736
Outstanding loan − end year 2	19 091
Third payment	10 000
	9 091
Interest at 10%	909
Outstanding loan − end year 3	10 000
Final payment	10 000
Outstanding loan − end year 4	—

21.1 Goodwill calculations
(a) Consolidated balance sheet:

The Cab Group balance sheet as at 31 March 19X0

	£000
Share capital	1500
Retained profits	500
	2000
Goodwill	200
Tangible assets	1800
	2000

Note that tangible assets are included on the basis of the fair value of the assets of Horse Ltd.

Balance sheets	*Amortised*		*Written off*	
	19X1	*19X2*	*19X1*	*19X2*
	£000	£000	£000	£000
Share capital	1500	1500	1500	1500
Reserves	510	525	330	365
	2010	2025	1830	1865
Tangible assets	1830	1865	1830	1865
Goodwill	180	160	—	—
	2010	2025	1830	1865

Profit and loss accounts				
Profit before taxation	300	330	320	350
Taxation	160	175	160	175
Profit after taxation	140	155	160	175
Dividends	130	140	130	140
Retained profit (deficit)	10	15	30	35

22.1 Definitions
(a) The *equity method* of accounting involves showing an investment in a company in the consolidated balance sheet at:
  (i) the cost of the investment; and
  (ii) the group's share of post acquisition retained profits and reserves of the company; less
  (iii) any amounts written off in respect of (i) and (ii) above.
  The investing group's share of profits is brought into the consolidated profit and loss account. SSAP 1 prescribes the 'equity method' for associated companies, while SSAP 14 prescribes the equity method where a subsidiary is excluded from consolidation because of lack of effective control, if all the other requirements for classification as an associate under SSAP 1 are met.

(b) *Acquisition accounting* is a consolidation approach where a business combination is accounted for as an acquisition. The difference between the fair value of the purchase consideration and the aggregate of the fair value of the separable net assets, both tangible and intangible, is identified as 'goodwill' and accounted for in accordance with SSAP 22. The results of the acquired company are only brought into the consolidated accounts from the date of acquisition.

(c) *Pooling of interests* is a consolidation approach where a business combination is accounted for as a merger. This means that the cost of a new investment is recorded in the acquiror's books as the nominal value of the shares issued plus the fair value of any additional consideration. On consolidation the book value of assets, liabilities and reserves is added together and any difference between the amount of the investment and the nominal value of the acquired shares is deducted from consolidation reserves if it is a debit balance, and shown as an unrealised reserve if it is a credit balance.

22.2   Merger accounting

Sid Ltd
Consolidated balance sheet 31 December 19X0

	Acquisition £	Merger £
Share capital:		
1 280 000 ordinary shares of 25p	320 000	320 000
Share premium	165 000	—
Reserves	300 000	345 000
	785 000	665 000
Fixed assets	270 000	270 000
Goodwill	120 000	—
Current assets	620 000	620 000
	1 010 000	890 000
Current liabilities	225 000	225 000
	785 000	665 000

Workings
Share premium – acquisition method:

	£
Market value 300 000 @ 80p	240 000
Nominal value 300 000 @ 25p	75 000
	165 000

23.1   Pensions costs

(a) The objective is that the employer should recognise the expected cost of providing pensions on a systematic and rational basis over the period during which benefit is derived from the employees' services.

(b) (i)   A defined contribution scheme is a pension scheme where the benefits are directly determined by the value of the contributions paid in respect of each member. Normally the rate of contribution is specified in the rules of the scheme.

(ii) A defined benefit scheme is one where the rules specify the benefits to be paid and the scheme is financed accordingly.

(iii) An experience deficiency is that part of the deficiency of the actuarial value of assets compared to actuarial value of liabilities which arises because events have not coincided with the actuarial assumptions made for the last valuation.

(c) Information given in the accounts should include:

(i) the actuarial method used and a brief description of the main actuarial assumptions;

(ii) the market value of scheme assets at the date of the valuation;

(iii) the level of funding expressed in percentage terms;

(iv) comments on any material actuarial surplus or deficiency.

24.1 SSAP 25

(a) Disclosure of geographical segmentation of turnover should be made on the basis of origin. Where materially different, turnover to third parties by destination should also be shown.

(b) In deciding whether a separate class of business is a distinguishable segment, factors to consider include:

(i) the nature of the products;

(ii) the nature of the production process;

(iii) the markets in which output is sold;

(iv) the distribution channels for products;

(v) the manner in which the entity's activities are organised;

(vi) any separate legislative framework relating to part of the business.

Index